Development
Director
↳ Connecticut
Law
Center

The Jossey-Bass Nonprofit and Public Management Series also includes:

HOW TO

WRITE
SUCCESSFUL
FUNDRAISING
LETTERS

MAL WARWICK

HOW TO

WRITE
SUCCESSFUL
FUNDRAISING
LETTERS

SAMPLE LETTERS · STYLE TIPS · USEFUL HINTS · REAL-WORLD EXAMPLES

JOSSEY-BASS
A Wiley Imprint
www.josseybass.com

Published by Jossey-Bass
A Wiley Imprint
989 Market Street, San Francisco, CA 94103-1741   www.josseybass.com

Chapter Nine: Excerpts from *How to Write, Speak and Think More Effectively* by Rudolf Flesch. Copyright (c) 1946, 1949, 1951, 1958, 1960 by Rudolf Flesch. Copyright (c) 1950 by Printer's Ink Publishing Corp. Copyright renewed. Reprinted by permission of HarperCollins Publishers, Inc.

Remaining credits are on p. 304.

Library of Congress Cataloging-in-Publication Data

Warwick, Mal.
    How to write successful fundraising letters / Mal Warwick.
        p.   cm.—(The Jossey-Bass nonprofit and public
management series)
Includes index.
    ISBN 0-7879-5652-X (alk. paper)
    1. Direct-mail fund raising. 2. Nonprofit
organizations—Finance. I. Title. II. Series.
    HV41.2 .W378 2001
    658.15'224—dc21   00–012115

Printed in the United States of America
FIRST EDITION
PB Printing   10 9

Contents

PART IV

The Letter Writer's Toolbox

Preface to the Revised Edition

Just in case you're curious how this revised edition is different from the first, I'll get that out of the way right off the bat:

- The book's contents have been completely reorganized into a more logical and smoothly flowing sequence (thanks to Johanna Vondeling, my eagle-eyed editor at Jossey-Bass).
- I've pored over every sentence, cutting a word here or there or adding some new insight that flitted through my mind.
- I've added fresh examples and some carefully selected new material.

And here's what I did *not* do in producing this revised edition: I did *not* add a whole lot of words. Readers of the first edition told me that one of that book's greatest virtues was its compact size and the ease with which they could refer to key points whenever the need arose. I chose not to run the risk of burying those key points in verbiage or superfluous examples. Besides, although I've been regarded as a radical most of my life, I'm a very *conservative* radical; I don't favor change for the sake of change alone. So if a paragraph I wrote for the first edition or an example I used struck me as equally relevant and instructive today, I left it alone. New isn't always better.

How This Book Is Organized

This revised edition is structured in four parts.

Part One begins where the writing of any fundraising appeal should begin: peering into the mind of the donor. These first five chapters examine the stuff of which successful fundraising is made:

- An appreciation for the broad range of motives that lead people to contribute money to good causes and important institutions
- An understanding of the dynamics in the relationship between the fundraiser and the donor
- Insight into the ways that donors view the fundraising letters they receive
- The characteristics of an effective fundraising letter

To put this understanding into a truly practical context, Part One concludes with a paragraph-by-paragraph tour through a successful appeal.

Part Two looks at the nuts and bolts. We'll approach the task of writing a fundraising letter from a strictly practical, down-to-earth perspective. In successive chapters in this part, we'll cover:

- What to do before you sit down to write a fundraising appeal
- The nine steps I recommend following in crafting a fundraising package
- The eight concrete cardinal rules that determine whether your appeal will be a success (or a dud), along with a self-assessment form that will help you evaluate the likely effectiveness of a fundraising letter in the light of these rules
- The practical guidelines of style and syntax I urge you to follow when you're writing a fundraising appeal—or, for that matter, any other prose that's meant to persuade the reader to act

The seven chapters in Part Three take you on a walking tour through the thickets of fundraising, visiting each of the most common types of fundraising letters to examine their unique characteristics and distinctive demands. In the course of Part Three, we'll study letters designed to do the following:

- Recruit a new member or donor
- Acknowledge a gift from a new donor
- Appeal for a special (additional) gift
- Request a year-end contribution
- Solicit a high-dollar-amount gift
- Persuade a donor to send a bigger gift
- Seek an annual gift

Part Four is where I invite you to steal my ideas as you might see fit. These resources are for your unregulated use—a bag full of treatments for the dread disease of writer's block:

- Sixty successful outer envelope teasers
- Fifty-four strong leads for fundraising letters
- Ninety ways to use the word *you* in a fundraising letter
- Sixty-three ways to handle awkward copywriting transitions
- Forty-one powerful ways to end a fundraising letter
- Fifty-eight ways to start a P.S. in a fundraising letter
- Fifteen ways how *not* to get results from your writing
- Ten other books to help you write successful fundraising letters

How You Can Use This Book

I'll feel fulfilled as a writer only if you absorb every word in this book with the loving care I invested in it. On a more practical level, however, I'm confident you will find *How to Write Successful Fundraising Letters* useful in at least three additional ways (as some readers of the first edition have told me they did):

- As a source of examples and inspiration when a writing task comes due and your mind won't stop thinking about everything other than fundraising
- As a quick-and-easy guide to the distinctive types of fundraising letters (found in Part Three)
- As a collection of crib sheets (the resources in Part Four) that will help you resolve some of those thorny letter-writing challenges

In any case, please use this book however you see fit. I wrote it for *you*.

Acknowledgments

The conventions of the publishing industry conspire to give the impression that one person alone writes a book. While there may be circumstances in which that's true, it's certainly not the case with this book. A number of people played roles in the conception and preparation of this book.

Stephen Hitchcock, as president of Mal Warwick & Associates, suggested I build a book around EditEXPRESS, a letter-editing service I offered from 1990 to 2000. This book has become far more than that. Nonetheless, Steve's imprint is visible on every page. His decade-old list of "reasons people give" was the starting point for my work on Chapter One. More important, Steve has been my writing mentor for more than a dozen years. Much of what he has taught me about writing for results is reflected in the following pages. He reviewed every chapter, page by page, painstakingly editing the most challenging parts. Also he has played a major role in freeing me from the burdens of the day-to-day management of Mal Warwick & Associates, so that I was able to undertake the time-consuming project of writing this book.

I'm indebted to the following EditEXPRESS clients for their gracious permission to reproduce here the work I performed for them:

- Co-op America, Washington, D.C. (Alisa Gravitz, Denise Hamler, Erin Gorman)
- Peace Action, Washington, D.C. (Peter Deccy, Monica Green, Carole Watson)

Three of my clients insisted on anonymity, so I've removed any evidence of their identity from the case studies and examples of my work for them.

With one exception, every letter included as an example in Chapters Ten through Sixteen was drafted by someone else. In many cases I don't know the identity of the author. I urge you to recognize that it was not I. Most of the time, my contribution was limited to playing the critic. (That's the easy part.)

The central theme of this book is that there are different types of fundraising letters and that each type presents unique challenges to the writer. To dramatize the unique aspects of each type of fundraising letter, I lead off the seven chapters in Part Two with illustrations from one nonprofit organization with an extensive and well-organized direct mail fundraising program. I wanted to make clear that a single charity may indeed need to write letters of all the types described in this book. To fill that bill, I turned to Bread for the World in Washington, D.C., a client of Mal Warwick & Associates since 1989. I owe special thanks to David Beckmann, Joel Underwood, Alice Benson, Diane Hunt, and their colleagues for their generosity and cooperativeness in granting permission for their materials to be reproduced in this book.

The lists in the resources in Part Four represent some of the best work of my colleagues at Mal Warwick & Associates. Significantly, ideas were suggested by staff involved in almost every phase of the creative and productive process: Stephen Hitchcock, Bill Rehm, Julie Levak, Deborah Agre, Judy Reimann, Marsha Mathews, Lissa Rosenbloom, Julie Weidenbach, Cherie Chavez, Christina Chavez, Sheila Bell, and Ramona Allen. Julie Levak and Deborah Agre won a free lunch at Berkeley's famed Chez Panisse Café for contributing more ideas to the lists than anyone else: seventy-one between the two. (You see? Writing fundraising letters *can* be fun!)

The freelance copywriting team of Deborah Block and Paul Karps generously took time out from a particularly busy season of their work on bread-and-butter fundraising projects to review the first draft of the manuscript. They paid particular attention to the case studies. Because of their sharp eyes and extensive knowledge of fundraising letters, they uncovered a great many inconsistencies. Their detailed critique helped me enormously in transforming a bunch of unrelated assignments performed over a three-year period into this book. I'm greatly indebted to them.

This book would not have seen the light of day without the help I received from Ina Cooper and Ramona Allen at Mal Warwick & Associates. Ina served as production coordinator, and Ramona faced almost daily assignments to scan or transcribe text and prepare seemingly endless rounds of photocopies. The hours they invested in this project may have equaled my own, and I'm very grateful to them.

Two other people have gone to great lengths to save me from my own excesses in preparing this revised edition. My editor, Johanna Vondeling, has been an unfaltering source of shrewd judgment about the structure and flow of this book. It is now much the stronger as a result of her efforts. Her fine editorial eye and sensitivity to style and syntax have made this job a great deal easier and more enjoyable for me.

My assistant at Mal Warwick & Associates, Kimberely Araña, cheerfully endured the deadly combination of my erratic schedule and the many, and often unpredictable, demands on her time that this project has occasioned. Her patience, thoroughness, and commonsense organizing skills helped keep me steady through this sometimes unsteadying process.

I owe special thanks, too, to the many readers of the first edition who encouraged me to think that this book was worth every bit of the time and effort I put into it. I hope you too will find this book to be helpful in your continuing effort to raise money for good causes and enduring institutions. I wish you the very best of luck.

Berkeley, California   Mal Warwick
December 2000

About the Author

MAL WARWICK is an internationally recognized consultant, author, and public speaker who has been involved in the not-for-profit sector for four decades. He has founded or cofounded four loosely affiliated companies that provide a wide range of fundraising and marketing services to clients throughout North America: Mal Warwick & Associates, a full-service direct mail fundraising firm; Share Group, one of the nation's leading telephone fundraising agencies; donordigital.com LLC, cofounded with Nick Allen to assist nonprofit organizations in using e-mail and the Internet for fundraising, marketing, and activism; and Response Management Technologies, which supplies data processing, donor file management, and laser-printing services to nonprofit organizations.

Warwick has written or edited ten books of interest to fundraisers, including *The Five Strategies for Fundraising Success* (Jossey-Bass, 2000) and the classic *Revolution in the Mailbox* (retitled and republished as *Raising Money by Mail*). He also edits *Mal Warwick's Newsletter: Successful Direct Mail, Telephone and Online Fundraising*.

Warwick's clients have included many of the nation's largest and most distinguished nonprofit organizations, as well as six Democratic presidential candidates. Together with his colleagues, he has raised more than $500 million during twenty-one years as a fundraiser.

Warwick served for ten years on the board of the Association of Direct Response Fundraising Counsel (the national trade association of direct mail fundraising agencies), including two years as its president. He is a member of the Direct Marketing Association Nonprofit Federation and the National Society of Fund Raising Executives and has spoken annually at the latter's conferences since the 1980s.

As a cofounder of Business for Social Responsibility, he served on its national board and executive committee in 1993, its first year. He cofounded a community foundation, the Berkeley Community Fund, in 1992, and has served on its board ever since. He also has been vice president of the Berkeley Symphony Orchestra since 1991.

Introduction
Why You Should Read This Book

I immodestly recommend that you read this book for a number of reasons:

- If you write fundraising letters for a hospital, a college or university, a museum, a health agency, a social service organization, a public interest advocacy group, or any other nonprofit that needs funds
- If you want to write letters that raise more money for your organization
- If you serve in a leadership role in a nonprofit organization as executive director, development director, or marketing director
- If you are a member of a nonprofit's board of directors and you want to measure the effectiveness of your fundraising appeals
- If you're involved in public relations, advertising, or marketing for a nonprofit organization or institution
- If you want to understand better how fundraising works
- If you want to learn how to write to get results
- If you want to be a more effective writer

If fundraising by mail is a science (a dubious proposition at best), its fuzziest, most inexact, least scientific aspect is writing the letters. There are those in the field who claim fundraising letters can be written by formula, but I'm not one of them. Writing this stuff is tough work, because what's effective for one organization may prove counterproductive for another. And what worked last year or last time may not work today.

The reality is that for most of us, writing of any sort is a royal pain in the neck. But there are ways to reduce the fuzziness and the pain and to raise the odds that your letters will bring in every nickel you need, and more. Talent helps, but experience counts for a lot too.

Over the years, I've read tens of thousands of fundraising appeals, written or edited thousands of those letters myself, and shared in the creative process as a manager or consultant in thousands of other mailings. All of this experience has given me a front-row seat in a never-ending "copy clinic"—a close-up view of what works and what doesn't (and sometimes even why). This book conveys what I've learned about writing fundraising letters.

In other books I've written, I've explored many of the elements of fundraising by mail—from choosing mailing lists to working with consultants, from measuring results to designing and producing packages, from strategizing to scheduling. This book isn't about any of those things. It's about *writing*. My topic here is the effective use of written English in the pursuit of charitable gifts.

Over my varied career, I've written newspaper stories, magazine articles, science fiction stories, and comic book scripts; ads for newspapers, magazines, radio, and television; sales letters, brochures, and pamphlets; technical manuals; speeches for others and speeches for myself—not to mention all those fundraising letters, plus eight other books about the craft of fundraising. I've written fiction and nonfiction, eulogies and humor, short pieces and long. I've written in three languages and translated from one to another.

Yet despite all this writing, I don't consider myself a particularly gifted writer. I'm no poet; my prose doesn't sing. I've written no unforgettable passage, contributed no timeless witticism to the language. But through long practice and difficult trial and error, I've learned to do one thing moderately well with my writing: *get results*. And there's just *one* result I want from this book: to help *you* write successful fundraising letters.

This book is a guide to the techniques and approaches that have proved successful for me—a tool chest of ideas and examples that will help you sharpen your own writing. If you prefer, look on it as a comprehensive review to help you gain perspective on the challenges you face as a writer of fundraising letters.

And there's one more result I hope to achieve with this book: I want you to enjoy reading it. I've found I do best what I enjoy the most—while those things I approach with deadly seriousness are least likely to turn out well. I suspect you too will find that the more fun you have when you write your fundraising letters, the more money you'll raise.

Why a Fundraising Letter Is Always More Than Just a Letter

Although the title of this book refers to fundraising letters, you'll see examples that aren't just letters. The reasons for this discrepancy are that most people refer to fundraising appeals as letters and the letter is almost always the most important component of an appeal. But the letter is never the only component of a fundraising package. Many other components of the package are important too. You'll need an envelope for your fundraising letter. And almost all the time you'll need at least two other items as well: a reply device (variously called a response device, coupon, card, form, or something else), plus an envelope to mail it back in. Without a reply device and an easy way to return it, most fundraising letters would generate precious few gifts.

Beginners at the craft of writing fundraising letters commonly treat these other components as afterthoughts. I hope after reading this book you won't do so. In fact, you may find you need to devote just as much thought to the reply device and the envelopes—both envelopes—as you do to the letter itself.

About the Letters Reproduced in This Book

Five of the seven case studies in Chapters Ten through Sixteen are drawn from the files of EditEXPRESS, a letter-editing service I offered from 1990 to 2000. To judge their value as illustrations, you need to understand how that service worked.

I operated EditEXPRESS as an editor of fundraising appeals, not as a writer of them. I took pains to make as few changes as possible in the letters I was sent to revise. My primary responsibility, as I saw it, was to increase the readability of the appeals. Although the writer or the fundraiser in me may have yearned to introduce new information—or even to take an entirely fresh approach—I usually contented myself by reshaping and rearranging the material I was given. (To get a sense of what I mean by this, take a look at the edited copy reproduced in Exhibit 1. That's the sort of thing I often do when I take on an editing job.) Most of the time, I'm told, that sort of copyediting has been good enough to achieve a significant improvement in results.

Why You Can Learn from the Case Studies— Even Though Your Organization Is Different

The causes and institutions represented in this book cover a wide range—from human services to the environment to lobbying against hunger. But what if your organization doesn't happen to fit into one of those categories? Or if it does fit, you're convinced it's really too different to benefit from the examples? In fact, you can learn a lot from fundraising letters written by other nonprofit organizations. There are three reasons I strongly believe this:

1. You can learn how the *fundamental rules of writing* apply (or don't apply) to the craft of writing fundraising letters. The fundamentals have nothing to do with your cause or your constituency.

2. By studying examples from other organizations, you can learn how the *special techniques of fundraising* and direct marketing can be put to work in fundraising letters. Those techniques change very little from one cause or constituency to another.

3. You can learn how to improve your fundraising letters if you *distance yourself* from the everyday needs and details of your organization's work. Often it's much easier to see the forest rather than the trees if you're looking into someone else's forest.

Take my word for that. I've been wandering around in other people's forests for a very long time.

In a sense, I worked on the first edition of this book for more than three years. In a larger sense, however, I started the project in 1979 when I founded my direct mail fundraising firm, Mal Warwick & Associates, or even in 1949, over half a century ago, when I wrote my first "fundraising" letter home from summer camp. I've put a lot into this book. I hope you get a lot out of it.

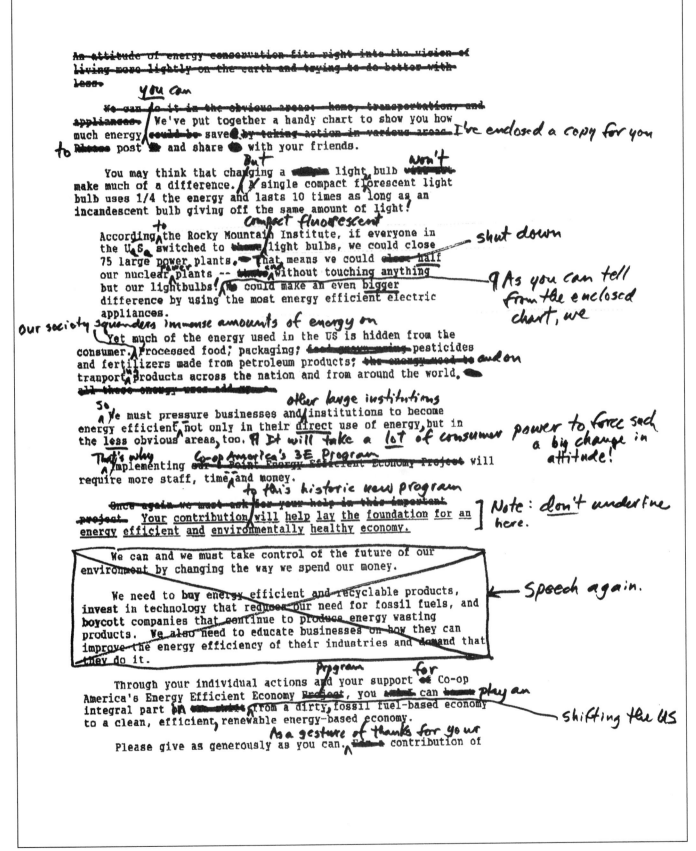

EXHIBIT 1 Editing Sample, One Page of Fundraising Letter.

Part I

Motivating Your Audience

These first five chapters examine the stuff of which successful fundraising is made:

- An appreciation for the broad range of motives that lead people to contribute money to good causes and important institutions
- An understanding of the dynamics in the relationship between the fundraiser and the donor
- Insight into the ways that donors view the fundraising letters they receive
- The characteristics of an effective fundraising letter

To put this understanding into a truly practical context, Part One concludes with a paragraph-by-paragraph tour through one successful appeal.

Why People Respond to Fundraising Letters

It's downright unnatural. Your fundraising letter must persuade the recipient to take an action that much of humanity thinks peculiar: to give money away.

To accomplish this seemingly unlikely objective, your appeal needs to be built on the psychology of giving. Forget your organization's needs. Instead, focus on the needs, the desires, and the concerns of the people you're writing to. Your job is to motivate them.

Commercial direct marketers frequently say that there are five "great motivators" that explain response: fear, exclusivity, guilt, greed, and anger. But I believe the truth is much more complex: that there are *at least* twenty-three reasons that people might respond to your fundraising letter. Any one of the twenty-three might suggest a theme or hook for your letter, and it's likely that several of these reasons help motivate each gift.

1. People send money because you ask them to.

Public opinion surveys and other research repeatedly confirm this most basic fact of donor motivation. "I was asked" is the most frequently cited reason for giving. Moreover, the research confirms that donors *want to be asked*. Focus group research also reveals that donors typically underestimate the number of appeals they receive from the organizations they support. These facts help explain why responsive donors are repeatedly asked for additional gifts in nearly every successful direct mail fundraising program. When you write an appeal, keep these realities in mind. Don't allow your reticence about asking for money make you sound apologetic in your letter.

2. People send money because they have money available to give away.

The overwhelming majority of individual gifts to nonprofit organizations and institutions are small contributions made from disposable (or discretionary) income. This is the money left over in the family checking account after the month's mortgage, taxes, insurance, credit cards, and grocery bills have been paid. Unless you're appealing for a major gift, a bequest, or a multiyear pledge, your target is this modest pool of available money.

For most families, dependent on a year-round stream of wage or salary income, the pool of disposable income is replenished every two weeks or every month. That's why most organizations appeal frequently and for small gifts. If your appeal is persuasive, your organization may join the ranks of that select group of charities that receive gifts from a donor's household in a given month. If you're less than persuasive or if competing charities have stronger arguments—or if the family just doesn't have money to spare that month—you won't get a gift.

For example, if you write me a letter seeking a charitable gift, you may succeed in tapping into the $100 or $200 I'll probably have "left over" for charity during the month your letter arrives. If your appeal is persuasive, I might send you $25 or $50—$100 tops—because I decide to add you to the short list of nonprofits I'll support that month.

Now you may have the mistaken impression that as a businessman, a snappy dresser, and an all-around generous fellow, I have a lot of money. You may even be aware I've occasionally made much larger gifts to local charities. But you're unlikely to receive more than $50 because that's all I have available *right now*. Those few larger gifts I gave didn't come from my disposable income stream. They came from other sources and required a lot of planning on my part.

3. People send money because they're in the habit of sending money by mail.

Charity is habit forming; giving by mail is a special variety of this benign affliction. When I became involved in direct mail fundraising in the late 1970s, I was told that only about one in four adult Americans were "mail responsive"—that is, susceptible to offers or appeals by mail. By the turn of the century, according to the Simmons Market Research Bureau, two out of every three adults were buying goods or services by mail or phone every year. Many purchases involved telemarketing—but there's no doubt Americans are now more mail responsive.

Surveys also reflect the growing importance of direct mail appeals in the fundraising process. Research shows that fundraising letters are the top source of new gifts to charity in America.

4. People send money because they support organizations like yours.

Your donors aren't yours alone, no matter what you think. Because they have special interests, hobbies, and distinctive beliefs, they may support several similar organizations. A dog owner, for example, may contribute to half a dozen organizations that have some connection to dogs: a humane society, an animal rights group, an organization that trains seeing-eye dogs, a wildlife protection group. A person who sees himself as an environmentalist might be found on the membership rolls of five or six ecology-related groups: one dedicated to land conservation, another to protecting the wilderness, a third to saving endangered species or the rain forest, and so on. There are patterns in people's lives. Your appeal is most likely to bear fruit if it fits squarely into one of those patterns.

5. People send money because their gifts will make a difference.

Donors want to be convinced that their investment in your enterprise— their charitable gifts—will achieve some worthy aim. That's why so many donors express concern about high fundraising and administrative costs. It's also why successful appeals for funds often quantify the impact of a gift: $35 to buy a school uniform, $40 for a stethoscope, $7 to feed a child for a day. Donors want to feel good about their gifts.

Your donors are striving to be effective human beings. You help them by demonstrating just how effective they really are.

6. People send money because gifts will accomplish something right now.

Urgency is a necessary element in a fundraising letter. Implicitly or explicitly, every successful appeal has a deadline: the end of the year, the opening of the school, the deadline for the matching grant, the limited press run on the book available as a premium. But the strong attraction in circumstances such as these is best illustrated if no such urgent conditions apply. If the money I send you this week won't make a difference right away, shouldn't I send money to some other charity that has asked for my support and urgently needs it?

7. People send money because you recognize them for their gifts.

You appeal to donors' egos—or to their desire to heighten their public image—when you offer to recognize their gifts in an open and tangible way: a listing in your newsletter; a plaque, certificate, lapel pin, or house sign; screen credit in a video production; a press release. If your fundraising program can provide appropriate and tasteful recognition, you're likely to boost response to your appeals by highlighting the opportunities for recognition in your letter or newsletter. Even if donors choose not to be listed in print or mentioned in public, they may be gratified to learn that you value their contributions enough to make the offer.

8. People send money because you give them something tangible in return.

Premiums come in all sizes, shapes, and flavors: bumper strips, gold tie tacks, coffee-table books, membership cards, even (in one case I know) a pint of ice cream.

Sometimes premiums (such as name stickers or bookmarks) are enclosed with the appeal; these so-called front-end premiums boost response more often than not and are frequently cost-effective, at least in the short run. In other cases back-end premiums are promised in an appeal "as a token of our deep appreciation" when donors respond by sending gifts of at least a certain amount. Either way, premiums appeal to the innate acquisitiveness that persists in the human race.

9. People send money because you enable them to "do something" about a critical problem, if only to protest or take a stand.

Today we are bombarded by information about the world's problems through a wide variety of channels. Although we may isolate ourselves inside triple-locked homes, build walls around suburbs, and post guards at gateposts, we can't escape from knowing about misery, injustice, and wasted human potential. Often we feel powerless in the face of this grim reality. Charity offers us a way to respond—by helping to heal the sick or balm troubled souls, teach new ways to a new generation, or feed the hungry. Your appeal will trigger a gift if it brings to life the feelings that move us to act, even knowing that action is never enough.

If you offer hope in a world drowning in troubles, your donors will seize it like the life jacket it really is.

10. People send money because you give them a chance to associate with a famous or worthy person.

There are numerous ways that the identity, personality, or achievements of an individual might be highlighted in a fundraising appeal. For example, that person may be the signer of the letter, the organization's founder or executive director, the honorary chair of a fundraising drive, a patron saint, a political candidate, an honoree at a special event—or simply one of the organization's members or clients. If the signer's character or accomplishments evoke admiration or even simply a past personal connection, your donors may be moved to send gifts in response. The opportunity to associate with someone who is well known or highly esteemed may offer donors a way to affirm their noblest inclinations—or compensate for what they believe to be their shortcomings.

11. People send money because you allow them to get back at the corrupt or the unjust.

There are too few outlets for the anger and frustration we feel on witnessing injustice and corruption in society. Both our moral sense and the secular law hold most of us in check, preventing expressions of violence or vocal fury that might allow us to let off steam. For many, contributing to nonprofit causes or institutions is a socially acceptable way to strike back. Whether your organization is a public interest group committed to fighting corruption in government or a religious charity devoted to revealing divine justice, it may help donors channel their most sordid feelings into a demonstration of their best instincts.

12. People send money because you give them the opportunity to "belong"—as a member, friend, or supporter—and thus you help them fight loneliness.

Your most fundamental task as a fundraiser is to build relationships with your donors. That's why so many organizations use membership programs, giving clubs, and monthly gift societies. The process of solicitation itself can help build healthy relationships. Shut-ins, for example, or elderly people with distant family and few friends, may eagerly anticipate the letters you send. Most of us are social animals, forever seeking companionship.

13. People send money because you enable them to offer their opinions.

The act of sending a gift to some nonprofit organizations might itself constitute a way to speak out. Consider, for example, the American Civil Liberties Union, or the Campus Crusade for Christ, or the Million Mom March; support for these groups makes an obvious statement about a donor's views. But almost any charity can offer donors an opportunity to state an opinion by including in an appeal an involvement device such as a membership survey, a petition, or a greeting card that might later be sent to a friend or family member. Although most donors may ignore the chance to offer suggestions, they may regard the invitation to do so as a strong sign of your respect and concern for them.

14. People send money because you provide them with access to inside information.

Even if your organization or agency isn't an institution of higher education or a research foundation, you still hold knowledge many donors crave. Nonprofit organizations are often on the front lines of everyday, hands-on research, gathering important data day after day from clients, visitors, or program participants. Their staff members are likely to be specialists, and often experts, in their fields.

Nevertheless, every nonprofit possesses information that is not widely known to the public and that donors may perceive as valuable. A loyal supporter may be vitally interested in the health and well-being of your executive director (who was ill lately), the progress of a project you launched last year (after a spectacular start), or what your field staff learned last month (three months after the hurricane).

Disseminating inside information, which is intrinsically valuable and thus constitutes a gift from you, also helps build strong fundraising relationships by involving your donors in the intimate details of your organization.

15. People send money because you help them learn about a complex and interesting problem or issue.

In most advanced industrial nations, education, health care, and the arts are regarded as largely government's responsibility to provide. By contrast, the traditional American response has been to meet important needs such as these principally through private, voluntary action. Nonprofit organizations in the United States tackle issues or problems that society otherwise ignores or undervalues. Don't think just of the private schools and colleges, nonprofit hospitals, museums, and symphony orchestras. Think about Mothers Against Drunk Driving, Disabled American Veterans, Planned Parenthood, the Nature Conservancy, and the hundreds of thousands of other organizations like them that are far less well known. Often these organizations are on the front lines of research or public debate on the most challenging, the most controversial, the most engaging issues. If that's true of your organization, the emphasis you place in your appeal on your special knowledge may help motivate donors to give.

Your donors may even perceive the appeal itself as a benefit. As research frequently reveals, donors regard the letters they receive from charities as a source of special knowledge. I believe that helps explain why long letters containing hard facts and intriguing ideas often outpull more emotional appeals.

16. People send money because you help them preserve their worldview by validating cherished values and beliefs.

The very act of giving affirms a donor's dedication to a charity's worthy aims. Donors support your organization's work because you act on their behalf, pursuing your mission with time and effort they could never bring to bear themselves. In this passionate pursuit, you act out their values and beliefs—the deep-seated convictions that lead them to join in your mission. But you must constantly remind them of the connection.

If your organization's mission is congruent with widely shared values and beliefs—a commitment to piety, for example, or saving dolphins, or promoting efficiency in government—you face an obvious marketing opportunity. But if your nonprofit is dedicated to an unpopular cause, you possess a similar (if unenviable) advantage: for that small number of donors willing to take a stand on an issue that others reject, the values and beliefs that make the act of giving a form of personal affirmation suggest to the fundraiser a language both may speak.

17. People send money because you allow them to gain personal connections with other individuals who are passionately involved in some meaningful dimension of life.

A charity is an intentional community of sorts—a cooperative venture, an institutional expression of a shared creed or common hopes. Your job as a fundraiser is to strengthen the bonds that tie your community together. Your greatest asset may be a person within your community whom donors may regard as an inspiring example: a selfless, dedicated staff member; a passionately committed trustee; a model client or beloved beneficiary of your work. If you bring such a person to life through your fundraising appeals, you enable your donors to live vicariously through him or her—and that can be a meaningful and rewarding experience for them, as well as profitable for your organization.

18. People send money because you give them the chance to release emotional tension caused by a life-threatening situation, a critical emergency, or an ethical dilemma.

The charitable impulse is often precipitated by special circumstances that cause pain, fear, or even embarrassment. Consider the enduring popularity of memorial gifts to commemorate the passing of friends or loved ones or the spontaneous outpouring of gifts to aid crime victims or the families of kidnapped children. People want to help relieve pain and suffering, if only because they share these feelings. And they want to respond to grave emergencies, if only because they fear death. Your appeal for funds may afford them an opportunity to ease their affliction.

19. People send money because they are afraid.

Fear motivates. The American public has been subjected to billions of fundraising letters expressly conceived to evoke fear. Fear of death. Fear of poor people or foreigners. Fear of social security benefit cuts. Fear of higher taxes. Fear of Democrats or Republicans, liberals or reactionaries. No Pollyannish view of human motivation can erase the evidence that vast sums of money have been raised by such appeals. Fear sells. Yet I believe with all my heart that it's often unseemly, at times ethically questionable—and ultimately counterproductive—to use this obvious stratagem.

Consider the would-be prophet who predicts Armageddon next year. Who will heed the prophet when next year has come and gone, and the world is still in one piece? A fundraiser who builds the case for giving on the worst-case scenario may be building on quicksand.

20. People send money because you allow them to relieve their guilt about an ethical, political, or personal transgression, whether real or imagined.

Guilt undeniably plays a role in prompting some gifts. Think of the $1 or $2 cash contribution mailed in response to direct mail packages containing name stickers or greeting cards, the belated membership renewals that follow a long series of increasingly insistent demands, or the millions of small gifts sent every year in response to photographs of skeletal children. Our complex society allows few of us the luxury of acting out of purely ethical motives. Compromise is woven through the fabric of our daily lives. The fact is that none of us is likely to feel guilt free at any time. Sometimes giving to charity, like coins thrown into the poor box in an earlier era, will help release the pressure.

Yet I believe guilt is highly overrated as a motivator; rarely will donors who are moved primarily by guilt prove loyal over the years, and larger gifts from them are relatively rare. As a fundraising strategy, guilt may be just as counterproductive in the long run as fear.

21. People send money because you give them tax benefits.

No list of motivating factors for charitable giving is complete without at least passing reference to tax benefits. Without question, the charitable tax deduction has played a major role in stimulating many large gifts and planned gifts because the benefits to the donor are substantial. (This is particularly true of gifts of artwork or other forms of appreciated property to such institutions as museums, because the tax laws are specifically structured to encourage such gifts.) However, many small donors also mistakenly believe they gain a great advantage from the tax deductibility of their gifts. That's why it's always advisable when requesting a gift to inform the donor that it may be deductible: it may not help, but it can't hurt.

Still, it's dangerous to construct an appeal exclusively on the basis of tax benefits, even an appeal to buy into a tax-reduction program such as a charitable remainder trust. Experts in planned giving advise that "donative intent"—the desire to help, to do good, to make a difference—is usually of far greater importance than any financial considerations.

And there are lots of tax-reduction schemes available to well-to-do people from institutions with no charitable purpose whatsoever.

22. People send money because they feel it's their duty.

Many of our religious traditions teach us that it's wrong to live life without observing our duty to others: to relieve their pain, enlarge their opportunities, or brighten their lives. There is also a secular belief, widely shared in the United States, that as citizens in a democracy, we have an obligation to help make things better for our fellow citizens. Those who benefit from military training may acquire a heightened sense of duty.

Not every nonprofit organization can appeal explicitly to donors' sense of duty (though many charities can do so). But duty may nonetheless play a role in inspiring the gifts they receive, for duty by its very nature is self-activating.

23. People send money because they believe it's a blessing to do so.

The Christian belief that "it is more blessed to give than to receive" is deeply ingrained in Western civilization and far from limited to practicing Christians. In the Jewish concept of *mitzvah,* for example, many Americans find justification for believing that doing good is its own reward. Clearly—at least in our idealized vision of ourselves—we Americans celebrate the notion of charity. Our self-image as "nice people" derives in no small part from our generous response to charitable appeals.

Now that we've got a handle on nearly two dozen of the reasons donors might respond to that fundraising letter you're writing, let's take a look at the dynamics at work when they find your letter in their mailbox.

2

How a Fundraising Letter Is Like a Personal Visit

Most of us who write letters to raise funds—or to sell products or services, for that matter—have a one-word answer to the question "How do you know whether that will work?" *Test.*

A German professor of direct marketing named Siegfried Vögele has *two* answers. He's just as firmly committed as any of us to the rigors of head-to-head testing to determine which of two or more variations in copy, design, or content will secure the best response. But Vögele can also cite chapter and verse from a realm of research that uses such devices as eye-motion cameras and machines that measure subtle changes in skin chemistry. This research, conducted over many years, has given him profound and detailed knowledge of the ways human beings react when they hold direct mail materials in their hands.

Many of us guess about these things; we have insights or hunches. Siegfried Vögele often *knows*.

Vögele has been practicing and teaching his craft in Germany since the 1970s. In 1980, he caused a sensation at the all-European direct marketing conference and has taught his Dialogue Method throughout Europe ever since. (Vögele asserts that a direct mail letter works when it successfully involves readers in a silent dialogue with the signer.) Thousands of marketers have attended his seminars, and articles based on his

like having a conversation w/ reader even though not physically there

eye-motion research have made their way to America. His *Handbook of Direct Mail,* published in German in 1984, has been translated into Italian, French, and English. In other words, the story's getting out. (Resource H provides details about his book.)

This chapter sets out the essence of Vögele's Dialogue Method as it applies to writing direct mail letters—and I'll carry the translation one step further into the realm of fundraising.

What Happens in a Personal Fundraising Visit

The doorbell rings. You trudge to the front door, switch on the porch light, and squint through the peephole.

Standing at your door is a young woman, nineteen or maybe twenty years old, scruffily dressed, a clipboard tightly gripped in one hand, and an eager smile pasted on her face. You may be thinking, "Is this another of those annoying canvassers? Do I have to write another check for twenty or twenty-five bucks to get her to leave? What group does she represent, and why are they bothering me? Am I *really* going to let this little pest inside my home?"

Nevertheless, you open the door, greet the young woman, and listen to her long enough to hear that she is representing a charity called [fill-in-the-blank]. Not only that, but something she says about how what [fill-in-the-blank] is doing relates to things you care about. Besides, she's a beguiling young person who appears to have a bright future. You sigh, open the door a little wider, and (still reluctant) let her into the house.

Now, perched on the edge of your living room couch, the young canvasser launches into her pitch for [fill-in-the-blank]. You're not listening closely, but you get the gist of it. Every so often you nod, smile, or gesture. Encouraged, she plunges ahead, keeping her eyes on you all the while she speaks, emphasizing this or that or the other thing as you demonstrate more interest (or less) by the way you nod your head, fold or uncross your arms, or even occasionally ask a question or venture a comment. There are lots of questions on your mind, but you pose few of them, not wanting to drag out this unwanted conversation. And although you don't understand or agree with everything the fundraiser says, when you frown, shrug, or lift your eyebrows in a questioning way, she slips in a quick answer or makes a reassuring statement, then quickly rushes on to the next point. All this goes on for a few minutes until the fundraiser says something that really catches your attention.

Fully engaged for the moment, you make a casual reference to an experience related to what she has just said and—just to be polite—you ask her a pointed question. With a rush, she launches into a detailed answer. It's interesting for a few seconds, but then your eyes start glazing over. Noticing your disengagement, the young woman makes some comment about the lateness of the hour and immediately makes her pitch: "So, can I count on you for a gift of $50 tonight to help [fill-in-the-blank]?"

Fifty dollars is far too much, so you demur, settling for $25 instead. (Truth to tell, you're just as interested in getting her to leave you alone as you are in helping [fill-in-the-blank].) The canvasser gratefully volunteers to wait while you retrieve your checkbook. She accepts your gift with effusive thanks and departs, leaving behind a thin sheaf of papers with the latest developments at [fill-in-the-blank] and a promise that soon you'll be hearing from them again so you'll know how your gift has been used.

Now, what has just happened here?

1. The canvasser got your attention by ringing your doorbell. You weren't expecting her, and as far as you're concerned, the evening would've been just as pleasant, if not more so, if she'd never shown up.

2. The moment you set eyes on her, barely conscious questions started welling up in your head in quick order: you wondered who she was, and why she'd come, and what she wanted you to do—and you answered most of those questions for yourself as quickly as they popped into your mind, because the answers were obvious.

3. The young woman was representing an organization that's working on an issue you care a lot about. If she'd asked your help for some other cause or to address some other issue, you might just as well have smiled as politely as you were able and wished her better luck with the neighbors.

4. Her manner or her appearance—combined with something about your own mood and circumstances—induced you to let

her into your home. You weren't planning to do so; it just happened. And you invited her in even though you knew perfectly well she was going to ask you for money.

5. Once inside, the young woman delivered her pitch, watching your body language all the while and answering every question you raised as responsively as she could, some more fully than others.

6. Something she said triggered a strong reaction in you—enough to provoke a comment of your own and a substantive question. Right away the fundraiser gave you all the details you asked for, and more.

7. As soon as she sensed your patience waning, she moved quickly to ask for a gift. She knew perfectly well you support the work of [fill-in-the-blank]: her challenge was to make you admit it.

8. You declined to contribute the full amount she requested but did agree to give something. Since you had taken up so much of her time, it seemed the least you could do. Anyway, [fill-in-the-blank] does such valuable work!

9. The canvasser didn't just take your money and run. She thanked you for your support, reassured you it will make a big difference, and promised you'll hear again soon from [fill-in-the-blank].

In short, you started the evening with absolutely no intention of giving a cent to [fill-in-the-blank]—or any other group for that matter, let alone a check for $25. You've done so anyway, and you feel pretty good about it!

Now let's consider a similar scene—one in which the appeal for funds comes by mail rather than in person. By comparing these two experiences we'll gain important insight into Vögele's Dialogue Method.

How People Decide Whether to Open Fundraising Letters

You've just gotten home from a tough day at the office. You toss the mail into a heap on the coffee table, grab something to drink from the refrigerator, and collapse into the easy chair, flicking on the TV with the remote control in one hand and pulling the wastebasket close to your chair with the other. Now, one or two deep breaths later, barely paying attention in the flickering glow of the television screen, you retrieve a handful of mail and begin the daily ritual.

Plunk! Into the wastebasket goes the fourth duplicate copy of the Spiegel catalogue. *Plunk!* Again, in one smooth, unhesitating motion: another credit card offer. And again and again: that health charity that reminds you of things you want to forget, a packet of discount coupons from a store you wouldn't visit if your life depended on it, a promise of untold wealth from Publishers Clearing House, a picture of pathetic little children. Now you come to the gas and electric bill—and something else that may be worth a glance: an envelope from [fill-in-the-blank], the people who do all that good stuff about whatchamacallit. At least they spelled your name right (unlike the catalogue merchant and the senders of some of the other pieces of mail). You know who it's from because the organization's name and address are right there in the upper left-hand corner, and, besides, there's a photo on the envelope that looks a lot like whatchamacallit. Anyway, it looks familiar.

Chances are that this is another fundraising appeal from [fill-in-the-blank]—but you never know for sure until you look inside. Maybe the group has something interesting to say, even if it is a solicitation.

Before you know it, you've turned over the envelope from [fill-in-the-blank], slit it open, and dumped the contents out onto your lap. *Now* there's no question what these people want from you: the self-addressed envelope with those telltale broad stripes and the reply card with a hefty check mark and a big bold "YES!" above a string of dollar amounts leave no doubt whatsoever this is a fundraising solicitation. But [fill-in-the-blank] is a fascinating group, and a photo and caption on the reply card give the impression this letter is definitely about whatchamacallit, so it's probably worth looking a little further.

Now let's take stock before we stumble deeper into the jungle of real-world fundraising. What's happening here, and how does it compare to the experience you've just had with that aggressive young canvasser?

1. You weren't expecting a fundraising letter from [fill-in-the-blank] any more than you were anticipating the young woman's visit to your home.
2. When you first glanced at [fill-in-the-blank]'s appeal, you weren't paying much attention at all—even less attention, no

doubt, than you paid that canvasser. (After all, she was standing right there.) Vögele estimates we devote no more than 10 percent of our attention to reading unsolicited mail.

3. Despite your lack of attentiveness, you noticed one thing without fail: the group spelled your name correctly. That young woman didn't know your name, but she looked you in the eye, accomplishing much the same end.

4. Something else about the letter caught your attention, triggering curiosity or concern—enough to motivate you to open the envelope and pull out the contents. What did the trick? The [fill-in-the-blank] name? That photo of whatchamacallit? It's hard to know (but ultimately doesn't matter) exactly what made the difference, just as your decision to open your front door to that canvasser was impulsive and difficult to analyze.

5. As you opened the envelope and dribbled the contents onto your lap, a stream of questions started flitting nearly unnoticed through the depths of your consciousness, much like those that came to mind as the fundraiser delivered her pitch in your living room. These questions included the obvious ones ("What's this about? What do they want from me? What's it going to cost me?"), and many of them were answered at a glance as you observed the contents of [fill-in-the-name]'s appeal. These casual little traces of wonderment or confusion are what Siegfried Vögele calls "unspoken readers' questions." As many as twenty such questions pop into the average reader's mind on picking up a direct mail solicitation.

But all this slips by with amazing speed. So far the whole incident—from your first glimpse of the [fill-in-the-blank] solicitation to your dumping the contents onto your lap—has taken a maximum of five to eight seconds.

To get a better sense of just how quickly five seconds flit by, follow the second hand on your watch, or count backward slowly by thousands. Those five *long* seconds spell the difference between the success or failure of a fundraising appeal. Tonight, for [fill-in-the-blank], they've been enough for a very good start.

Now, let's pick up the trail of our story again.

How a Fundraising Letter Is Like a Face-to-Face Dialogue

Taking a sip of your drink, then turning up the volume on the television set, you now fish out [fill-in-the-blank]'s letter from the jumble on your lap. Dangling it before you between thumb and forefinger, you glance at the front page. Briefly you take in a dramatic little photo in the upper right-hand corner and note that the letter contains short paragraphs, subheads, and underlining. Then you quickly flip the letter over to the back page to see who's writing to you.

Your eyes temporarily fix on the signature and the typed name below it, then drop down onto the postscript; it's only three lines long, so you read it through. Sure enough, [fill-in-the-blank] is hoping you'll send money to do something new about whatchamacallit. A whole new round of questions rushes to the surface—questions such as, "How are they going to pull that off again? Will my twenty-five bucks make a difference? Are they going to send me something if I mail them a gift?" So now you scan the subheads and underlined words in the letter at a rapid rate, *first on the last page*, then, very briefly, on the two interior pages, and finally on the first page again.

Now you begin reading the letter's opening sentence. It's the beginning of a story, and before you know it you're hooked. You read first one longish paragraph, then another—but that's enough. You're satisfied. [Fill-in-the-blank] is doing exactly what you'd hoped, and you're just as eager to be part of the act this year as you were before. Out of long-ingrained habit, you grab the reply card and scan it to be sure you didn't misunderstand what [fill-in-the-blank] expected of you. Satisfied there was no miscommunication, you add the reply card to [fill-in-the-blank]'s postage-paid return envelope and drop them on top of the gas and electric bill: both will go into the "bills to pay" file. You'll write both checks next Saturday—or so, at any rate, that's what you say to yourself.

Let's pause here to take stock again, reviewing what's taken place from the perspective of Siegfried Vögele.

1. You were still largely inattentive—after all, you had a drink in one hand and a TV set blaring—but something about the letter from [fill-in-the-blank] persuaded you to turn it over for a second look

rather than toss it into the wastebasket along with the day's direct mail losers. Was it that photo on the first page? The way those short paragraphs, subheads, and underlining suggested the letter would be quick and easy to read? No doubt both factors helped.

2. Take a careful note: your eyes may have skipped through quite a number of words in scanning the first page of the letter, but you didn't actually read anything. The first words you read were the signature; the first element of text, the postscript. In other words, *the P.S. was the lead of this letter.* Siegfried Vögele says his eye-motion research reveals that the postscript is the first text read by more than 90 percent of all direct mail recipients.

3. But what was it you saw on the final page of the letter that motivated you, first to read the P.S. and then to scan the subheads and underlining? Was it the easy-to-read format and accessible language—or was there something genuinely involving in what you read? Was [fill-in-the-blank] making it worth your while to read on—by answering *your* unspoken questions with carefully crafted subheads, addressing *your* concerns through judicious underlining, spelling out the advantages *you* would receive by supporting their work? Vögele says yes: that only by answering *your* silent questions through such devices as these will a solicitation be involving enough to induce you to read on. If the letter doesn't answer those questions in the most obvious and accessible way, it's unlikely to be read at all.

4. Notice that the first time you read a complete block of copy was when you took in the P.S. The second time was after you read the opening sentence of the letter and learned it was interesting enough to engage you; then you read one or two complete paragraphs—and *that* was the point where you were finally hooked. In Vögele's way of looking at these things, there are two stages in a reader's involvement in a direct mail letter. As soon as you read one full block of text from beginning to end, you passed from the first stage to the second and final stage. At that precise moment, you began to participate in the "comprehensive second dialogue." Here's how Vögele describes the process: "We answer unspoken readers' questions in a simple, easily understood way, first through a short 'dialogue' which makes the reader aware of the benefit to himself, then through a [second and] more

detailed 'dialogue' built along the same lines as a real personal sales conversation."

5. But what was it that caused you to glide so smoothly from the "short dialogue" to the "comprehensive second dialogue"? Vögele would say many factors contributed—everything in the content, language, and format that made the letter easy to read, accessible, informative, and directly responsive to *your* concerns. All are examples of the response boosters he calls "amplifiers": little signs and gestures of positive reinforcement that help the reader spot encouraging answers to his unspoken questions.

In Vögele's lexicon, "filters" are the polar opposite of amplifiers. They're the negative forces that come into play in a direct mail package: the elements of formatting or contents that make the package hard to read, uninteresting, off-putting.

Amplifiers provide you with little yesses to answer those unspoken questions. Filters produce no's.

The canvasser used her own arsenal of amplifiers by speaking intelligently (but not over your head), answering your questions (whether vocalized or not), watching and responding to your body language, and shutting up quickly when your patience flagged.

She skillfully moved you to answer yes to your own unvocalized questions—again and again and again. She avoided all the little traps (or filters)—the distractions, the boring lists of facts, the self-centered emphasis on [fill-on-the-blank]'s needs. Instinctively she knew those missteps were a surefire way to lead you to answer your own unspoken questions with no—over and over again. Whoever wrote that letter for [fill-in-the-blank] did much the same thing, guiding you to answer yes far more often than you answered no.

As Vögele sees it, getting to that big YES!—a check mark on the reply form, along with a check—is merely a matter of helping the reader answer yes a lot more frequently than he answers no.

But something else was going on here, too, something much more basic: *both fundraisers—the letter writer no less than the canvasser—took pains to engage you in a dialogue.* They answered *your* questions (spoken or not). They both went out of their way to involve you in a conversation— silent and one-sided in the case of the letter but nonetheless involving.

Neither the young woman nor the writer of the letter was engaged in a monologue, preoccupied with [fill-in-the-blank]'s needs and problems. Both made the effort to *relate the organization's needs to you*—the listener or the reader—in a style, language, and presentation format that subtly moved you to adopt [fill-in-the-blank]'s needs as your own.

Answering Your Reader's Questions Before They're Even Asked

The trick to this craft, Siegfried Vögele tells us, is to anticipate the questions that will be on the reader's mind and answer those questions clearly and forcefully. He admonishes us to pay extra special attention to those questions that highlight the advantages the reader will enjoy (what we call *benefits*). Your answers must find their way into photos or drawings (and accompanying captions) or into subheads or underlined phrases or words—because those are the items in your letter that the reader will notice before actually reading what you've written.

Much of the skill that a letter writer brings to the task, then, is to catalogue the questions readers are sure to ask and artfully weave the answers into the letter. Vögele says there are two types: basic questions—those that involuntarily leap to mind when someone picks up any fundraising letter—and product questions—those that relate specifically to your appeal and might not come to mind if your reader were instead examining an appeal from some other charity. Although Vögele's terminology is derived from the experience of commercial direct marketing, both categories of readers' unspoken questions have their equivalents in the realm of fundraising.

Here are some of the basic questions that donors or prospective donors might ask themselves when they pick up one of your fundraising letters:

- Where did this letter come from?
- What's inside the envelope?
- Who wrote this letter?
- Who signed this letter?
- Where did they get my address?
- What do they know about me?

- Why are they writing to me specifically?
- How much money do they want from me?
- Should I even bother to read this letter?
- Can they prove what they say?
- What happens after I respond?
- Do I have to sign anything?
- Do I have to put a stamp on it?
- What would my spouse think about this?
- What would my friends think?
- Can this wait?
- What would happen if I don't do anything?
- Can I throw this thing away?
- Have I received this before?
- Will they put my name on another mailing list?
- What's the catch?

Now consider some of the many product questions that might leap into your reader's mind at the first sight of your fundraising letter:

- Have I heard of this organization before?
- Have I given to these people before?
- Do they get any government funds?
- Do they really need my help?
- What difference will it make if I respond?
- Are they going to send me a newsletter?
- Will I get lots of other solicitations from these people?
- Will they expect me to give them money every year?
- How much of this gift will actually be used the way they say?
- How is this different from what other groups do?
- Are they going to send me a thank-you?
- Have they been doing this kind of work for very long?
- Is there a local branch of this organization?
- How do I know they're honest?
- Who runs this organization?
- Is there anybody famous who supports them?
- Is there a deadline?
- What do I have to do to fill out the reply card?
- Is there a better solution for this problem?

These questions are actually quite straightforward. Questions of both types are a natural human response to any unsolicited appeal, whether it comes by mail or in person. In a face-to-face visit, the fundraiser intentionally confronts the most promising of these questions and tries to provoke yet more questions, knowing that engaging a prospect in dialogue is the straightest path to a gift. In a written fundraising appeal, too, the skillful writer seeks to anticipate these readers' unspoken questions, knowing that the more directly readers' true private concerns are met, the more involved they'll become in silent dialogue.

The Four Waves of Rejection

If the writer doesn't properly anticipate and answer the reader's unspoken questions, instead of a preponderance of little yes's that add up to one big beautiful YES! the no's have it, Vögele says—and *plunk!* goes that letter. Rejection can come at any moment, he warns us. There are four possible stages in which the reader might give up on you.

Wave One

You've got up to twenty seconds to engage the reader—just long enough for her to open the envelope, examine the contents, and decide whether to spend any more time with your letter. Vögele refers to this as the "first run-through." In this stage, you face your first and biggest hurdle; if your letter survives this test, the greatest danger is past. If, instead, the reader concludes, "I've never heard of these people before," or "I already sent them money this year," or simply "I'm not interested"—or any one of a thousand other possible excuses not to proceed—your appeal may well end up in the wastebasket. Most do. Even letters to your most loyal and generous donors may suffer this ignoble fate: few people have the time or the inclination to read everything they receive in the mail.

Wave Two

If your appeal survives the first wave of possible rejection, your chances of securing a gift are greatly improved, but you don't have a lock on a gift. All that's happened, from Vögele's perspective, is that your reader has found satisfactory answers to the first round of silent questions. Now, reading more thoroughly, the reader looks for answers to a whole new round of questions. Previously the reader has looked only at the pictures, read the subheads, and cruised through the underlined text. Now comes the true test: what you've written (or failed to include) in the blocks of text. What the reader encounters here must respond to questions and spell out the benefits she will receive as a result of giving a gift. If the blocks of text in your letter don't speak to the reader and if your text fails to provoke a preponderance of little yesses, chances are your appeal will make its way into the trash in this second throw-away wave.

Wave Three

Even if your letter survives the second wave of rejection, there's yet more potential trouble in store for you—for starters, the "filing-away or archive wave." If your letter succumbs to the near-universal human fondness to put off until later what could just as easily be done right now, it won't find its way into the trash—at least not immediately. But, Vögele points out, time acts as a filter: the reader who was impressed enough with your appeal to put it away for later reference may no longer remember why she was so moved after a week or a month has gone by. The effect achieved is little better than a big fat NO! Rarely will archived appeals result in donations.

Wave Four

Vögele distinguishes between the phenomenon of "archiving" (or filing away) and what he terms "putting to one side." The difference lies in the reader's intentions: in putting aside your appeal, the reader has resolved to do something but can't quite decide what that will be. This may happen because you've presented her with a decision to make, a question to answer, a form to fill out, a comment or greeting to write—or because she simply doesn't have enough money in her checking account at the moment. Vögele estimates that 50 percent of the solicitations that are "put to one side" will ultimately get lost. He explains: "One day, they may well end up in the wastebasket too, even if the advantage offered in them was once recognized. In the meantime, a long period of time has elapsed. New pictures and information have taken precedence."

The Solution

Here's the key: the faster you get your reader to respond, the more likely she will. That puts an enormous burden on the first twenty seconds of your letter's exposure to the reader's indifference. So let's conclude by going back to the beginning of this process: the first twenty seconds.

A Closer Look at the First Twenty Seconds in Your Letter's Public Life

Vögele divides the crucial first twenty seconds into three phases:

Phase One, before the envelope is opened—eight seconds on average. During this time, recipients turn over the envelope, note how it's addressed, read the return address and any text, look for a way to open the envelope, and finally tear it open.

Phase Two, lasting approximately four seconds. The reader picks up and examines the contents. Even before she has read a single word, the materials have immediate impact on her. She unfolds them, forming a general impression of what they contain.

Phase Three, another eight seconds. In what Vögele refers to as the first run-through, the reader examines the pictures and headlines, finding short answers to her silent questions. If the writer has done a good job, the reader is now fully engaged in the short dialogue.

Remember that the writer's objective is to involve the reader by persuading her to *read* some of the blocks of text in the letter—to become involved in the comprehensive second dialogue. "This means you need to get your reader's interest long before the twenty seconds are up," Vögele warns. The recipient will continue reading only if the benefits *to her* are obvious within the first few seconds. And that's why he insists a letter needs to "express the advantages to the reader by using pictures and headlines" and underlined words and phrases.

Now let's take a break from the quantifiable certainties of German research and venture into the realm of qualitative research—by taking a close look at what donors really think about fundraising letters.

What Donors Really Think About Fundraising Letters

Some years ago, as I was writing the first edition of this book, I took time out to observe a focus group in Los Angeles. For two hours I cringed behind a two-way mirror while ten people sat around a table, picking apart a direct mail fundraising letter for Camp Fire Boys and Girls. I was present because the leadership of Camp Fire had retained my firm to help launch a nationwide direct mail fundraising program.

The letter those people were salvaging was one I'd edited less than a week before. I'd thought the letter was pretty good to begin with, but I was convinced my brilliant editing had lifted it into the ranks of the fundraising hall of fame. Indeed, one of my senior associates went out of his way to congratulate me on my fine work, and for the first time ever, Camp Fire staff approved the text without changing a single word. They *loved* the letter. Nevertheless, Camp Fire had agreed that before mailing the letter, we would test our draft copy in focus groups and not rely exclusively on our own instincts. The Los Angeles group was the second of two organized exclusively for that purpose.

The group consisted of seven women and three men, diverse in age, ethnicity, religion, and income level as well as occupation: among them were a couple of retired people, a housewife, a teacher, a banker, and two business owners. Half had completed at least four years of college; most had done volunteer work in the past three years.

Despite their differences, these ten people had one crucial element in common: in interviews over the telephone, they said they had previously contributed money by mail to human service organizations such as the Girl Scouts, Boys' Town, Special Olympics, City of Hope, or Red Cross. In other words, they seemed to us like good prospects to support Camp Fire.

Now here's what happened.

How Ten People Reacted to My Pride and Joy

Under the skillful guidance of a professional moderator, the participants quickly warmed up to the subject at hand by discussing their views of direct mail fundraising and youth programs. They revealed what they knew—mostly what they *didn't* know—about Camp Fire. Prodded by the discussion leader, they cited examples of "good letters" from charities (ones that were "interesting" and contained "local examples so you can see the money at work"). Their biggest concern about fundraising letters was "authenticity." They were worried about getting sucked into scams "like you hear about on TV."

The group analyzed what was then Camp Fire's tagline—"The first fire we light is the fire within"—which most of them seemed to like. (A typical comment: "I'm not sure what it means, but I like it.") Then they critiqued one of our two candidates for the outer envelope design. That envelope featured the Camp Fire logo, name, address, and tagline along with smaller type reading "recycled paper," plus a much bolder and larger teaser: "Inside: Our free gift to you." Here's what the members of the focus group had to say about the envelope:

"'Recycled paper.' I like that."
"Pretty good as an envelope."
"Camp Fire caught my attention. The logo."
"I focused on 'Inside: Our free gift.'"
"There might be too much on it."
"It's very feminine. Like Camp Fire *girls*."

"You get the feeling there's something they're going to tell you about
    the spark [which was nowhere to be found on the envelope]."
"'Free gift'? I like that."
"They want something."
"I'd throw this away."
"Why are they offering a free gift?"
"I'd open it."
"So would I."
"I'd toss it."
"You think you have to send a gift and then they'll send something."

The reviews were mixed, but not too bad for starters. Then the moderator passed out copies of the one-and-a-half-page fundraising letter intended to be mailed in that envelope and asked the group to read it. This was the letter I'd edited, actually a version of a much longer letter my firm had drafted. My hunch was that a shorter letter would be better received in the market we expected to mail for Camp Fire, because appeals from many national charities already competing in that market were typically short.

Here's what the group had to say about the letter:

"I would throw it away."
"There's nothing in there that says anything about the free gift."
"There's not enough information in there."
"How are they going to teach kids to "'be somebody'" [the promise
    made in the text of the letter]?
"I don't know Camp Fire."
"I think it's very wordy."
"How do I know it's an authentic program?"
"It didn't sell me."
"There are a lot of programs out there that are trying to do the same
    thing."
"I'd rather contribute to an L.A.-based organization. I'd contribute if
    it said kids in L.A. would be helped."
"The letter just doesn't flow very well."
"I don't like this 'Dear Caring American [the salutation].' Leave
    that out."

"Are these kids from poorer areas, or is this like the Boy Scouts?"
"Is *kids* acceptable? Shouldn't you say *children*? *Teens*? *Youth*?"
"This doesn't sound like Camp Fire. There's nothing camp-y here."
"They've been in business for over fifty years. Why don't they say that?"
"They need an 800-number. A hotline or somewhere you can call."

At various points along the way, the moderator turned the group's attention to specific elements in the letter copy:

- The letter's headline: "I'm gonna be dead by the time I'm 18."
  "It's not big enough."
  "It wouldn't mean anything unless I read the rest."
- The name we'd chosen for contributors of $12 or more: "Leadership Circle."
  "Too long a name."
  "Do I become a member?"
- The title we promised to early respondents: "Charter Member."
  "It sounds like the group [Camp Fire] is new."
  "I'm not important enough to be a Charter Member."
  "This letter's going to 10 million people."
  "Just ask me for the money."
  "Does it mean they'll expect more money next year?"

To clinch matters, the moderator asked the group, "If you received this letter in the mail, would you consider making a contribution?" The unanimous response: "No."

Oh, ignominy! Oh, pain and suffering!

But am I glad that answer came from a focus group, and not from an equally uncaring public—after Camp Fire spent a small fortune mailing 50,000 copies of the letter all over the country!

Why Did We Set Up That Exasperating Focus Group, Anyway?

Now listen to a few of the comments about the *four-page* version of our Camp Fire appeal our firm had drafted. That version led with a gripping story about an inner-city child whose life was turned around by Camp Fire:

> "I personally like this. I would give."
> "It gives you an actual person."
> "It's lovely."
> "The lead grabs you—real hard."

A similar sentiment had prevailed the evening before in a focus group assembled in Tulsa, Oklahoma. I'm told the Tulsa group had a somewhat different take on the first letter: they were much more familiar with Camp Fire, were much less critical of the copy, and showed none of the Los Angeles's group's cynicism about charity. But emphasis and nuances aside, there's no question that both groups favored the longer letter instead of the shorter one, and by a huge margin.

Camp Fire didn't go to all the trouble and expense of organizing focus groups merely to choose between two versions of one appeal. Hearing unguarded comments from representative prospects helped us fine-tune our copy. We were able to answer major questions we hadn't anticipated and clear up ambiguities in the copy and artwork, any one of which might have a profound impact on the results. In other words, we learned in advance what our readers' unspoken questions were likely to be and made changes in the copy to answer those questions. For example, each of the following comments was helpful in making final copy revisions:

> "How come there are boys as well as girls?"
> "What makes this organization different? What are they going to do?"
> "Are there Camp Fire programs here in Los Angeles?" [There are.]
> "What is AIDS counseling? As a parent, I would be very interested in knowing what approach they take."
> "If it were Girl Scouts, we wouldn't be as critical. We see them here."
> "Teaching kids how to survive. This is a key point."
> "It doesn't tell exactly where the money goes—like, '30 percent to this.'"
> "What's it going to do for my city?"

What Those Ten People Taught Me (All Over Again)

So lest you too stumble into the wilderness of indifference—armed only with a pitiful little one-and-a-half-page fundraising letter—please keep the following lessons in mind:

Donors need lots of information to be persuaded to send gifts by mail. They may say they want to read only short letters, but what they really crave are answers to their questions. And questions produce doubt or disinterest, the parents of inaction. If it takes an extra page or two to answer every question you can anticipate, increase the budget and stifle your natural tendency to keep your message short and sweet. The results will vindicate you.

Donors are skeptical. It's best to head them off at the pass by volunteering information about the unique character, the impact, and the cost-effectiveness of your work. And they want proof you're really doing the things you say you're doing. Abundant details—facts—will get that point across.

An appeal is too long only if it doesn't convey the information that donors want. My one-and-a-half-page version was "wordy" because it lacked the particulars of the four-page letter. The longer version was *not* wordy.

Human interest sells—and probably doubly so in human service appeals. A story, especially about children, is a great way to humanize a fundraising letter. That is what we did in the longer letter.

If there's a way to misunderstand your message, donors will find it. They'll miss important points if you don't emphasize them. They'll be thrown off by awkward transitions, unfamiliar words, poor word choices, and attempts to gloss over details. Words matter.

Format and design affect understanding. In a fundraising letter, the only tools you've got are words, numbers, typography, pictures, paper, and ink. Use them all wisely; you have no other way to establish your credibility by mail.

Most of the time, I remember all those lessons when I sit down to work on a fundraising letter. Yet I still sometimes write letters that don't work well.

Raising money by mail is an endlessly tricky business, and no amount of knowledge will equip a fundraiser to avoid occasional unpleasant surprises. But experience, insight, and market research like the focus group reported in this chapter can all help narrow the uncertainties and enlarge the odds of success.

Focus groups may not be cost-effective for your organization, and they're certainly not needed for every fundraising letter. But friends, family, and coworkers can informally evaluate your writing and the design of your package. That way, you too might find you're not achieving the effect you thought you were.

Now that we've examined what really happens to fundraising letters when donors receive them in the mail, let's examine the characteristics of an effective fundraising letter—one that takes account of the insights we've gained through focus groups and other techniques that cast light on the whims and foibles of the human beings who read our appeals.

Characteristics of
an Effective Fundraising Letter

Most fundraisers apparently think fundraising letters are all pretty much the same. Here's how their definition of a fundraising letter seems to run: "A fundraising letter is an appeal from a nonprofit organization, describing needs and requesting charitable gifts to fill them."

Right?

Wrong! Wrong on every count.

So banish that ill-conceived and misleading definition from your consciousness. Better yet, copy it down onto a sheet of scratch paper, cross it out with bold strokes of your pen, slice it up with scissors, and deposit the whole mess in the nearest wastebasket.

Now you're ready to get started on the right foot! Read this next part carefully:

An effective fundraising letter possesses three attributes:

1. **An effective fundraising letter is an appeal from one person to another.**

2. **An effective fundraising letter describes an opportunity for the recipient to meet personal needs by supporting a worthy charitable aim.**

3. An effective fundraising letter invites the recipient to take specific and immediate *action*.

I'm sure you noticed that one all-important word is missing here: *money*. Money—a request for a charitable gift—is an indispensable element in the overwhelming majority of fundraising letters. Omit that request for funds, and your letter will fail the most basic test of effectiveness. What's worse, you'll almost certainly fail to raise much money.

But the action requested in a fundraising letter doesn't always consist of sending money, at least not right away. The specific action requested might be to complete and return a survey; to use a set of stamps, name stickers, or greeting cards; or to authorize regular bank transfers. There are hundreds of possibilities. The letter writer's first responsibility when writing for results is to determine what that action is. And understanding that duty leads to what I call the Fundamental Law of Fundraising Letter Writing:

> *When you set out to write a fundraising letter, make sure you know precisely to whom you're writing and why—and be certain your letter makes that point just as clear to them as it is to you.*

That "point"—the equation that expresses the who, what, why, when, and how of your appeal—is what I've fallen into the bad habit of calling the *marketing concept*. I'll discuss this all-important notion in more detail in Chapter Six, where I sum up the central message of this book. For starters, though, let's take a stab at a working definition:

- The marketing concept embodies the *purpose* you're writing: to secure a gift of $500 or more, for example.
- The marketing concept identifies the *person* to whom you're writing: to extend the previous example, a donor who has previously given your organization at least one gift of $100 or more.
- The marketing concept incorporates the *benefits* the person you're writing to will receive as a result of responding—in this example, great satisfaction from knowing how much your organization can accomplish with $500 or more, plus special recognition for giving such a generous gift.

The Fundamental Law, then, is to work out the marketing concept before you write a single word—and then to be sure every word you write speaks to that concept.

Fundraising Letters: One Size Won't Fit All

Fundraising letters are of many different types, serving a broad variety of ends and thus involving a great many different marketing concepts. To write an effective appeal, you must first determine the target audience and specific purpose you want to serve:

- Are you writing to people who have never before supported your organization, asking them to join? That's an *acquisition* (or prospect) letter. I cover that topic in Chapter Ten.
- Is your letter to be mailed to new members or donors, welcoming them to your organization? I call that a *welcome package*; others may describe it as a welcome packet or kit, or even a new-donor acknowledgment. Chapter Eleven takes up this subject.
- Are you writing to previous donors, appealing for additional gifts for some special purpose? That's a *special appeal.* You'll find examples in Chapter Twelve.
- Are you writing to proven donors at the end of the year? That's a *year-end appeal.* The topic is covered in Chapter Thirteen.
- Are you writing to some of your most generous donors, seeking large gifts? I refer to an appeal of that sort as a *high-dollar letter,* the subject of Chapter Fourteen.
- Is the specific purpose of your letter to induce previous donors to increase their support? If so, you're writing an *upgrade appeal.* You'll learn about that topic in Chapter Fifteen.
- Are you writing to your new and regular supporters to ask them to renew this year's annual gift or membership dues? Then you're writing a *renewal.* That's the theme of Chapter Sixteen.

The case studies in Chapters Ten through Sixteen that contain examples of all seven of these types of fundraising appeals will prepare you for many letter-writing challenges—but hardly all of them. There are important types of fundraising letters that don't appear in this book—for example, monthly sustainer requests, upgrades or renewals, lapsed-donor reactivation letters, planned giving letters, cultivation letters, and dozens more. No author can anticipate every need you may face. No book can supply you with models to follow in every contingency.

But in spite of such great variety in fundraising letters, the most productive fundraising appeals I've read share six qualities:

1. *Clarity.* There's no doubt or ambiguity about the writer's intent or what the reader is asked to do. The message is delivered in unmistakably clear and simple terms that rule out guesswork. Early on, the reader gets the point of the appeal, and that point never wavers throughout the package.

2. *Cohesiveness.* Every component of the package works with every other to reinforce the message. If the message is complex—as, for example, in an appeal that combines a petition with a request for money—the close connection between the two is absolutely clear. The message isn't mixed. This means, for example, that an appeal for funds shouldn't be muddied by including a catalogue or a flier that offers merchandise for sale or an update on a project discussed in an earlier appeal.

3. *Authenticity.* From beginning to end, the appeal is credible. The style and approach of the letter fit smoothly with what readers are likely to know about the signer, and the text includes enough revealing personal information to drive home that fit. Similarly, the nature of the appeal fits smoothly with what readers know about the organization and its work. In short, it's natural for *this* signer and *this* nonprofit to be sending *this* particular appeal. For instance, a Hollywood starlet, no matter how popular, might not be the most credible signer of an appeal from a research institute.

4. *Ease of response.* The appeal contains everything the reader might need to respond without a moment's delay after reviewing the appeal. At a minimum, the package includes a clearly marked response device and a preaddressed response envelope, and there's no doubt that these two items are included exclusively for the purpose of responding to the appeal. In direct mail, the fundraiser's job is to make it easy for the reader to

respond. Experience shows that if it's not easy, the recipient is likely to set the appeal aside and never respond at all.

5. *Appropriateness.* The message is calculated to be of interest to the intended reader, and the appeal requests assistance of a sort that the reader might naturally be assumed to be able to provide. For example, I might write an extraordinarily interesting letter about the cuisine of Kyrgyztan, but I would be unlikely to generate much response to my appeal unless I were writing to people with either a demonstrated interest in exotic cuisine, or a fascination with Kyrgyztan, or, even less likely, both. In other words, it's always important to write to the audience.

6. *Engaging copy.* There's something inherently intriguing about this appeal in the story it tells, the character of the request (or offer) it makes, or the language in which it's written. It's interesting and holds the reader's attention. Sometimes this can be accomplished with a clever outer envelope teaser (which is appropriately followed through inside the package). Sometimes a fascinating personal story about a recipient of the agency's help connects with the reader on a deeply emotional level. Sometimes a writer's style is so fresh and compelling that the reader is inexorably drawn through the copy. Whatever it is, something catches the reader's attention—and holds it.

From a mechanical perspective, however, the only things common to all appeals are an *offer* (or proposition) that incorporates the ask, if any, as well as the benefits to the donor, and the *case*, which is the argument that justifies the offer and spells out the benefits. If the appeal is framed as a letter, as are almost all successful fundraising efforts, it's likely to include a salutation and signature that clarify the relationship between the letter signer and the person to whom the letter is addressed, a lead that starts off the letter, a close that ends it, a P.S., and a response device (or reply device) that the donor may use to return a gift. That's about it.

Many fundraisers relate these elements to a formula, insisting there's a standard structure or sequence a writer may follow in constructing an appeal. I disagree. To understand how to write successful fundraising letters, you must study appeals that have worked well, determine what made them successful—and then put them aside and focus on your own donors and your own organization. Your fundraising letters will be successful only if they reflect what's unique about your organization and uniquely attractive to your donors.

To bear down hard on this important point, let's take a stroll through the pages of a single well-written fundraising letter. By accompanying me on this paragraph-by-paragraph tour in the next chapter, you'll gain an overview of the approach I'll spell out later in more detail. In the process, you'll gain insight about how to frame the unique attractions of your own organization in ways that will be compelling to your donors.

A Leisurely Tour Through One Successful Appeal

We'll meander slowly, paragraph by paragraph, through a four-page fundraising letter and its companion package components in an excellent example of the fundraiser's craft. Before we embark on our journey, however, I urge you to read the whole package in its entirety (Exhibits 5.1 through 5.5). As you do, weigh it against the six characteristics of successful appeals that I discussed in the previous chapter: clarity, cohesiveness, authenticity, ease of response, appropriateness, and engaging copy.

My colleague and friend Bill Rehm wrote this fundraising appeal for the San Francisco Conservatory of Music in 1993. The conservatory had retained our firm to assist it in building its membership base, part of a broader development strategy to lay the foundation for a significant capital campaign several years hence.

The Outer Envelope

1. My eyes leap first to the signature in the upper left-hand corner (called the *corner card*). Colin Murdoch, the president of the conservatory, signed the appeal inside, and printing his signature on the envelope (in blue ink, to contrast with the red of the logo and return address)

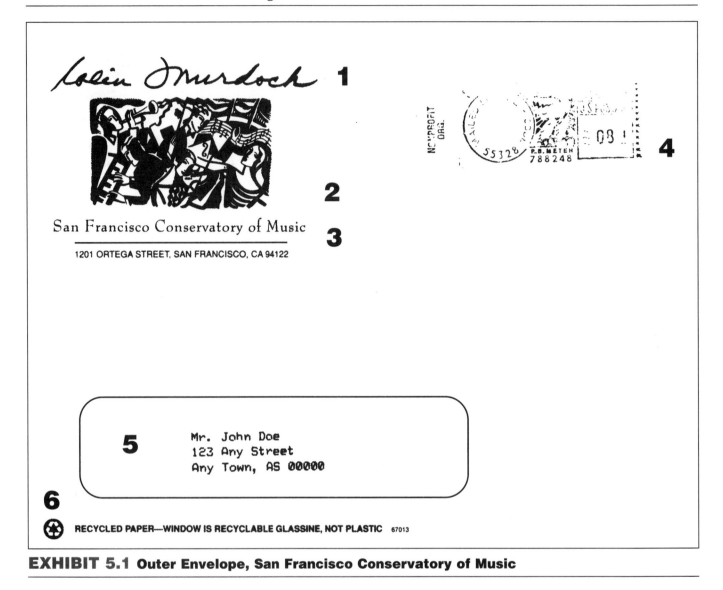

EXHIBIT 5.1 Outer Envelope, San Francisco Conservatory of Music

lends a personal touch that previous testing suggests may improve results—regardless of how well-known he is.

2. With the same glance, I take in the extraordinary woodblock print in the corner card: the conservatory's logo.

3. The typefaces used in the conservatory's name and address are consistently repeated throughout the contents of the package, as they should be. A typeface can be an organization's signature as surely as the most distinctive logo design.

4. A postage meter has been used instead of a postal indicia (that is, a permit imprint). Testing sometimes shows that metered postage out-

pulls an indicia (but both are usually far less successful, though not necessarily less cost-effective, than first-class stamps).

5. Now, *you and I* may have noticed all four of the features of this envelope I've already enumerated, but a recipient of this appeal is much more likely to have found her eyes leaping first to the mailing label. Why? Because, research shows, she'll notice her own name before anything else. So she sees a so-called Cheshire label, a strip of plain paper machine-affixed to a card inside that shows through a glassine (recyclable) window, revealing a computer-imprinted name and address plus a five-digit key code (upper right in the window) and a postal bar code. The bar code enabled the conservatory to mail this particular envelope at a savings of three cents off what was then the standard nonprofit bulk rate (8.1 cents versus 11.1 cents).

6. The envelope advertises "recycled paper," though testing may show that using recycled paper doesn't improve results, even among donors who describe themselves as environmentalists. So what? As my grandmother would have said, "What can it hurt? And it might help!" Besides, it's the right thing to do.

The Letter

Page One

7. The size of the page, 7 by 10 inches, is important. This so-called Monarch letter has a personal touch to it, because it's notably smaller than standard business size (8½ by 11 inches), much more like personal stationery. And there's that lovely logo again. It appears above the address—a street address, not a post office box—and a telephone number. Nowadays we might add a web site address as well. Using the conservatory's actual address, telephone number, and web site address may help inspire confidence in me as a prospective donor. It may also lead me to pay an unexpected visit or place a telephone call out of curiosity or suspiciousness—but that's very unlikely.

8. The use of "Thursday afternoon" is a copywriter's conceit. Still, it may subliminally convey an illusion that the letter bears a specific date. There's no real date here because this appeal was mailed via bulk rate, making it likely that at least some of the letters will be delivered two weeks or longer after the mail date.

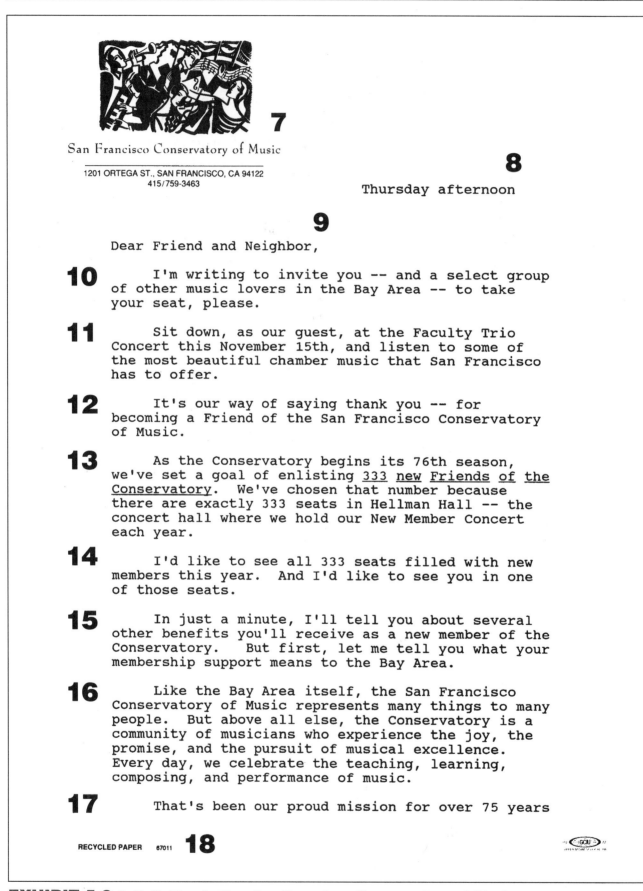

San Francisco Conservatory of Music

1201 ORTEGA ST., SAN FRANCISCO, CA 94122
415/759-3463

7

8

Thursday afternoon

9

Dear Friend and Neighbor,

10   I'm writing to invite you -- and a select group of other music lovers in the Bay Area -- to take your seat, please.

11   Sit down, as our guest, at the Faculty Trio Concert this November 15th, and listen to some of the most beautiful chamber music that San Francisco has to offer.

12   It's our way of saying thank you -- for becoming a Friend of the San Francisco Conservatory of Music.

13   As the Conservatory begins its 76th season, we've set a goal of enlisting <u>333</u> <u>new</u> <u>Friends</u> <u>of</u> <u>the</u> <u>Conservatory</u>. We've chosen that number because there are exactly 333 seats in Hellman Hall -- the concert hall where we hold our New Member Concert each year.

14   I'd like to see all 333 seats filled with new members this year. And I'd like to see you in one of those seats.

15   In just a minute, I'll tell you about several other benefits you'll receive as a new member of the Conservatory.   But first, let me tell you what your membership support means to the Bay Area.

16   Like the Bay Area itself, the San Francisco Conservatory of Music represents many things to many people. But above all else, the Conservatory is a community of musicians who experience the joy, the promise, and the pursuit of musical excellence. Every day, we celebrate the teaching, learning, composing, and performance of music.

17   That's been our proud mission for over 75 years

RECYCLED PAPER   67011   **18**

EXHIBIT 5.2 Solicitation Letter, San Francisco Conservatory of Music

Page two **19**

20 -- ever since the Conservatory was first founded by pianists Ada Clement and Lillian Hodghead in 1917.

21 Today, the San Francisco Conservatory of Music is one of the most respected institutions of music education in the country, offering instruction to more than 1,500 students ranging from pre-school to post graduate levels.

22 Conservatory students, faculty and guest artists perform more than 300 concerts on campus each year.

23 And over the past seventy-five years, the Conservatory has trained some of our country's most brilliant musicians -- violinists Isaac Stern and Yehudi Menuhin, pianist Jeffrey Kahane, and guitarist David Tanenbaum, to name just a few.

24 The Conservatory's faculty of 78 professional musicians are drawn from some of the finest musical organizations in the country, including 32 musicians who are currently playing with either the San Francisco Symphony, the San Francisco Opera, or the San Francisco Ballet.

25 It goes without saying that all of us at the Conservatory share a love for music. But more than that, we possess the desire to help talented and motivated students realize their dreams.

26

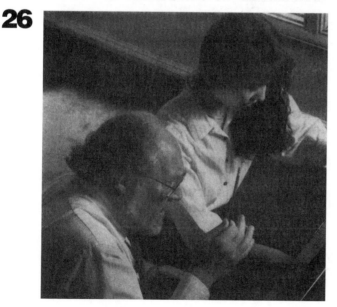

With a student-faculty ratio of just six to one, teachers give special attention to every student.

EXHIBIT 5.2 Continued

28   I see our role at the Conservatory as one of helping to nurture and develop the creativity, skill, and genius residing within each musician.

29   I also see it as the responsibility of the Conservatory to share the music we help create with the community.

30   Through the Conservatory's Community Service Program, our students give more than 400 performances each year. We bring music to hospitals, convalescent homes, day care centers, retirement homes -- reaching people who otherwise would never have the pleasure of hearing live classical music.

31

Conservatory students contribute to our community by performing more than 400 free concerts each year.

32   The San Francisco Conservatory of Music has a long, proud tradition of teaching and providing musical excellence to the Bay Area. And, I assure you, this will continue to be our overriding mission in the years ahead.

33   But the Conservatory is only as great as its supporters. Tuition and fees cover just 59% of our annual budget. The remainder must come from generous individuals in our community.

34   Currently, we have a very special group of Friends -- people like you -- who help support the Conservatory with a tax-deductible membership contribution each year.

35   That's why I hope you'll accept my invitation to become a Friend of the San Francisco Conservatory

EXHIBIT 5.2 Continued

Page four

36 of Music today -- and support one of San Francisco's oldest and most respected institutions.

37 When you become a Friend of the Conservatory, you'll receive all these membership benefits:

- **38** o A subscription to At the Conservatory, the monthly newsletter and calendar of events.

- **39** o Free tickets to the special Faculty Trio Concert for new members on November 15.

- **40** o Free attendance at the "Friends Only" Tour and Concert in January, 1994.

- **41** o Membership discounts for Conservatory concerts throughout the year and special discounts for Conservatory extension classes.

- **42** o Advance ticket purchase for the Sing-It-Yourself Messiah concerts at Davies Symphony Hall this December.

43 Perhaps the greatest benefit you'll receive, though, is knowing you're helping to ensure that students will continue to get the best musical instruction available.

44 So please, right now while everything is in front of you, take a minute to write your tax-deductible check and send it to the San Francisco Conservatory of Music.

45 With many thanks.

46 Sincerely,

Colin Murdoch

Colin Murdoch
President

47 P.S. To reserve your free ticket to the Faculty Trio Concert at the Conservatory's Hellman Hall on November 15, we must receive your membership contribution by November 8. Please send your gift today. Thank you very much.

EXHIBIT 5.2 Continued

9. "Dear Friend and Neighbor" is a neat variation on the standard "Dear Friend"; it's a signal that this appeal was mailed only locally. This is, in its way, a form of personalization, shortening the distance between the conservatory and me. However, since this letter is *not* addressed to me personally, it's obviously not personalized within the generally accepted meaning of that term. This is a bulk appeal, mailed in quantity, and there's no way around that.

10. In its five opening words, "I'm writing to invite you," this appeal simply and directly establishes the basis of a relationship between the signer and me. (Most people who receive this letter probably will flip to the bottom of page 4 to view the signature, to see who is sending the letter, and to read the P.S. But let's be orderly about this, and stick to our paragraph-by-paragraph story.) The opening sentence (the *lead*) identifies me in two important ways—as a music lover and a resident of the San Francisco Bay Area—and seizes my attention with an unfamiliar request: to take a seat.

11. The second paragraph quickly explains that unfamiliar request with specifics: *what* (a concert), *when* (on a particular day), and *where* (in San Francisco), in time-honored journalistic fashion. You'll note too that the conservatory is appealing to my love for chamber music. (How do they know that? They don't, of course. But they know how popular chamber music is among classical music lovers.)

12. Now Colin Murdoch makes clear exactly why he's writing this letter to me. He wants me to become a "Friend" (and since I receive lots of letters like these, I've got a pretty good idea what he means).

13. Now come more facts—details that tell me this is a letter about something specific. Numbers and capitalized words capture my interest because they supply information that answers questions I may have about a topic that (as we've already established) is of general interest to me. The unusual number "333" is itself engaging, because it's unexpected.

14. That intriguing number is repeated. And so are the words *you* and *I*, each for the third time so far. This is not an impersonal institutional appeal. It's a letter from Colin Murdoch to me. You'll also note that "333 new Friends of the Conservatory" is underlined—the only underlining on this page, so it really stands out. A different writer might have chosen different words to emphasize, but what's most important here is that underlining is used sparingly, to lessen the impression this is simply one more direct mail appeal.

15. There's *you* again: three more times. And *me* counts as a form of *I.* Just as important, the concept of membership, broached in each of the two preceding paragraphs, is introduced in terms of its benefits, both to me and to the area where I live (not San Francisco, you'll notice, but the entire, and much larger, Bay Area).

16. In this seven-line paragraph—the longest on all four pages of the appeal—the conservatory is described in emotional and conceptual terms, not as brick and mortar. Murdoch is connecting with me where I really live—on the plane of values: joy, promise, excellence, teaching, learning, music.

17. Note that only one line of this paragraph appears on this page: that's a device to draw my eye onto the second page.

18. There's that "recycled paper" again.

Page Two

19. This letter consists of two sheets of paper that form four pages. The notation "Page two" at the top helps orient me, minimizing the possibility I'll be confused (and thus less likely to send a gift).

20. Take note of specifics again. Facts and figures (used with reasonable restraint) heighten reader interest.

21. This reference to the conservatory's nationwide reputation helps establish credibility. The additional facts lend authority to the reference, making it more than a boast.

22. Here's a significant and surprising fact. Most concertgoers are aware that 300 performances per year is a very large number for any arts group.

23. More facts here, and interesting ones at that. These names, familiar to classical music lovers, help reinforce my interest while enhancing the credibility of the appeal.

24. Facts again (numbers). By now, I'm really getting acquainted with the conservatory.

25. We're back to values and abstracts again: *love, desire, talented, motivated, dreams.* This fellow Murdoch isn't sending me a term paper. He's connecting with me about things that matter.

26. This intense and charming photograph and its handwritten caption convey important facts about the conservatory and its work. They also lend added human interest to the appeal.

Page Three

27. The words "Page three" reassure me that I'm on the right page. But I haven't been hit over the head with a "Next page, please" or the equivalent on the bottom of page 2. (No doubt some direct marketer has tested that obnoxiously condescending device and found it improves response. I tend to avoid using it. I doubt it makes much difference other than to serve as one more subtle but unwanted reminder that an appeal is really, after all, just an impersonal direct mail letter sent to large numbers of people.)

28. Again, Colin Murdoch reveals his personal feelings. He uses the lofty language that gets to the heart of the subject: the teaching of music.

29. Continuing in the first person, Murdoch now reveals the outward-looking dimension of the conservatory's mission: relating to the community—*my* community.

30. I see that by supporting the conservatory, I won't just be helping to bring out the genius in future world-class performers. I'll also help support my community's social safety net.

31. This photograph depicts an obviously diverse group of school children, and the caption repeats the number 400. The effect is to drive home the point that the conservatory serves far more than its own students and faculty or affluent concertgoers like me. Those 400 concerts are free.

32. Now we're back to values again: tradition and musical excellence. Even the word *mission* connotes passion and an orientation to values.

33. Citing the central financial fact about the conservatory brings me back into the picture once again. There's little doubt in my mind that I'm (supposedly) one of those "generous individuals."

34. Any doubt I may have is now quickly dispelled: Murdoch is talking about "people like" me. But the contribution he wants is more than simply that. It's "tax deductible," it buys me a "membership," and it's to be annual.

35. That, obviously, is what Murdoch means when he asks me to become a "Friend." But I'm going to have to go on to the next page to learn whether there's some qualification or exception to his request.

Page Four

36. There is no exception here—just another argument for supporting the conservatory: its long and respected institutional history.

37. Here, in the first underlined words since the phrase on page 1, Murdoch introduces the subject of membership benefits. (Note that the words are individually underlined. Some people prefer continuous lines, but I think the underlining of spaces distracts the eye from the message and focuses it on what's less important: the fact of the underlining itself. It also eliminates the spaces between words, which readers use to "swallow" words and phrases one bite at a time.)

38. As a "Friend," I'll receive a monthly newsletter and calendar. Murdoch cites the newsletter's name, emphasizing the unstated promise of events I may want to attend at the conservatory.

39. In fact, I'll receive free tickets to a specific concert—one that's coming up very soon.

40. More free tickets, and another event that's not too far off.

41. I'll get discounts—not only on admission to other concerts but for extension classes too. Here's a potentially important benefit that piques my curiosity. (I gave up trying the clarinet in fifth grade, but maybe I could learn it after all.)

42. Now—underlined again and deliberately placed last in the series, where it's most likely to be remembered—is a membership benefit that could well be the most attractive of all: the conservatory's wildly popular sing-along *Messiah* concerts at San Francisco's elegant Symphony Hall.

43. Despite all these tangible benefits of membership, Murdoch rushes to remind me I'll get something even more valuable: the satisfaction of knowing I've helped achieve something I value highly: the teaching of good music.

44. If I'm tempted to set this appeal aside and make my mind up later about whether to respond, Murdoch's suggestion that I do it now may have no effect on me, but at worst it's a throwaway line. And I'm reminded once again that my gift will be tax deductible, a fact that may be of special interest to me since the end of the year is fast approaching.

45. Ever hopeful, Murdoch thanks me.

46. He signs off "Sincerely," rather than a more formal "Yours truly" or a flamboyant "See you at the Conservatory!" He is, after all, the president of a respected institution. His flowery signature has an artful flair; it's printed in dark blue ink, to set it off from the typed text and reinforce the illusion of personal (or, rather, business) correspondence.

47. As you'll remember, most readers read the P.S. first. This P.S.

makes good use of that opportunity. It restates the date of the fast-approaching faculty concert and, for the first time, lays out a specific deadline for membership contributions. To be sure I'll beat that deadline, I may really have to mail in my gift *today*, as I'm asked to do. (Although I rarely recommend including specific dates in letters written to recruit new members—or, for that matter, in any other letters mailed at bulk rate—this case is an exception. The appeal was mailed within a narrow region and likely to be delivered well in advance of the concert date. And conservatory faculty and students perform so frequently that similar offers can be made almost any time of the year.)

Lift Letter

48. Yes, that intense-looking fellow in the upper right-hand corner photo is the renowned cellist Yo-Yo Ma. Classical music lovers probably know that. It's likely to be the photograph that first catches attention. That's what the eye-motion studies reveal. Then your eyes swept leftward to take in the musician's name, and finally down to the salutation and lead. This musical celebrity has signed what is called a "lift letter"—a brief, supplementary letter or note that strengthens the main appeal by emphasizing an important endorsement (as in this case) or providing significant information not found in the main letter.

49. While Colin Murdoch addressed me as a "Neighbor," Yo-Yo Ma finds common cause with me as a "Music Lover." It's a flattering reference. (He obviously never heard me play clarinet!)

50. From this first paragraph until the fifth and last, this testimonial lift letter from Yo-Yo Ma is a credibility-building exercise. It means a lot for one of the world's most illustrious concert performers to write about the conservatory's "high standards."

51. Similarly, it's useful—and impressive—for a celebrity in the world of music to name several of the conservatory's faculty members, who are far less likely to be known to the readers of this appeal. (I, for one, knew none of the three names cited.)

52. In a longer letter, Mr. Ma might have revealed how frequently he visits the conservatory and how much time he spends there, thus establishing his authority as a judge of the conservatory's participation in the Bay Area community. In this context, I'm not impressed with the claim he makes in this paragraph.

48

YO-YO MA

49 Dear Friend and Music Lover,

50   Some of the finest cello teaching in the country today takes place at the San Francisco Conservatory of Music, where high standards are combined with an openness to new trends.

51   The San Francisco Conservatory of Music has a sense of tradition in the best sense of the word. Generations of great cello teachers from Margaret Rowell to Bonnie Hampton and Irene Sharp have nurtured some of the finest young cellists today.

52   The Conservatory is a working community -- it not only functions as an institution, but it participates as a vital member of the Bay Area community.

53   The high standards, tradition and a sense of community are the reasons why the San Francisco Conservatory of Music continues to be such a strong, creative force in producing the next generation of musicians.

54   I urge you to support this fine institution.

55   Sincerely,

Yo-Yo Ma

EXHIBIT 5.3 Lift Letter, San Francisco Conservatory of Music

53. He's back on more solid ground in this paragraph, speaking about musical tradition and the "next generation of musicians."

54. Most celebrities try to get off easy in lift letters like this one, omitting explicit endorsements such as the last paragraph. But without such a direct statement, a lift letter's value is limited. Now I know that Yo-Yo Ma really wants me to lend a hand. (His appeal would have been even stronger if he had written, "I urge you to join me as a Friend of the San Francisco Conservatory," thus leaving not a shadow of a doubt about his own deep commitment.)

55. He signs off "Sincerely," his name alone sufficing to identify himself. His signature, like Colin Murdoch's, is printed in dark blue ink to set it apart from the typewritten text.

The Reply Device

56. "BRAVO!" What an appropriate variation on the more commonly used "Yes!" (The applause line is printed in dark red, as are the check boxes and suggested gift amounts; the logo, name, address, and telephone number; and the headline below the line of dashes near the bottom. That bottom portion is tinted a gentle shade of red. All the text and every other element on this reply device is printed in black.)

57. In three terse sentences, the response device sums up the essence of "the offer" spelled out in Colin Murdoch's letter.

58. I'm offered three choices here. (Unfortunately, I have to read the text at the bottom of this reply device closely to be certain "Regular Membership" really entitles me to all the benefits I'll get as a "Friend" of the conservatory. It might have been better to label the $40 option "Friend of the Conservatory" and devise a new name for the $100 option, while spelling out special benefits for the higher level of support. But no appeal's perfect.)

59. Here I'm reminded of the deadline, November 8. It's also clear to me that the offer of free tickets to the Faculty Trio Concert is a serious one: this is an excellent and appropriate use of a premium in membership acquisition.

60. Here's the Cheshire label (noted in paragraph number 5, describing the outer envelope).

61. That wonderful logo again!

62. I'm reminded, for the third time, that my gift will be tax deductible.

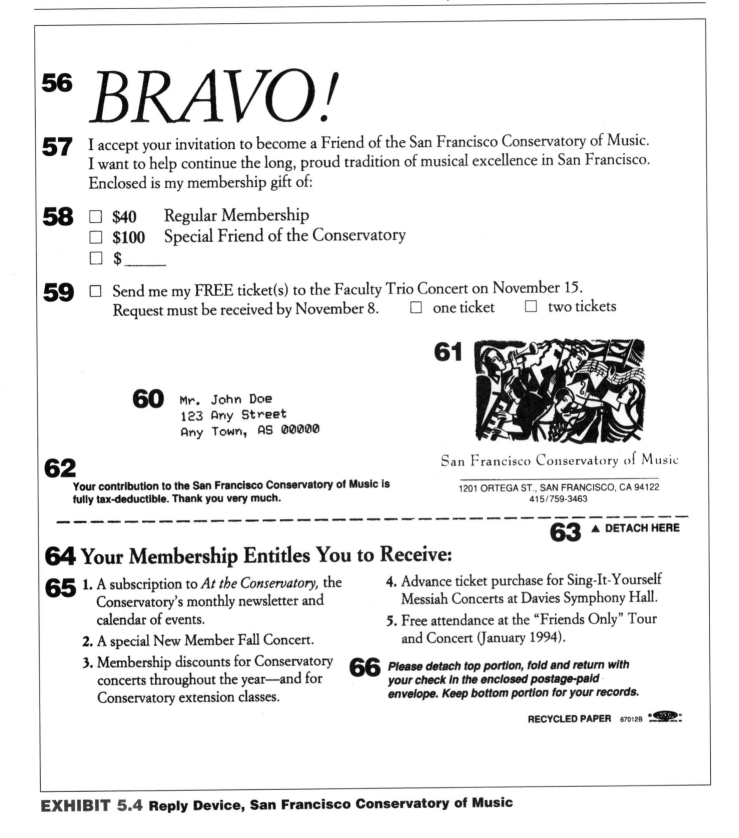

56 *BRAVO!*

57 I accept your invitation to become a Friend of the San Francisco Conservatory of Music. I want to help continue the long, proud tradition of musical excellence in San Francisco. Enclosed is my membership gift of:

58 ☐ $40 Regular Membership
☐ $100 Special Friend of the Conservatory
☐ $ _____

59 ☐ Send me my FREE ticket(s) to the Faculty Trio Concert on November 15. Request must be received by November 8.   ☐ one ticket   ☐ two tickets

61

60 Mr. John Doe
123 Any Street
Any Town, AS 00000

San Francisco Conservatory of Music
1201 ORTEGA ST., SAN FRANCISCO, CA 94122
415/759-3463

62
Your contribution to the San Francisco Conservatory of Music is fully tax-deductible. Thank you very much.

63 ▲ DETACH HERE

64 Your Membership Entitles You to Receive:

65 1. A subscription to *At the Conservatory*, the Conservatory's monthly newsletter and calendar of events.

2. A special New Member Fall Concert.

3. Membership discounts for Conservatory concerts throughout the year—and for Conservatory extension classes.

4. Advance ticket purchase for Sing-It-Yourself Messiah Concerts at Davies Symphony Hall.

5. Free attendance at the "Friends Only" Tour and Concert (January 1994).

66 *Please detach top portion, fold and return with your check in the enclosed postage-paid envelope. Keep bottom portion for your records.*

RECYCLED PAPER   67012B

EXHIBIT 5.4 Reply Device, San Francisco Conservatory of Music

63. It's almost always wise to include instructions such as "Detach Here." Certainly I could figure out that the reply device is perforated along the line of dashes, but it's courteous to relieve me of the (admittedly very slight) burden of determining that for myself. Instructions of this sort also reinforce the action-oriented nature of direct mail appeals.

64. Now any lingering doubt that I might not actually receive the wonderful benefits that Colin Murdoch's letter described is totally dispelled.

65. Those benefits are listed, described in the same words as in the letter.

66. The last thing I want to do when signing up for a membership in the conservatory is to fumble around with unfamiliar slips of paper of odd shapes and sizes, so I'm pleased to be told exactly what to do.

Reply Envelope

67. Once again I'm reminded that my gift to the conservatory entitles me to membership, with its attendant benefits. This handwritten tagline is printed in dark blue, like that of the signatures on both letters.

EXHIBIT 5.5 Reply Envelope, San Francisco Conservatory of Music

68. "Recycled paper" again!

69. This five-digit code helps production staff and envelope printers keep this envelope apart from those used with hundreds of other projects.

70. These vertical ruled lines are for the electronic scanning equipment used by the U.S. Postal Service to route the mail.

71. The indicia and the horizontal ruled lines are for the naked eye: unmistakable signs that this envelope is, as the words to the left explain, "Business Reply Mail." It will cost the conservatory approximately 40 cents per envelope returned.

72. The envelope is addressed to the conservatory. In a more personal appeal—a membership renewal letter, for example—it might be appropriate to type Colin Murdoch's name above the institutional name. Its omission here is not a significant oversight: I would find it a little difficult to believe that the president of the San Francisco Conservatory of Music would be opening envelopes containing new memberships. Still, typing Murdoch's name on the reply envelope would reinforce the personality of this appeal; on balance, I would favor doing that.

73. This bar code enables the U.S. Postal Service to sort returning envelopes with minimal human intervention: the vertical lines are computer language for the letters and numbers contained in the address.

What You Can—and Can't—Learn from This Example

This fundraising letter for the San Francisco Conservatory of Music is a singular appeal; it was written for a particular purpose on behalf of a particular organization at a particular time. As a result, there are several ways this letter may not work well as a model for your own fundraising efforts. The package was written to acquire members, whereas most fundraising letters are written to proven donors. The letter is benefit driven, even to the point of offering prospective members admission to a specific performance, and most nonprofits have to reach far to come up with tangible donor benefits. There's a celebrity lift letter, a device that's appropriate for most nonprofits only in unusual circumstances.

Nevertheless, it's worthwhile for you to study this package so closely because it does its job so well. I chose this fundraising letter because its varied contents illustrate how to meet so many different letter-writing challenges and, more to the point, because it dramatizes how different a particular fundraising letter can be from every other fundraising letter. There's no question what the conservatory is offering. The marketing concept couldn't be clearer.

A Shorter Journey Through a Letter That Doesn't Work Well

By contrast, let's take a look at an appeal that's much closer to the dysfunctional definition of a fundraising letter that I referred to at the beginning of the previous chapter (Exhibit 5.6).

A. Glance at the outer envelope. You can't miss the return address rubber-stamped in the upper left-hand corner or the incomplete (and, in many parts of the country, undeliverable) address on the mailing label. The only thing this envelope has going for it is a first-class stamp. But you probably guessed, just as I did, that the reason this was mailed first class was one of the following: (1) the quantity wasn't large enough to qualify the appeal for bulk mail, (2) the organization didn't have or couldn't get a nonprofit bulk mailing permit, or (3) the list was in such bad shape the organization couldn't bundle the mail properly to suit postal personnel.

B. Now take a look through the text on the first page. It has its positive points: short paragraphs, white space, underlined subheadings, language that's clear and relatively readable. But there are precious few personal pronouns anywhere in sight—except for *we* a few times—and the rest is argumentative and rhetorical. It's not even really clear this is an appeal for funds because I'm asked if I can "assist in other ways." But there's no way I can tell how my "financial contribution"—or any other sort of help I might give—is connected to anything else in this letter.

C. The second page continues in the same vein, compounding the problems of the first page: more statistics, more rhetoric, a laundry list of organizations (some of them little known), a dual signature—and *no ask*. It's hard to imagine a letter better calculated *not* to raise money.

D. Apparently the Federal Jobs Program outlined in the top two-thirds of this reply device is the principal program of the organization that sent this appeal, although I'm forced to guess that's really the case.

Only at the bottom of the page do I find a way to respond to the letter (assuming I'd be so inclined). You'll note it's called an "Endorsement Form." However, there's no way for me to indicate my endorsement (for the Federal Jobs Program? the Campaign to Abolish Poverty?). There's also no suggested gift amount and no return address (in case the form becomes separated from the letter or the return envelope).

E. This rubber-stamped little reply envelope doesn't inspire confidence. Major gift fundraisers speak of an organization's readiness to receive big gifts. This organization doesn't appear ready to receive little gifts.

Building Relationships

Throughout the journey you've just completed, you must have recognized the emphasis I placed on the relationship between the conservatory and the donor. Relationship building is the essence of good fundraising; the biggest rewards come with time.

To gain perspective on the techniques that will allow you to use fundraising letters to maximum advantage in strong, long-term building relationships with your donors, please join me now in Part Two, "The Letter Writer's Plan of Action."

EXHIBIT 5.6. Campaign to Abolish Poverty Appeal: (a) Outer Envelope

Campaign to Abolish Poverty

942 Market Street, #708, San Francisco, CA 94102 ● Ph: 415-397-4911 Fx: 415-434-3110

November 6, 1992

Dear Friend:

Electing Bill Clinton President certainly creates new opportunities in Washington, D.C. The pendulum is beginning to swing in the opposite direction.

But it remains to be seen how much difference Clinton will make, particularly for the poor and near-poor. If history is any guide, strong grassroots pressure will be necessary to push Clinton beyond his election-year program.

The Campaign to Abolish Poverty (CAP) aims to push the pendulum as hard as possible. Our current focus is to build support for the Federal Jobs Program -- a proposal to create two million new, permanent, public service jobs -- as a first step toward ending poverty in this country.

We urge you to help this effort by sending a financial contribution now, and letting us know if you can assist in other ways.

Clinton has committed himself to a number of good positions. But there is a downside to most of them.

Jobs

On the one hand, for example, it is encouraging that Clinton proposes federal funding for public works jobs. But he's only talking about one-shot infrastructure repair -- temporary jobs which largely would exclude women, minorities and low-income people who need them the most.

We need to persuade Clinton and Congress to support <u>sustained</u> federal funding for local human service jobs -- jobs for which the poor and near-poor would qualify, with relevant on-the-job training.

Tax Reform

It is also positive that Clinton advocates increasing taxes on the wealthy. But his proposal would roll back only one-fifth of the tax breaks received by the top 2% of all households during the last fifteen years. If these families with annual incomes over $200,000 paid 34% of their income in federal taxes, as they did in 1977, $80 billion in addition to the $20 billion targeted by Clinton could be generated.

We need to persuade Clinton and Congress to restore 1977 tax rates for the wealthy. All other income groups are now paying higher federal taxes (including payroll taxes). The wealthy could pay what they paid in 1977 without undue hardship.

EXHIBIT 5.6. Campaign to Abolish Poverty Appeal: (b) First Page

Military Spending

Clinton's proposals for reductions in the military budget are inadequate. **We need to persuade Clinton and Congress to move in the direction of a 50% cut in military spending,** which could free almost $150 billion per year to help put Americans to work.

Federal Jobs Program

In consultation with a wide range of recognized experts and community organizations, CAP has developed a specific program -- the **Federal Jobs Program** -- that would appropriate $50 billion to create two million permanent public service jobs, paid for by higher taxes on the wealthy and reductions in the military budget (see enclosed).

A broad range of community-based organizations, community leaders, and elected officials have already endorsed this program, including American Friends Service Committee, Catholic Charities of San Francisco, California Legislative Council for Older Americans, Coleman Advocates for Children and Youth, San Francisco Lawyer's Committee for Urban Affairs, and Maryland United for Peace and Justice. Considering that we have been gathering endorsements only since early October, this support is very encouraging.

But in order to influence the next session of Congress, the Campaign to Abolish Poverty and its membership must broaden its base and press its case effectively in Washington. We have recently begun encouraging discussions with a number of national organizations with lobbyists in Washington to build support for our jobs program.

The desperation and misery experienced by growing millions of Americans compel us to make this effort and to continue until economic security for all is established as a human right.

So please give what you can financially, and if possible contribute time and energy as well. Please complete the form enclosed and return it with your tax-deductible donation as soon as possible.

With your help, we have a chance.

Sincerely,

Wade Hudson

Wade Hudson
Chair

Barbara Arms

Barbara Arms
Director

EXHIBIT 5.6. **Campaign to Abolish Poverty Appeal: (c) Second Page**

FEDERAL JOBS PROGRAM

Purpose: To appropriate $50 billion to create 2 million new public service jobs in both urban and rural areas, as the first step toward guaranteeing every adult the opportunity to work at a living wage. Each year, funding should increase by 20% until these jobs go begging due to lack of applicants.

Types of Work: These funds shall be used to hire workers in repair/maintenance/ rehabilitation of publicly-owned facilities, conservation/rehabilitation/ improvement of public lands, child care, health care, in-home caregiving, education (including tutorial services), peer counseling, housing and neighborhood improvement, recreation, arts programs, community centers, and other vital public services.

Wages: Wages shall range from $7-$12 per hour, plus benefits, and shall be indexed to inflation. The compensation for these positions shall not be less than the prevailing compensation for individuals employed in similar occupations.

Allocation of Funds: Two and one-half percent of all funds shall be allocated for Native American tribes and Alaska Native villages. Remaining funds shall be allocated by the Secretary of Labor to the states based upon the number of people living in poverty in each state.

Administration: The Secretary of Labor shall distribute the funds to the states for distribution to local governments. The cost of administration shall be no more than the standard for similar programs. Each recipient of funds shall be responsible for ensuring equal employment opportunities, equal pay for equal work, and the full participation of traditionally underrepresented groups, including women and racial and ethnic minorities.

Displacement: The following shall be prohibited: a) any displacing of current employees, including partial displacement such as a reduction in the hours of nonovertime work, wages, or employment benefits; b) impairing of existing contracts or collective bargaining; c) filling of openings created by related layoffs or terminations; or d) infringing on promotional opportunities of current employees.

Oversight: Prior to submitting its plan to the State, each eligible entity shall conduct an open public review and comment process, and during the year, shall conduct at least one public hearing to receive input into its evaluation process. Workers hired by these funds shall be encouraged to participate in this review process.

Source of Funds: The funds needed for this program shall come from increasing personal income taxes on the richest 2% of households and from reducing the military budget.

ENDORSEMENT FORM

___Please find enclosed a check for _____ (made payable to: Campaign to Abolish Poverty) to help with building support for the Federal Jobs Program. (Contributions are tax-deductible.)

___I would like to volunteer some time to help.

___Please send me more information about CAP and the Federal Jobs Program.

Name (print) _____

Organization (if any)_____

Address _____

City_____State_____Zip_____

Day Phone_____Eve Phone_____Fax_____

EXHIBIT 5.6. Campaign to Abolish Poverty Appeal: (d) Reply Device

CAMPAIGN TO ABOLISH POVERTY
942 MARKET STREET #708
SAN FRANCISCO, CA 94102

EXHIBIT 5.6. Campaign to Abolish Poverty Appeal: (e) Reply Envelope

Part II

The Letter Writer's Plan of Action

It's nuts-and-bolts time. In this part, we'll approach the task of writing a fundraising letter from a strictly practical, down-to-earth perspective. In successive chapters, we'll cover these topics:

- What to do before you sit down to write a fundraising appeal
- The nine steps I recommend you follow in crafting a fundraising package
- The eight concrete Cardinal Rules that determine whether your appeal will be a success (or a dud), along with a self-assessment form that will help you evaluate the likely effectiveness of a fundraising letter in the light of these rules
- The practical guidelines of style and syntax I urge you to follow when you're writing a fundraising appeal—or, for that matter, any other prose that's meant to persuade a reader to act

What to Do Before You Write
Any Fundraising Letter

How do you get started writing that fundraising letter that's due at the printer's next month?

You *think*.

Effective writing begins with clear, uncluttered thinking. Before you set down on paper a single word of your next fundraising appeal, you must understand precisely to whom you're writing, why you're writing, and what you're writing. That's what the following twenty questions are about. Asking yourself these questions won't guarantee you'll write a better letter (much less a more successful letter), but they will help you think clearly about the task at hand and focus your writing on the specific points you most need to make.

Answering these questions will enable you to construct a powerful marketing concept, the idea that's at the core of any piece of writing conceived to produce results. The marketing concept is a tapestry woven of need, opportunity, and circumstance. It's the pure essence of the message you're conveying. Or think of it as an executive summary of your letter.

The marketing concept is at the heart of the dialogue that Siegfried Vögele describes (see Chapter Two). Incorporated into it are the answers to many of your readers' unspoken questions.

Never forget this: the words you write will obtain the objectives you desire *only* to the extent that those words convey a marketing concept powerful enough to motivate your donors. You must appeal to them clearly and unambiguously, which requires that you begin with an absolutely clear understanding of why you're writing a letter in the first place. That's where the twenty questions start.

The Twenty Important Questions You Need to Ask Before You Begin Writing

First, Think About Why You're Writing This Particular Letter

1. What is the purpose of your appeal? To acquire new donors or members? Solicit larger gifts or major gifts? Urge your donors to consider planned giving? Reactivate lapsed members or donors? Or meet any of a multitude of other specific fundraising needs?

Now, Think About the People You're Writing To

2. What do the people you're writing to have in common with each other? For example, do they share a powerful experience: an earthquake, religious conversion, new citizenship, a crushing personal loss? Are they patriotic, or dedicated to a particular cause? Are they all likely to be concerned about family values?

3. What fact, or facts, may be true about almost all of these people— facts to distinguish them from the rest of the world's population? Are they all over the age of sixty? Do they all live in a single community? Were they all once patients in your hospital? Are they all women? Baby boomers? Donors? Nondonors? Members?

4. What do you know about the feelings of the people you're writing to? Are they likely to be angry (or elated) about a recent turn of events in the world or in your local community? Have recent economic setbacks made life more difficult for them, or changes in tax laws made them more comfortable? Are they likely to be skeptical about charity? Concerned about declining family values? Fearful of old age?

5. What's the relationship of these people to your organization? What do they know about you, your organization, or the issue or problem you're addressing? What *don't* they know? What do they *want* to know? Have they been contributing regular gifts for several years and

demonstrated interest, even commitment, to your agency? Is the typical reader of the letter you're about to write a longtime subscriber to your newsletter or a new donor who lacks basic information about your work? Is there likely to be a personal relationship between the readers and your executive director or a member of your board?

6. Consider the typical recipient of your letter. What experiences, feelings, and thoughts is that person likely to have that would help her understand the issue or problem you're addressing? Is it likely that this typical reader will feel very deeply, based on her own personal experience, about some issue or problem that underpins your agency's work? For example, if you serve the homeless, is she likely to come into contact with homeless people on a daily basis—or almost never? Put yourself in her position, and think how she might think and feel about the challenges your organization faces every day.

7. What leads you to believe that the typical person you're writing to will respond favorably? Does she have a long history of supporting your agency or, at least, other organizations like yours? Has she expressed interest in knowing how she might help? Is there some personal connection, such as a child who was a patient, a parent who benefited from your services, or an old school tie? Is this a time of crisis, and have earlier appeals to the same or similar groups amply demonstrated that people like those you're writing to now are likely to respond?

Now, Think About What You'll Ask People to Do

8. What is it exactly that you want recipients to do? Renew their memberships? Send larger annual gifts than they did last year? Join an exclusive giving club? Commit to making monthly gifts via electronic funds transfer? Support a special new project? Respond to an emergency with an additional $10 or $15?

9. What is the minimum amount of money (if any) that you hope to receive from each recipient? Few other questions are more important in appeals sent by mail. The amount of your *ask*, particularly the minimum amount, will often predetermine the amount you receive. A prospective donor may be incredulous at a request for $1,000, while a long-loyal supporter thinks the same sum too small. (That's one reason why the same appeal usually can't be sent to both prospective and proven donors.) To be successful, your appeal must ask for a specific amount, and that must be the *right* amount.

10. Is there anything else you want recipients to do right now? Will your appeal ask for a cash contribution and nothing more? Or will you request a three-year pledge, a monthly commitment, a signature on a credit card authorization form—or something entirely different? For example, will your appeal include an "involvement device" such as a postcard to the governor, a membership survey, or an offer to supply information about wills and bequests?

Now, Think About the Circumstances in Which You're Writing This Appeal

11. What problem, need, issue, or opportunity prompts your agency to send this appeal? Be specific; don't state the need as simply that "funds are tight" or "we need money." Think about the particular set of circumstances that makes it necessary for your agency to raise funds right now. Is there a profoundly exciting new opportunity that your organization wants to meet by launching a new program? Has there been an unanticipated demand for your services—or a shortfall in funding from corporate and foundation donors? Is a trustee or a friendly foundation offering a challenge grant (or willing to do so)?

Think About the Person Who Will Sign the Appeal

12. What is the signer's name? It's dangerous to draft an appeal not knowing who will sign it. A fundraising appeal—a letter from one person to another—is most powerful when it reflects the personal views and feelings of both people—the sender and the receiver. The appeal will be most effective if you can bring it to life with a relevant anecdote or two, or a typical statement that will ring true—something that might cause a knowledgeable reader to nod and say, "Yes, that's ol' Fred in a nutshell, all right!"

13. What is the connection between the signer and the problem, need, issue, or opportunity that prompts the appeal? If the signer is your president or executive director, the connection may be obvious—and rife with possibilities to bring that opportunity to life. If the signer is instead someone who has no day-to-day connection with the events or circumstances that prompt your appeal, think about what might move the signer to write an emotional appeal at this particular time. Is there something in his past: his education, his childhood, his experience as a soldier at war, his business achievements?

14. What is the connection between the signer and those who will receive the appeal? Do they share the experiences of a generation? For example, are most of them over the age of fifty-five—or under forty? As loyal members of a single organization, have they shared a particular event or intense experience: the death of a president, a Superbowl victory, the landing on the moon, the fall of the Berlin Wall? Or are they all well-to-do, or members of a particular community? Have they received similar honors, attended the same school, watched the same shows on television?

15. What are the signer's feelings and thoughts about the problem, need, issue, or opportunity that underlies the appeal? If you don't know the answer to this question, ask it. Sometimes the signer—even an in-house, staff, or board signer—can suggest a powerful line of argument or an evocative story that will bring your appeal to life. Emotional copy is usually more effective than intellectual copy, but a powerful fundraising letter is built on ideas and facts as well as feelings. Look for both to flesh out your appeal.

Consider What Benefits People Will Get If They Respond to Your Appeal

16. List all the tangible benefits, if any. Are you offering a newsletter, for example, or discounts on products or services, or the promise of invitations to events with celebrity supporters? Or have you enclosed a premium such as a bookmark, name stickers, photographs, or a calendar?

17. List the intangible benefits of sending a gift in response to your appeal. Will donors help you change the course of human history, or save the life of a tiny child? Will they be ensuring that their values and beliefs will be passed along to generations of descendants or raising the quality of life in their community? Will donors gain salvation, learn about a headline-grabbing issue, prevent the abuse of pets?

Now, Why Do the Readers of Your Appeal Need to Respond Right Now?

18. Is there an especially urgent need or opportunity that justifies this appeal? Is Thanksgiving approaching, and with it increased demand for the hot meals your agency serves to the poor? Is a regional war about to

break out, shutting down communications with your field office? Is the congressional debate drawing to a close? Will the board of directors be forced to shut the program down soon if funding goals aren't met?

19. <u>Is there a deadline by which you must receive responses?</u> For instance, have you arranged—or can you arrange—a challenge grant with an imminent deadline? Is the end of the calendar year approaching, and with it the opportunity for donors to save on this year's taxes? Is Easter special to your organization, representing a traditional time for your supporters to demonstrate their compassion for the less fortunate?

20. What will happen if you don't receive responses before that deadline? Will you lose the challenge grant? Will poor people go hungry? Will children be turned away from the door to your agency? Will small animals die, or the supply of autographed books run out, or people with AIDS suffer needless pain?

How to Write a Marketing Concept

Once you've answered those twenty questions, sum up all this information in one paragraph. Be as specific and precise as possible, and write the paragraph in the first-person singular (just as you'll have to do when you write the letter itself). Address it to that one typical individual who will be receiving your letter. This paragraph will be the marketing concept for your appeal. Once you've written it, the rest of your job will be easy.

Keep in mind that the marketing concept is not the letter itself or even its opening paragraph; it's simply a way to get started. Others might call it the "copy platform." It's the foundation on which you'll construct your appeal. It's what you'll write about: facts, information, feelings, circumstances—that is, specifics. The marketing concept is the skeleton on which you hang them all together. In writing your letter, you'll put flesh on those bones.

To help you get the hang of it, here are examples of two typical marketing concepts:

Because you've been so generous to The Center in the past, you've heard from me from time to time about exciting new developments here. I've told you before how far we stretch your contributions to serve the underserved in the Community. Now, a renewal gift from you of as little as $25 will go twice as far as before! Your $25 will help house the homeless children of the Community by enabling The Center to buy $50 or more worth of lumber and tools—because your gift will be matched, dollar for dollar, by an anonymous donor through The Center's new Matching Gift Program. That way, you'll get double the satisfaction from your act of generosity—and bring new hope to twice as many of your neighbors in the Community.

You may not know me, but I'm sure you're familiar with the Museum, which has been the centerpiece of my life during the past twenty years of my tenure as its Director. I'm writing to you, a fellow resident of The City, because I want you to be among the first to know about the Museum's unique new Charter Membership program. As a person who appreciates the finer things in life, you'll cherish for many years to come each magnificent issue of our new bimonthly magazine on the visual arts. You'll receive the magazine absolutely free of charge as a Charter Member of the Museum. And you'll have the satisfaction of knowing that your Charter Membership contribution of $45, $75, $150, or more will help us to showcase the exciting work of emerging new artists in our region.

Often, but not always, the reply device restates the marketing concept in a successful direct mail fundraising package. That's why many experienced direct mail copywriters (myself included) tackle the reply device first when they set out to write a package.

To get a stronger grip on this point, study the reply devices in Exhibits 6.1 through 6.5. You'll soon get the gist of the marketing concept behind each of the fundraising appeals from which these response forms were selected. They stare you right in the face. That's what your marketing concept needs to do every time you write an appeal!

Remember always that your reader has only twenty seconds to get the message. (Think back to Siegfried Vögele's eye-motion research.) If your message—the central reason that your readers should respond—isn't clear at a glance, there's little chance your letter will be read at all, much less generate contributions.

Join me now on a step-by-step journey through the route I usually take when setting out to write a fundraising letter.

Heal the Bay — *New Member Enrollment Form*

SIGN ME UP as a member of Heal the Bay. Use my support to protect our bays and beaches, and to keep the pressure on government agencies and polluting corporations to clean up their act. Enclosed is my tax-deductible gift of:

☐ **$25** Friend ☐ **$35** Advocate ☐ **$50** Supporter ☐ **$100** Benefactor ☐ **$**_____

* Please consider a gift at this level or higher

Your contribution is tax-deductible. Thank you for your support.

As a Heal the Bay member, you will receive our educational quarterly newsletter and be invited to our many special events throughout the year.

Be sure to check out the latest beach conditions on our website: www.healthebay.org. Just click on the Beach Report Card and select your favorite Beach.

2701 Ocean Park Blvd., Suite 150
Santa Monica, CA 90405
Tel 310.581.4188
Fax 310.581.4195
E-mail htb@healthebay.org
www.healthebay.org

Heal the Bay ®

RECYCLED & RECYCLABLE / PRINTED WITH SOY INK   93182

EXHIBIT 6.1 New Member Enrollment Form, Heal the Bay

JOIN THE MILLION MOM MARCH FOUNDATION

Yes, Donna, I agree. I'll join you and thousands of mothers, fathers, and others who participated in the Million Mom March in a continuing effort to put a stop to gun trauma—once and for all. Count me in as a member of the Million Mom March Foundation. I am enclosing my tax-deductible membership gift in the amount of:

☐ **$20** ☐ **$25** ☐ **$35** ☐ **$50*** ☐ **$100** ☐ **$250** ☐ **$1000** ☐ **$**_____

* You will receive a Million Mom March T-shirt with your gift of $50 or more.

My e-mail address is:

Your gifts are tax-deductible to the full extent allowed by law.

_____

Please complete and return this form with your check to the Million Mom March Foundation, Membership Services Department, 2550 Ninth Street, Suite 1065, Berkeley, CA 94710. If you prefer, call 1-888-989-MOMS toll-free, or visit us online at www.millionmommarch.com.

☐ **Send me information about joining a Million Mom March chapter near me.**

☐ **I am interested in starting a chapter of the Million Mom March.**

☐ **Please send me e-mail alerts about gun issues in my state and community.**

MILLION MOM MARCH FOUNDATION

Sensible gun laws, safe kids

RECYCLED & RECYCLABLE / PRINTED WITH SOY INK   65022M

EXHIBIT 6.2 New Member Enrollment Form, Million Mom March Foundation

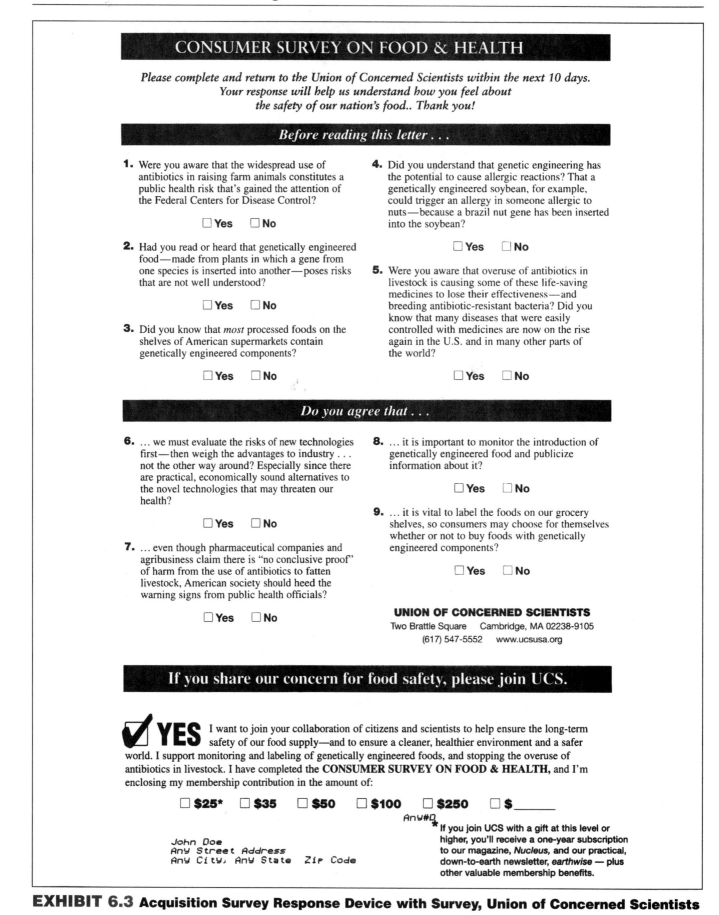

CONSUMER SURVEY ON FOOD & HEALTH

Please complete and return to the Union of Concerned Scientists within the next 10 days.
Your response will help us understand how you feel about
the safety of our nation's food.. Thank you!

Before reading this letter . . .

1. Were you aware that the widespread use of antibiotics in raising farm animals constitutes a public health risk that's gained the attention of the Federal Centers for Disease Control?

☐ **Yes** ☐ **No**

2. Had you read or heard that genetically engineered food—made from plants in which a gene from one species is inserted into another—poses risks that are not well understood?

☐ **Yes** ☐ **No**

3. Did you know that *most* processed foods on the shelves of American supermarkets contain genetically engineered components?

☐ **Yes** ☐ **No**

4. Did you understand that genetic engineering has the potential to cause allergic reactions? That a genetically engineered soybean, for example, could trigger an allergy in someone allergic to nuts—because a brazil nut gene has been inserted into the soybean?

☐ **Yes** ☐ **No**

5. Were you aware that overuse of antibiotics in livestock is causing some of these life-saving medicines to lose their effectiveness—and breeding antibiotic-resistant bacteria? Did you know that many diseases that were easily controlled with medicines are now on the rise again in the U.S. and in many other parts of the world?

☐ **Yes** ☐ **No**

Do you agree that . . .

6. . . . we must evaluate the risks of new technologies first—then weigh the advantages to industry . . . not the other way around? Especially since there are practical, economically sound alternatives to the novel technologies that may threaten our health?

☐ **Yes** ☐ **No**

7. . . . even though pharmaceutical companies and agribusiness claim there is "no conclusive proof" of harm from the use of antibiotics to fatten livestock, American society should heed the warning signs from public health officials?

☐ **Yes** ☐ **No**

8. . . . it is important to monitor the introduction of genetically engineered food and publicize information about it?

☐ **Yes** ☐ **No**

9. . . . it is vital to label the foods on our grocery shelves, so consumers may choose for themselves whether or not to buy foods with genetically engineered components?

☐ **Yes** ☐ **No**

UNION OF CONCERNED SCIENTISTS
Two Brattle Square   Cambridge, MA 02238-9105
(617) 547-5552   www.ucsusa.org

If you share our concern for food safety, please join UCS.

✔ **YES** I want to join your collaboration of citizens and scientists to help ensure the long-term safety of our food supply—and to ensure a cleaner, healthier environment and a safer world. I support monitoring and labeling of genetically engineered foods, and stopping the overuse of antibiotics in livestock. I have completed the **CONSUMER SURVEY ON FOOD & HEALTH,** and I'm enclosing my membership contribution in the amount of:

☐ **$25*** ☐ **$35** ☐ **$50** ☐ **$100** ☐ **$250** ☐ **$_____**

Any#Q

* If you join UCS with a gift at this level or higher, you'll receive a one-year subscription to our magazine, *Nucleus,* and our practical, down-to-earth newsletter, *earthwise* — plus other valuable membership benefits.

John Doe
Any Street Address
Any City, Any State   Zip Code

EXHIBIT 6.3 Acquisition Survey Response Device with Survey, Union of Concerned Scientists

R.S.V.P.

Yes, Raúl, count me in!

To celebrate the growing respect Latinos now command in U.S. society, I will proudly join you as the newest Associate of the *National Council of La Raza.*

John Doe
123 Anystreet
Anytown, Usa 12345-6789

I am pleased to support your continuing efforts to raise the profile of the Latino community nationally and to provide vital services to millions of less fortunate Hispanic Americans.

Enclosed is my tax-deductible gift in the amount of:

☐ $20   ☐ $25   ☐ $35*   ☐ $50   ☐ $100   ☐ Other $_____

N C L R

* With a gift of $35 or more, you will be entitled to all the privileges and benefits of an Associate of the National Council, including a free one-year's subscription to the quarterly Hispanic journal, Agenda, and periodic alerts on important legislative matters.

☐ Please inform me about information available to Associates by e-mail.
   My e-mail address is: _____

NATIONAL COUNCIL OF LA RAZA

Please return this card along with your check payable to *"NCLR"*.

THANK YOU VERY MUCH FOR PLAYING YOUR PART IN ADVANCING THE WELL-BEING OF THE HISPANIC COMMUNITY!

48022D   Recycled and recyclable/printed with soy ink

DETACH HERE AND KEEP THIS FOR YOUR RECORDS

Gift Amount $ _____   Date _____
Check # _____

P.O. Box 97249
Washington, DC 20077-7414

N C L R

NATIONAL COUNCIL OF LA RAZA

EXHIBIT 6.4 New Member Enrollment Form, National Council of La Raza

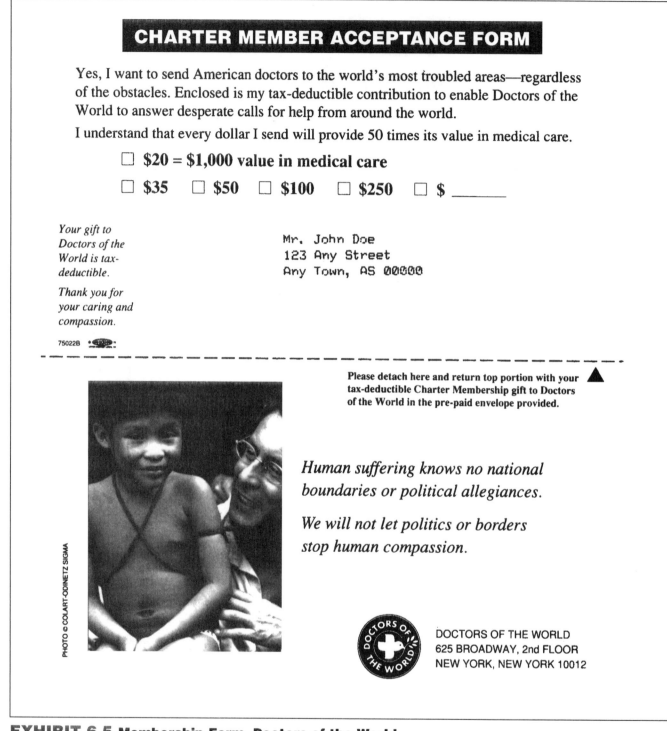

CHARTER MEMBER ACCEPTANCE FORM

Yes, I want to send American doctors to the world's most troubled areas—regardless of the obstacles. Enclosed is my tax-deductible contribution to enable Doctors of the World to answer desperate calls for help from around the world.

I understand that every dollar I send will provide 50 times its value in medical care.

☐ **$20 = $1,000 value in medical care**

☐ **$35**　☐ **$50**　☐ **$100**　☐ **$250**　☐ **$** _____

Your gift to Doctors of the World is tax-deductible.

Thank you for your caring and compassion.

75022B

Mr. John Doe
123 Any Street
Any Town, AS 00000

PHOTO © COLART-ODINETZ SIGMA

Please detach here and return top portion with your tax-deductible Charter Membership gift to Doctors of the World in the pre-paid envelope provided.

Human suffering knows no national boundaries or political allegiances.

We will not let politics or borders stop human compassion.

DOCTORS OF THE WORLD
625 BROADWAY, 2nd FLOOR
NEW YORK, NEW YORK 10012

EXHIBIT 6.5 Membership Form, Doctors of the World

Eight Steps Toward Successful Fundraising Letters

Not long ago, a man who has been raising money by mail for more than thirty years bragged to me that he rarely spends more than an hour or two writing a fundraising letter—and he has been responsible for some big winners. Some of the most successful appeals he has ever written, he claimed, took no more than forty-five or sixty minutes of work.

You may choose to believe his claim or not. (I, for one, am skeptical.) But you won't hear me making similar assertions. I've been known to spend hours—even, occasionally, days—wrestling with a marketing concept before I set a single word down on paper.

In other words, I sometimes spend just as long thinking about what I'm going to write as another writer might require to do the job from start to finish. It's usually time well spent, as far as I'm concerned. Once I know what I'm going to write, the rest goes much more smoothly (at least most of the time).

Developing the marketing concept is just the first of eight steps I take when writing a fundraising letter, but it may occupy half or three-quarters of all the time I spend on a project.

The eight-step sequence I follow may not work for you. In fact, you may believe you're better off working like my colleague Stephen

Hitchcock, who swears he writes *in order to* think (rather than the other way around). I suspect the truth is that Steve simply thinks a lot faster than most of the rest of us. You may too. Nevertheless, I hope you'll try it my way at least once. You might even like it!

So let's run through the eight steps, one by one. Assume that you've been assigned the task of writing a simple, straightforward special appeal to the active donors of a charity called "Hope Is Alive!" Here is the way I recommend you go about the project.

Step 1: Develop the Marketing Concept

Write a complete marketing concept, so you'll understand the offer you'll be making in the letter. Writing this concept down will force you to decide how much money to ask for, who will sign your letter, and whether you'll include a donor involvement device (such as a survey), a premium, or a deadline—all the things you're writing the letter about. In this case, let's say you've determined that the marketing concept runs as follows:

> As Executive Director of Hope Is Alive! I've written you many times in the past about the terrible challenges faced by the homeless in our city. Now I'm writing to you, as one of our most loyal and generous supporters, to tell you about a challenge that's a wonderful **opportunity**: two members of the Board of Trustees have volunteered to match your gift on a dollar-for-dollar basis if we receive it before January 15—up to a total of $10,000. The money raised in this Challenge of Hope will be used to outfit our new shelter, so that thirty more homeless families can find a warm and secure place to sleep in the difficult weeks still to go before winter ends.

Now you're *almost* ready to start writing the appeal itself.

Step 2: Determine the Contents of Package

Exactly what are you going to write? A long letter or a short one? A window envelope with text (a "teaser") on the outside or a businesslike, "closed face" (no window) envelope with no printing except the name Hope Is Alive! and the return address? In other words, it's time to determine how your marketing concept will be implemented as a fundraising package. What will the appeal consist of? In preparing this particular appeal, you might decide the following components are adequate to the task:

- A Number 10 closed-face outer envelope printed in black on the front only, with the addressee's name and address laser-printed on the front and mailed first class with a postage stamp
- A two- or three-page letter, 8½ by 11 inches, printed in two colors, one side only on two (or, if necessary, three) sheets, with page 1 laser-personalized and subsequent pages printed to match but not personalized
- A reply device, approximately 3¼ by 8½ inches (to fit unfolded in a Number 10 envelope), printed on one side only, in two colors, on card stock, with name, address, and the ask amounts laser-personalized
- A Number 9 business reply envelope printed in one color on one side only

I suggest you write all this information down on a sheet of paper. Label it something like "Contents of Package." And take the time necessary to describe in some detail the paper stock and other specifications for each of the items you've decided to include in the package.

These are never casual choices. You've settled on a closed-face outer envelope with no teaser because you reason that committed donors will be inclined to open an appeal from Hope Is Alive! without an extravagant promise on the envelope. You've picked a two- or three-page letter with no brochure or other graphic enclosures because the story of the matching gift challenge is easily told and the January 15 deadline fosters a sense of urgency that might be undermined by a photo brochure that takes time, trouble, and expense to design and print.

Note how much closer you're getting now to knowing exactly what you're going to write. If you were writing a package to acquire new members rather than solicit support from proven donors, you might feel the need for a longer letter, a bigger reply device (to accommodate a full listing of membership benefits perhaps), plus a brochure or other insert, and maybe a premium such as name stickers as well. You might also find laser personalization is impractical in such a member acquisition package (because it's unlikely to be cost-effective). Before you actually write a letter, you need to know such things for two reasons: (1) the person in charge of getting the letter printed and mailed will need to secure printing and lettershop bids and (2) you need to know the space limitations you'll be facing when you write.

Even what might seem like inconsequential details can make a big difference in the way you go about writing a letter. Take, for example, the way the choice of printing technology affects the choice of minimum suggested gift levels in the letter. The choice of laser personalization on the reply device and the first page of the letter allows you to ask for gifts commensurate with each individual's giving history, since those amounts appear in the same computer file as the names and addresses. However, if you don't laser-personalize the letter's subsequent pages, you can't repeat the specific ask amounts printed on page one. If the final page of the letter is to be reproduced on an offset printing press rather than a laser printer, any ask amounts printed there will all be identical—something of a disadvantage, since it's customary and advisable to repeat the ask close to the end of an appeal.

But now your choices have been made. You know what you're writing, and you're ready to start.

Step 3: Draft the Reply Device

Drafting the reply device may take no more than a minute or two, since you've already written a complete marketing concept. And as you write the device, you may find yourself fleshing out the marketing concept. For instance, if there are to be several different ask levels or segments in your appeal for Hope Is Alive! now's the time to think through the implications. A gift of $500 might require a dramatically different justification from one of $25. Waiting until later to figure that out might oblige you to do a lot of rewriting.

But this appeal, I've said, is simple and straightforward. So let's assume different versions of the letter aren't needed for different segments. The language on the reply device, then, will read somewhat as follows:

Yes, I'll help meet the Challenge of Hope! so that thirty more homeless families can find a safe, warm place to sleep in the difficult weeks remaining before winter ends. To beat the January 15 deadline—so my gift is matched dollar-for-dollar by the Trustees—I'm sending my special tax-deductible contribution in the amount of:

☐$*[Last + 50%]* ☐$*[Last + 25%]* ☐$_____

Step 4: Write the Outer Envelope

Here's the point where I'm likely to get hung up all over again, even after developing a gem of a marketing concept. If a letter I'm writing requires an outer envelope teaser—one of those brassy, cute, provocative little half-statements and promises—I might find myself dithering for hours before I can get past this crucial fourth step in the process. I can write two thousand words in the time it takes me to devise a really good teaser. More often than not, I have to settle for one that's less than ideal.

Yet a teaser can entice the reader to open the envelope, which nothing else may be able to bring off. A teaser that's doing its job will challenge, question, or intrigue the reader, drawing her more deeply into the silent dialogue that later may give birth to a gift.

Like everything else in a fundraising package, the outer envelope teaser must be appropriate to its type. For example, it's hard to imagine how any of the following teasers could be used on an outer envelope for a donor acquisition package: "It's time to renew!" "Special Bulletin for Members Only," or "Your newsletter is enclosed." All of these are teasers as surely as the most outrageous come-on for a "free gift" or a petition to the president of the United States. So are such seemingly off-handed statements as "First Class Mail" or "Official Documents."

Often the best teaser is no teaser at all. Fundraising letters are almost always crafted to mimic personal letters, so teasers may well cheapen or undermine the effect the writer hopes to achieve. In fact, extensive testing suggests that response isn't necessarily higher when you use a teaser, even when it seems eminently appropriate to do so. I believe that only *really good* teasers have the intended effect. Teasers that fall short of the mark probably have no effect whatsoever—or, worse, they may persuade the reader *not* to open the envelope. After all, for most people, teasers are a dead giveaway for what all too many reflexively look on as junk mail.

The outer envelope in Exhibit 7.1, an oversized (9 by 12 inches) closed-face carrier, was part of a high-dollar fundraising package. The envelope bears first-class stamps, and the only words in sight are those in the address and the corner card, where the return address appears. There was no teaser in the generally accepted sense of that term. But for that appeal, at that time, the absence of a teaser was the best possible come-on. Words calculated to call greater attention to the contents or otherwise hype the appeal would likely have depressed response rather than boosted it. That's why I regard the teaser in Exhibit 7.1 as the best ever, bar none.

Let's assume that you've decided the appeal you're crafting for Hope Is Alive! will be mailed in a closed-face, personalized outer envelope with no teaser. You're ready to move along to the fifth step.

Step 5: Write the Lead

If the opening paragraph of a letter doesn't engage the reader's attention, he's unlikely to read further. Research shows the lead of the letter has higher readership than any other element but the outer envelope copy and the P.S. The lead paragraph—a simple sentence, more often than not—is one of the most important elements in a fundraising letter, which may help explain why the lead is another one of those points where I've been known to clutch.

You won't clutch, however. You know *exactly* how you're going to lead off your letter for Hope Is Alive! You'll begin with a brief, inspiring story about a six-year-old client of the agency who personifies everything that's best about its work—something like this:

> Jennifer just <u>knew</u> things were going to get better. Molly told her so.
>
> Jennifer was only six years old, and she'd spent most of those years on the streets. Drifting from town to town with a dad who could never find work that lasted. No school. No friends, really. No pretty clothes like the other girls she saw sometimes.
>
> But one day Jennifer and her dad showed up at our Front Street shelter. Molly D'Alessandro was on duty and greeted the new arrivals. You might say it was love at first sight.

While you're engaged in writing this lead, you might find it convenient to write the close of the letter as well. Just as the lead ought to be directly connected to the outer envelope teaser, if any, the close

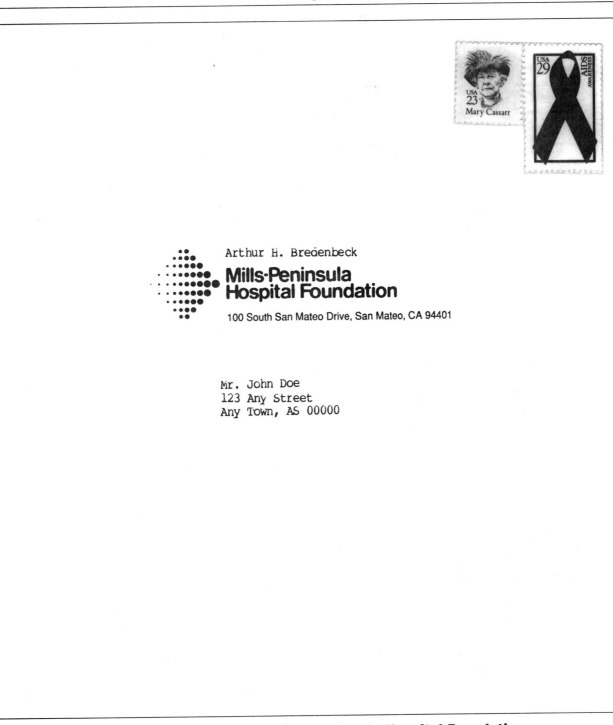

EXHIBIT 7.1 Exemplary Outer Envelope, Mills-Peninsula Hospital Foundation

should relate to the lead. If you began by asking a question, answer it now. If you started by challenging the reader, refer to the challenge again, and note how the offer you've made will enable the reader to respond in a meaningful way. Complete the circle; round out your letter with a satisfying close. In this case, you'll want to be sure that Jennifer and her dad and Molly D'Alessandro all figure in the way you wind up the letter.

Step 6: Write the P.S.

We've learned from Siegfried Vögele that the postscript is the real lead more than 90 percent of the time because that's where readers usually turn first. This step deserves your full attention.

After a lot of thought, you've decided to use the P.S. to emphasize the deadline for receipt of matching gifts in the trustees' challenge grant campaign. The postscript would go something like this:

P.S. Your gift will be matched dollar-for-dollar—but only if we receive your check by January 15. In this difficult winter, please help us outfit the new shelter and take thirty more homeless families off the streets!

This P.S. conveys three of the strongest elements of the appeal—the deadline, the dollar-for-dollar match, and the thirty families who will benefit—at just the place in the letter that's bound to have the highest readership of all.

Now you're ready to move along to the body of the letter itself.

Step 7: Consider Subheads and Underlining

Do you remember Vögele's observations about the behavior of real-world direct mail recipients—how they skip about the text, glancing at a phrase here and a highlighted word or two there? If so, you'll want to decide at the outset what points to highlight visually within the body of the letter.

The items to underline or to feature in subheads aren't necessarily the ones you think will break up the text at the most convenient intervals or help convey your tone of voice. Rather, subheads and underlining must *appeal directly to the reader.* Ideally, such emphasis is used to spotlight donor benefits, tangible or intangible—the payoff to those who respond to the appeal with contributions.

Let's assume you've decided that subheads are inappropriate for the appeal you're writing for Hope Is Alive! Perhaps they're out of character for the signer, the executive director, who tends to be a bit stuffy, or you think subheads detract from the upscale image the agency wants to convey. There's still an easy way for you to accept the benefits offered in your appeal, answer readers' unspoken questions, and make your letter easier to read: by underlining. Do it sparingly on only a few key words and phrases. If possible, choose them before you write the body of the letter. One way you can determine which points warrant underlining (or subheads) is to outline the letter before you write it. If you construct your outline paying particular attention to the benefits you're offering, the appropriate words and phrases may jump off the page.

In this case, you'd be likely to decide that among the points requiring underlining are two important ones:

> If you respond by January 15, _your gift will be matched dollar-for-dollar._
>
> With your generous support, Hope Is Alive! will be able to open the new shelter on time—and _thirty homeless families will be off the streets_ for the rest of the winter.

Instead of emphasizing Hope Is Alive!'s $10,000 budget to outfit the new shelter, you've wisely chosen to stress the thirty homeless families who will have a warm and secure place to sleep. Obviously your readers will care much more about Jennifer and her dad and the other families than about an agency's budget!

Step 8: Write the Text (At Last!)

This is the easy part. You've already written the reply device; you've developed the lead, the close, and the P.S.; you've drafted the principal underlined points. What else is there to do? A game of fill-in-the-blank.

Take care, though; it's all too easy to stumble off-course in the stretch. Tell the story you started about Jennifer and Molly, but don't turn it into a novelette. Make sure the story shows the benefits the reader will receive if she accepts your offer: that Jennifer now has hope for a better life, and so will dozens of other good people trapped in terrible circumstances. Stick to the points you selected for emphasis by underlining.

You picked those points because they answer the unspoken questions you know your reader will have—and because they emphasize the benefits that you hope will motivate the reader to send a gift without delay. If you stay on this course, Hope Is Alive! will raise its $10,000, and those thirty families will be off the streets. You, the author, will be a hero. And so will everyone who responded to your appeal.

In the next chapter let's recap the essentials by reviewing what I call the Cardinal Rules of Fundraising Letters.

The Cardinal Rules of Fundraising Letters

In many ways, the techniques required to write an appeal for funds share a lot with any other sort of writing that's intended to persuade or otherwise produce results. But there are guidelines that apply specifically to writing fundraising letters. I call these axioms the Cardinal Rules of Fundraising Letters.

The Cardinal Rules

To illustrate the eight rules spelled out below, I'll refer to the direct mail package in Exhibits 8.1 through 8.6. It's an appeal mailed by St. Joseph's Indian School of Chamberlain, South Dakota; the letter was one of several efforts to secure an additional gift from one of my newsletter's correspondents in the year after we sent the school an unsolicited $15 check. The appeal isn't without flaws, but it does illustrate the eight rules.

Rule 1: Use I and You (But Mostly You)

You should be the word you use most frequently in your fundraising letters. Your appeal is a letter from one individual to another individual, not a press release, a position paper, or a brochure.

St. Joseph's Indian School
Chamberlain, South Dakota 57326

October 30, 1992

Dear Friend,

You are a dream catcher.

The Lakota (Sioux) believe that good dreams and nightmares float in the air, and that a special willow frame strung with sinew can screen out nightmares and let only good dreams pass through.

They call the ornament a dream catcher and put one in every tipi and on the cradle board of every baby.

The other evening I was walking through the William House, one of our childrens' homes. I peeked in on some of the younger kids who were already asleep. I watched the children sleeping and dreaming peacefully.

Sweet dreams are something new for so many of the children. They've come from such troubled homes — and nightmares are far more common on the reservations. I thought about the Lakota (Sioux) dream catcher and my thoughts turned to you.

You protect our children from nightmares. You save them from poverty, illiteracy, and despair — a nightmare fate that befalls so many Native Americans on the reservations.

You bring them good dreams — of a bright future as well-educated, young adults with a purpose and strong values. And you help make those dreams come true. You are a dream catcher!

Because you are a guardian of good dreams for the children of St. Joseph's, we want you to have a special gift. I've enclosed a Thanksgiving Card that features the Lakota dream catcher.

I hope you'll keep this card to bring good dreams to yourself and your family, or pass it on to bring good dreams to a faraway loved one at Thanksgiving.

Because so many of our friends are interested in Lakota traditions, we have ordered a small number of

EXHIBIT 8.1 Letter, St. Joseph's School Appeal

Lakota dream catchers in antique brass.

If you can send a special gift today of $25 or more, I'd love to send you one of these unique ornaments as a special gift from the children of St. Joseph's.

These highly detailed dream catchers make wonderful gifts for children and new parents, and make unique Christmas Tree decorations.

In any event, please send a gift today of whatever you can afford to bring dreams of hope to the children of St. Joseph's. Without people like you, their lives would be a nightmare.

Thanks!

Yours in Christ,

Bro. David Nagel
Director

P.S. Thanksgiving is a special, happy time around here. It's one of the few times when America remembers all the gifts Native Americans gave to this country — and how little they received in return. Please remember the children of St. Joseph's when you offer thanks over your Thanksgiving dinner. We'll be praying for you.

EXHIBIT 8.1 Continued

Dreams of Hope for the Children

2150050. 079

Mr. Karps:
Send a gift today of $25 or more, we'll send you a beautiful antique brass Dream Catcher ornament as a special gift from the children of St. Joseph's.

Mr. XDakIX Karpx
XOX KdtX48 X7X
XOOKtaXnX XiDtx,x oxXx 94x40x08X7x

IIIluulullllundulllulluuulldulululludu

YES!

I want to be a dream catcher to help bring dreams of hope to the children of St. Joseph's.

2150050. 079

Enclosed is my gift of:

( ) $25   ( ) $15   ( ) $48   ( ) $_____

( ) I have enclosed a gift of $25 or more, please send an antique brass Lakota dream catcher ornament.

Please make your tax-deductible gift payable to St. Joseph's and mail it with this slip. Use the other side for your prayer requests and intentions. Please be sure the return address on the reverse side shows through the window of the enclosed envelope.

St. Joseph's Indian School Chamberlain, South Dakota 57326

EXHIBIT 8.2 Reply Device St. Joseph's School Appeal

PRAY FOR ME

Dear Brother David, I am in need. Please pray for the following intentions.

☐ For the health of my loved ones   ☐ For my peace of mind

☐ For the strength of my marriage   ☐ For my children

☐ Other _____   ☐ For my health

_____

_____

☐ Please send information about your Charitable Gift Annuity.

**Please be sure this address
shows through the window
of the enclosed envelope:**

ST. JOSEPH'S INDIAN SCHOOL
CHAMBERLAIN SD 57326

EXHIBIT 8.2 Continued

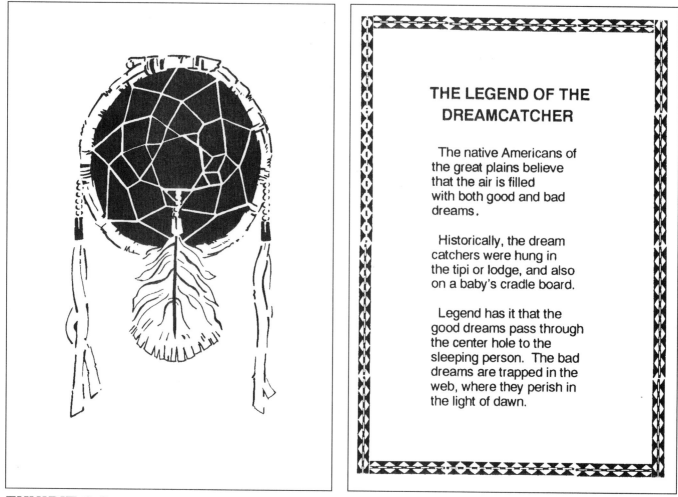

THE LEGEND OF THE DREAMCATCHER

The native Americans of the great plains believe that the air is filled with both good and bad dreams.

Historically, the dream catchers were hung in the tipi or lodge, and also on a baby's cradle board.

Legend has it that the good dreams pass through the center hole to the sleeping person. The bad dreams are trapped in the web, where they perish in the light of dawn.

EXHIBIT 8.3 Dreamcatcher Premium, St. Joseph's School Appeal

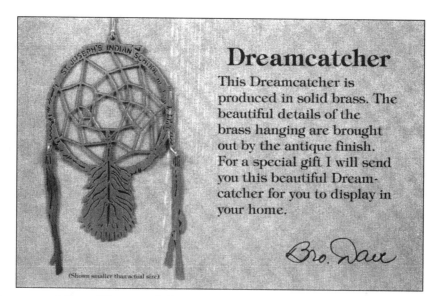

Dreamcatcher

This Dreamcatcher is produced in solid brass. The beautiful details of the brass hanging are brought out by the antique finish. For a special gift I will send you this beautiful Dreamcatcher for you to display in your home.

Bro. Dave

(Shown smaller than actual size)

EXHIBIT 8.4 Dreamcatcher Thanksgiving Card, St. Joseph's School Appeal

make a note!

It's Time For
A Little
End Of The Year
Pre-Planning

You may discover that a timely charitable contribution this time of the year could increase your personal joy of helping the Lakota boys and girls at St. Joseph's and play an important role in reducing your income taxes.

With a little PRE-PLANNING NOW, you may pleasantly learn that you have more charitable gift possibilities than you realize!

One of the ways, as you know, to save on your taxes and do some good at the same time is with a gift to charity. Those who have adequate deductions to itemize, may include their gifts as charitable deductions.

Perhaps you have found in the past that you did not have enough deductions to benefit by itemizing. However, a Larger-Than-Usual gift this year, might enable you to hoist your deductions and allow you to itemize as you benefit from a tax savings.

As we advance toward the final months of 1992, it is wise to begin making plans for gifts that could help you before the year ends.

THIS IS AN IDEAL TIME OF THE YEAR TO CONSIDER A ST. JOSEPH'S CHARITABLE GIFT ANNUITY.

If you have been "thinking about" an annuity but kept putting it off — NOW, BEFORE THE YEAR'S END — is a good time to find out how our Gift Annuity works.

Keep in mind, it is a Gift as well as an Investment! With a St. Joseph's Gift Annuity you are giving to some of the neediest children in our country as well as guaranteeing yourself a lifetime income. PLUS, you are allowed definite tax advantages the year the gift is made. About 45 to 50 percent of your initial gift is considered a charitable deduction by the IRS, and as we pay you, part of your annuity is not taxed.

Our Gift Annuity program is very simple: you give a specified amount ($1,000 or more) to the school and we in turn pay you a FIXED rate of return for as long as you live. The older you are the higher the return. You may be interested in the Single Life contract only — or perhaps the Joint Life plan may be best (even if rates are a bit lower) if you are married.

If you are between the ages of 50 to 65, you might like to investigate our Deferred Gift Annuity plan. With this type of annuity, you contribute your gift right away and claim the Charitable Deduction portion the year it is given. However, your income payments do not begin until a later-specified time, perhaps the year you retire. In the meantime, your gift

is safe and accruing interest. This is a very useful plan for individuals or married couples who could use the Charitable Deduction during their working years but will not need the income until they retire.

You may wish to consider exchanging appreciated stocks or bonds for a St. Joseph's Charitable Gift Annuity. This can be a wise way to make a gift, which may eliminate some of your capital gains tax, and earn a charitable deduction the year the gift is made.

Now as the year is rapidly ending it is an excellent time to find out more about a St. Joseph's

Charitable Gift Annuity. Fill out the attached coupon and return it to us. We would be delighted to send you a personalized proposal before the year ends.

EXHIBIT 8.5 Charitable Gift Annuity Brochure, St. Joseph's School Appeal

REMEMBER

1) Donations made to St. Joseph's on or before December 31 are deductible this year if you itemize.

2) A gift that is larger-than-usual might enable you to itemize for your 1992 taxes.

3) Consider a gift of appreciated stocks and avoid capital gains tax or receive a considerable savings if exchanged for a Charitable Gift Annuity.

4) This is a beautiful time of the year to give a memorial gift in honor of a loved one while making a charitable gift to us.

5) The IRS allows a charitable deduction for gifts of property such as antiques, artwork, jewelry, and any type of collection if we can actually use it for the school. The deduction would be for the fair market value of the object given.

6) The joy and satisfaction of making a major type gift to the Lakota boys and girls at St. Joseph's Indian School.

It is always wise to consult your tax advisor before any final contribution is made that may affect your tax outcome.

Special Gifts
St. Joseph's Indian School
P.O. Box 100
Chamberlain, SD 57325-0100

Dear Brother David,

Please use the following information to calculate my Gift Annuity benefits. I understand that I am under no obligation and this personalized proposal is FREE.

☐ Immediate Gift Annuity   ☐ Deferred Gift Annuity (payments to begin year_____)

Amount of Gift Being Considered: $_____ (Minimum Annuity Amount $1,000.)

Frequency of Payment Desired: ☐ Annual   ☐ 2 Times/Year   ☐ 4 Times/Year ($5,000 Min.)   ☐ Monthly ($10,000 Min.)

Name (Mr., Mrs., Miss) _____

Address _____

City _____ State _____ Zip. _____

Telephone _____

☐ We are interested in a Two (Joint) Annuity plan.

Birth Date: Month_____ Day_____ Year_____

Name of Second Annuitant: _____

Birth Date: Month_____ Day_____ Year_____

Relationship of Second Annuitant: _____

Please Note: For proposed annuitant(s) less than 50 years of age, we write only Deferred Payment Annuities—payments typically to start at age 65. (All information is confidential.)

EXHIBIT 8.5 Continued

EXHIBIT 8.6 Outer Envelope and Reply Envelope, St. Joseph's School Appeal

Studies on readability supply the fundamental reason the words *you* and *I* are important: they provide human interest. Stories, anecdotes, and common names (and capitalized words in general) have some of the same effect, but the most powerful way to engage the reader is by appealing directly to her: use the word *you*.

In the St. Joseph's Indian School fundraising letter (Exhibit 8.1), notice how Brother David Nagel uses these powerful personal pronouns to establish intimacy:

> You are a dream catcher. . . .
>> I peeked in on some of the younger kids who were already asleep. . . .
>> You protect our children from nightmares. You save them from poverty, illiteracy, and despair. . . .
>> I hope you'll keep this card to bring good dreams to yourself and your family. . . .

Note that the singular "Dear Friend" is used here—and the same singular salutation appears even if the letter is addressed to a married couple. (Only one person at a time reads a letter.) Abolish the plural *you* from your vocabulary (as in "Dear Friends," for example). Try to avoid the royal *we* too; it smacks of condescension and will detract from the personal character of your appeal.

Use of the singular will require that you stick to a single letter signer. You'll cause yourself two problems by using more than one signer. First, you won't be able to enliven your letter with the personal details and emotional asides that might come naturally in a letter from one person to another. And second, with multiple signers, you'll sacrifice suspension of disbelief: your reader's willingness to accept that your letter is actually a personal, one-to-one appeal.

Think about it: how am I as the receiver of this letter to believe that two or three busy people who don't live together or work in the same office have collaborated in writing a fundraising letter to me? Which one of them typed the letter? (*Or was it really someone else?*) Did they both *actually* sign it? These are not questions you want your readers to be asking!

When to Break Rule 1

You may write a letter in the first-person plural *if*—and only if—there's a special reason to do so—for example, if the letter is to be signed by a married couple, or your organization's two venerable cofounders, or a famous Republican and a famous Democrat. Even in such exceptional cases, however, I advise you to craft the letter *as though it were written by only one* of the two signers, in much the same manner as one of those annual family letters that arrive by the bushel every December. Something like this: "When Bob and I agreed to co-chair this fundraising drive, it was absolutely clear to both of us that we'd have to turn first to the agency's most loyal and generous donors—people just like you."

Rule 2: Appeal on the Basis of Benefits, Not Needs

Donors give money because they get something in return (if only good feelings). To tap their generosity, describe what they'll receive in return for their money—such benefits as lives saved, or human dignity gained, or larger causes served. And don't be shy about emphasizing tangible benefits. Donors may tell you they give money for nobler reasons, but premiums often make a difference. (Most donors read your letters in the privacy of their own homes. They don't have to admit their own mixed motives to anyone—not even themselves.)

Look at how Brother David bases his request for funds to the St. Joseph's Indian School on the benefits to the donor, both tangible and intangible:

> If you can send a special gift today of $25 or more, I'd love to send you one of these unique ornaments as a special gift from the children of St. Joseph's.
>
> These highly detailed dreamcatchers make wonderful gifts for children and new parents, and make unique Christmas Tree decorations.
>
> In any event, please send a gift today of whatever you can afford to bring dreams of hope to the children of St. Joseph's. Without people like you, their lives would be a nightmare.

When to Break Rule 2 If you're sending a genuine emergency appeal, you'd be foolish not to write about your organization's needs—and graphically so. But if it isn't a real emergency (and you'll really be in trouble if you habitually cry wolf), then write about benefits, not needs. In the long run, you'll raise a lot more money that way.

Rule 3: Ask for Money, Not for "Support"

Almost always the purpose of a fundraising letter is to ask for financial help. Be sure you do so clearly, explicitly, and repeatedly. The ask shouldn't be an afterthought, tacked onto the end of a letter; it's your *reason* for writing. Repeat the ask several times in the body of the letter as well as on the reply device. It may even be appropriate to lead your letter with the ask.

Note in the St. Joseph's appeal that the ask appears twice in the letter and twice again on the reply device (Exhibit 8.2). Notice, too, how clear and explicit the requests for funds are: "Send a special gift today of $25 or more," "Please send a gift today of whatever you can afford," "Send a gift today of $25 or more," and "Enclosed is my gift of . . . "

When to Break Rule 3 Many direct mail packages are structured not as appeals for funds but as invitations to join a membership organization. Others feature surveys or other donor involvement devices. In these cases, deemphasize the financial commitment, and highlight membership benefits—or stress the impact of completing the survey or mailing the postcard you've enclosed.

Rule 4: Write a Package, Not a Letter

Your fundraising letter is the single most important element in the mailing package, but it's only one of several items that must fit smoothly together and work as a whole. At a minimum, your package will probably include an outer (or carrier) envelope, a reply envelope, and a reply device in addition to the letter. When you sit down to write, think about how each of these components will help persuade donors to *send money now*. Make sure the same themes, symbols, colors, and typefaces are used on all elements, so the package is as memorable and accessible as possible. And be certain every element in the package relates directly to the big idea or marketing concept that gives the appeal its unity. (We spoke about marketing concepts in Chapter Six.)

Notice that the St. Joseph's Indian School package contains seven components:

- Outer (carrier) envelope
- Two-page letter (Exhibit 8.1)
- Reply device (Exhibit 8.2)
- Photograph in full color of the dreamcatcher premium (Exhibit 8.3)

- Dreamcatcher Thanksgiving card (Exhibit 8.4)
- Charitable gift annuity brochure (Exhibit 8.5)
- Outer envelope and reply envelope (Exhibit 8.6)

Examine these components carefully, and you'll see several earmarks of a successful effort to package the contents of this appeal in a unified way:

- Theme. The dreamcatcher theme, the big idea in this appeal, is emphasized on every component of the package except for the brochure on gift annuities and the nearly text-free reply envelope.
- Subtext (or underlying theme). The subtext of gift giving is explicit almost everywhere and implicit everywhere else. There's no mistaking that this is an appeal for funds, but it's couched as an exchange of gifts.
- Color. Although you can't see them in this book's black-and-white reproduction, the colors used on the outer envelope, the letter, and the reply device are identical: black text with bright orange accenting and imagery. (The brochure is printed in red and black.)

When to Break Rule 4 Sometimes it pays to spend a little extra money on a package insert that doesn't directly relate to the marketing concept. For example, a premium offer might be presented on a *buckslip*—an insert designed to highlight the premium—but the offer might not appear anywhere else in the package (with the possible exception of the reply device). Often, in fact, a buckslip works best if it doesn't use the same color and design as other package elements so that it stands out more clearly.

Rule 5: Write in Simple, Straightforward English

Use compact, powerful words and short, punchy sentences. Favor words that convey emotions over those that communicate thoughts. Avoid foreign phrases or big words. Minimize the use of adjectives and adverbs. Don't use abbreviations or acronyms; spell out names, even if their repetition looks a little silly to you. Repeat (and underline) key words and phrases.

Brother David's simple, unadorned language, free of pretense, in his letter (Exhibit 8.1) helps convey the strength of his appeal: "good dreams and nightmares," "the younger kids," "You bring them good dreams," and "to bring dreams of hope to the children."

When to Break Rule 5 A letter that could have been written by a twelve year old might not look right bearing the signature of a college president or a U.S. senator, so follow this rule judiciously. But don't make the mistake of confusing big words, complex sentences, and complicated thoughts with intelligent communication: the most literate fundraising letter needs to be clear and straightforward.

Rule 6: Format Your Letter for Easy Reading

The eye needs rest, so be conscious of the white space you're leaving around your copy:

- Indent every paragraph.
- Avoid paragraphs more than seven lines long, but vary the length of your paragraphs.
- Use bullets and indented paragraphs.
- In long letters, try subheads that are centered and underlined. Underline sparingly but consistently throughout your letter— enough to call attention to key words and phrases, especially those that highlight the benefits to the reader, but not so much as to distract the eye from your message.

Take another look at the St. Joseph's appeal in Exhibit 8.1. Notice that not a single paragraph in the body of the letter is longer than five lines (and there's only one that long). Only the P.S. exceeds that limit, with seven lines. Every paragraph is indented the standard five spaces, although the letter is printed on Monarch-sized paper. There are neither underlining nor bulleted points in Brother David's appeal, but they aren't needed here; the letter is short enough and sufficiently appealing. It's easy to read.

When to Break Rule 6 Don't mechanically follow this rule. Some special formats, such as telegrams or handwritten notes, have formatting rules of their own. Don't ignore them. Remember that you want the reader to believe—or at least to *act* as though she believes—that you've sent her a telegram, a handwritten note, or a personal letter (or whatever else the communication might be).

Rule 7: Give Your Readers a Reason to Send Money NOW

Creating a sense of urgency is one of your biggest copywriting challenges. Try to find a genuine reason that gifts are needed right away: for example, a deadline for a matching grant or an approaching election date. Or tie your fund request to a budgetary deadline so you can argue why "gifts are needed within the next 15 days." There is *always* a reason to send a gift now. And the argument for the urgency of your appeal bears repeating—ideally, not just in the text of your letter but also in a P.S. and on the reply device.

There are several ways Brother David builds a sense of urgency in his appeal for the children of St. Joseph's Indian School:

- The emphasis on Thanksgiving in an appeal dated October 30 provides a natural and easily understood deadline.
- The brochure headlining "It's Time for a Little End of the Year Pre-Planning" (Exhibit 8.5) sets a fallback date, December 31, thus laying down a second line of urgency.
- Brother David's comment that "we have ordered a small number of Lakota dreamcatchers" implies that the supply could run out quickly, leaving the donor *without* "wonderful gifts for children and new parents."
- The topic of "poverty, illiteracy, and despair," set out in the letter, is freighted with urgency all its own.

When to Break Rule 7 Be very careful about fixed deadlines if you're mailing by bulk rate, which might delay delivery by two weeks or more. (Instead of giving a date, use a phrase like "within the next two weeks.") Don't overuse the same arguments for urgency, lest your credibility suffer. And try not to depend on deadlines based on actual dates in large-scale mailings to acquire new donors: the value of those letters will almost always be greater if you can continue to use the same letter over and over again.

Rule 8: Write as Long a Letter as You Need to Make the Case for Your Offer

Not everyone will read every word you write, but some recipients will do so, no matter how long your letter. Others will scan your copy for the information that interests them the most. To be certain you push *their* hot buttons, use every strong argument you can devise for your readers to send you money now. And to spell out every argument may mean writing a very long letter; it may also mean repeating what you've written to the same donors many times in the past. But don't worry about boring your readers by restating your case: research repeatedly reveals that even many of the most active donors remember very little about the organizations they support.

Brother David's appeal for St. Joseph's is only two pages long. If all the information contained in the two inserts devoted specifically to the dreamcatcher offer were to be included in the letter rather than printed as separate items, the appeal would run to three pages. (It's much better the way it is.) Still, this letter doesn't convey enough information about St. Joseph's to answer the questions that might occur to a *prospective* donor who has never before heard of the school. (For starters: "How many kids attend the school? Where is Chamberlain? Does all the money come from donors like me, or does the government pay too?") This appeal was mailed to a previous donor who presumably has had those questions answered.

When to Break Rule 8 Not every organization and not every appeal calls for a long letter. A well-known organization with a readily identifiable purpose—the American Red Cross, for example, or a prominent children's hospital—might be able to make its case with only a sentence or two. Similarly, in writing to your proven donors, you can sometimes state the argument for a straightforward membership renewal or special appeal in just a few words. "It's time to renew your membership" is a good example.

Three More Things to Keep in Mind

If you follow the eight rules I've just described, you won't go far wrong when you write your next fundraising appeal. But I suggest you also keep in mind the psychology of the position you've placed yourself in as the signer of your letter. You might want to consider the following as three additional rules of writing fundraising letters:

- "You" (the signer) are an individual human being, with hopes, fears, convictions, and experiences. Look at how Brother David takes up that challenge, writing about "sweet dreams," "nightmares," "despair," "loved ones," and "wonderful gifts." This is no masterpiece of self-revelation, but it gives a sense of a man who is engaged in his work and feels strongly about the children at the school.
- "You" are writing to one person, the addressee, who has hopes, fears, convictions, and experiences too. Notice how Brother David appeals directly to the donor's feelings: "You bring them good feelings," "to bring good dreams to yourself and your family," "Without people like you, their lives would be a nightmare."
- Regardless of its mission, your organization addresses human needs on many levels, intangible as well as concrete, emotional as well as practical. Those are the things people care about. Remember that Brother David doesn't write about budgets, fiscal years, and funding shortfalls. He writes about *the kids*—their dreams, their nightmares.

Rating Your Writing

Some people think that writing fundraising letters is pure art. Others insist the work is simply a matter of building on well-known formulas. Judging from the hundreds (sometimes thousands) of fundraising appeals I see every year, they're both wrong. There's precious little art in evidence. And if formulas really work in writing fundraising letters, they're not well known because their influence doesn't show either.

Without a formula for success, most level-headed folks would be likely to think that there is no systematic way to assess the effectiveness of a fundraising letter. But as a life-long contrarian, I maintain that there are two ways to do so:

The standard way. Just mail the letter, and you'll see how well it works. However, if you've been doing a little too much of that and with too little to show for it, you might try using the following method to review your work before the market renders its own, possibly costly, opinion.

My way. With my cardinal rules as a point of departure, I've developed a simple self-assessment form for a fundraising appeal, reproduced as Exhibit 8.7. (Note that in the course of converting the cardinal rules into a method of evaluation, I've lent more weight to some factors and less to others.) If this is a formulaic approach, so be it. It works for me.

Let's move on to Chapter Nine, where we'll examine some of the more general considerations that come into play when you're writing for results.

Rate the package on each criterion by circling the rating, with 5 = best, 0 = worst.

Cardinal Rule Number	Criterion	Rating	Weight	Total
1	Speaks *to* the reader, *from* the signer. Uses the singular personal pronouns, *you* and *I*.	0 1 2 3 4 5	× 2 =	
2	Talks about benefits, not needs.	0 1 2 3 4 5	× 3 =	
3	The "offer" is unmistakably clear. Benefits to donor are compelling. Asks for a specific amount of money or other explicit act.	0 1 2 3 4 5	× 5 =	
4	Unified into a whole package, with components reinforcing each other.	0 1 2 3 4 5	× 2 =	
5	Powerful writing style: short words, emotion, short sentences, short paragraphs, no ten-dollar words, foreign expressions, abbreviations, acronyms. Uses Anglo-Saxon, not Latin.	0 1 2 3 4 5	× 2 =	
6	Formatted and designed for easy reading. Uses white space, indents, bullets, underlining, a P.S. Looks like a typewritten letter.	0 1 2 3 4 5	× 1 =	
7	Establishes urgency by making the case to take action *now*.	0 1 2 3 4 5	× 2 =	
8	Letter is as long (or as short) as necessary to make the case. Must address all the unspoken questions a reader is likely to have.	0 1 2 3 4 5	× 1 =	
9	Outer envelope commands attention, provokes curiosity.	0 1 2 3 4 5	× 3 =	
10	Response device makes it easy to take action.	0 1 2 3 4 5	× 2 =	
11	Effectively uses color, graphics, white space to emphasize essentials: benefits, deadline, call to action.	0 1 2 3 4 5	× 1 =	
	TOTAL			

Total the 11 ratings. (Remember: 0 × 5 = 0!) Then, to evaluate your score, turn to the next page.

EXHIBIT 8.7 Rating Your Writing Worksheet

How to evaluate your score

With as many as 5 points available for each of the eleven criteria, and weighting factors that total 24, a perfect score is 120 points. You may translate a numerical score into a letter grade as follows:

Rating	Letter Grade	Meaning
110–120	A+	No more need be said.
100–109	A	Give that writer a pat on the back!
80–99	B	Shows lots of promise.
60–79	C	Needs some improvement.
30–59	D	Requires a lot of work. Maybe better to start from scratch!
0–29	F	Uh-oh!

EXHIBIT 8.7 Continued

You're Writing for Results— Not for a Pulitzer Prize

My brother has never forgiven me. Art was eighteen and about to enter his first year of college. He has since become a respected psychiatrist and taught at universities that rival any I've ever attended. But back then—to my mind, at least—he was just my snot-nosed younger brother. And Art was absolutely, positively guaranteed to stumble over freshman English—or so everyone else in our family was convinced.

Since I was three years older than my brother and a veteran of hundreds of essays, letters, stories, reviews, and critiques, not to mention a few political speeches, our mother pressed me into service during that summer of 1962. As a former English teacher, she was suffering from acute embarrassment in addition to her maternal fear for Art's future.

"Make yourself useful for a change," she told me. "Help your brother. Teach him how to write."

This assignment pleased neither Art nor me, but orders were orders. (Our parents were still paying the bills, after all.) With mutual ill will, we took up our new roles: I as a teacher, he approximating the role of the obedient younger brother.

Things went from bad to worse after I gave Art his first assignment: a 500-word essay entitled "How to Tie Your Shoelaces."

Art wrote and then rewrote that essay at least a dozen times, each successive draft a mosaic of my notations in red, blue, and black pencil. The essay was finished only after painful daily sessions stretching over several weeks. Along the way, there were countless changes in word order and sentence structure. We discarded adjectives and adverbs, shifted prepositions, changed verbs, and thumbed through *Roget's Thesaurus* for sparkling new nouns. But when the job was complete and we were ready to proceed with the second assignment, it was obvious that what Art had learned about writing had little to do with any of the changes we'd made in his labored drafts. The essence of what he learned (and I "taught") was this:

- To write clearly and effectively, the writer must *think* before setting pen to paper (or, more likely now, fingers to the keyboard). Clearly written communication is nothing more—and nothing less—than a reflection of disciplined, logical thinking.
- When writing to achieve results, the writer must *make things easy for the reader.* Unless held at gunpoint or facing the loss of a job, the reader has no obligation to the writer and nothing to fear. The reader is free to abandon what she or he is reading and turn to something more personally rewarding—like badminton or Beethoven, for example.
- The *right* word is not necessarily the most colorful or even the most precise. The right word is the strongest, the most expressive word—the word that communicates the writer's meaning most effectively.
- A skillful writer can make any subject interesting, amusing, or at least palatable.

Perhaps I'm kidding myself. Art may never have learned those four things at all. Or his freshman English teachers might have forced some discipline into his writing where I'd utterly failed. But I cherish the thought that my brother's subsequent academic success had at least a little to do with my drillmaster's brand of summertime writing instruction.

Like so many of the other times in my life when I thought I was helping someone else, I was really helping myself a lot more. That summer, acting in the belief that a good teacher needs to be thoroughly familiar with his text, I reread Strunk and White.

If you're not familiar with this legendary little volume, I suggest you pick up a copy and devour it. If you already know the book, reread it before you start your next writing job. Its title is *The Elements of Style,* its coauthors William Strunk, Jr., and E. B. White. It's readily available in inexpensive paperback editions throughout North America, and—perhaps best of all—*The Elements of Style* is truly a *little* book. My 1950s-vintage paperback version is all of seventy-one pages long.

Some writers claim they can get along quite well without Strunk and White or any other grounding in the basics of writing. I'm told there are hugely successful advertising and public relations copywriters who learned everything they know on the job. I'm skeptical of this assertion, which I ascribe largely to the self-promotion that's so common among people who traffic in myths. But for the sake of argument, let's accept the claim that copywriters can learn their craft even if they're ignorant of the fundamentals of English style. That doesn't mean it's a good idea to violate all the rules. In fact, I believe the copywriter's life will be easier—and probably more successful—if it starts with training in the basics. That brings us to Dr. Rudolf Flesch.

Rudolf Flesch's Rules of Effective Writing

Generations of Americans have turned to Rudolf Flesch for advice on effective writing and speaking, and no wonder. Flesch's books, written decades ago, contain insights as fresh today as when they were newly written. I especially recommend *How to Write, Speak and Think More Effectively* (an inexpensive and widely available paperback available from NAL/Signet and described in Resource H). Flesch's "Rules of Effective Writing" are well worth reading in full, but here's the gist of them:

- Write about people, things, and facts.
- Write as you speak.
- Use contractions.
- Use the first person.
- Quote what was said or written.
- Put yourself in the reader's place.
- Don't be too brief.
- Plan a beginning, middle, and end.

- Go from the rule to the exception and from the familiar to the new.
- Use short forms of names.
- Use pronouns rather than repeating nouns.
- Use verbs rather than nouns.
- Use the active voice.
- Use small, round figures.
- Be specific. Use illustrations, cases, and examples.
- Start a new sentence for each new idea.
- Keep sentences and paragraphs short.
- Use direct questions.
- Underline for emphasis.
- Make your writing interesting to look at.

These aren't arbitrary rules of taste or style. They're the result of Flesch's studies of readers' reactions to written material.

Rudolf Flesch is the all-time master of the study of readability, which means the likelihood that what you've written will actually be understood (and possibly remembered) by your readers. Flesch held sway in an era when numerical measurements inspired more faith than they do in today's skeptical society, but his charts, graphs, and scores are still useful.

Flesch found, for example, that two key indicators of the readability of writing were the number of syllables per 100 words and the average length of a sentence (expressed in number of words).

I won't go into the precise way Flesch defined these two measurements. You can read it yourself in his book (and I hope you will). But look at how Flesch interprets these measurements:

Description of Style	Syllables per 100 Words	Average Sentence Length (number of words)
Very easy	123	8
Easy	131	11
Fairly easy	139	14
Standard	147	17
Fairly difficult	155	21
Difficult	167	25
Very difficult	192	29

In Flesch's lexicon, "very easy" writing is to be found in comic books. "Standard" writing is the earmark of such magazines as *Time,* and "very difficult" writing is found in scientific and professional journals.

This chapter averages eleven words per sentence, according to my word processor—pretty easy reading, Flesch would say. Judge for yourself whether you find my writing readable.

But short words and short sentences alone won't make your writing easy to read. Flesch insists (and I agree) that a factor of equal importance is the human interest in what you write. Human interest is a function of the proportion of personal words (such as personal pronouns and proper names), the frequency with which quotations are used, and the extent to which you engage the reader by challenging, questioning, or directly addressing her.

Flesch's suggestions about how to increase readability are equally useful. Here are some of them:

- Focus on your reader.
- Focus on your purpose.
- Break up sentences and paragraphs.
- Find simpler words.
- Help your reader read (emphasize, anticipate, repeat, summarize).
- Learn to cut unnecessary words.
- Rearrange for emphasis.
- Write to be read aloud.
- Rearrange for emphasis.
- Don't write down to your reader.

To write for results, you'll need to do more than polish your writing style. Writing for results is different from writing meant merely to describe or report to the reader. Let's take a look at the differences now.

How Writing for Results Is Different from Writing to Describe or Report

There are at least nine differences between writing for results and writing merely to describe or report, all of which might prove to be crucial elements in your fundraising or sales letters.

1. *Colloquialisms.* Writing for results requires you to use everyday language and patterns of speech because you need to communicate readily, without delay or complication and without forcing the reader to work for understanding. There are exceptions to this rule, but, like much else that can be said about writing for results, the exceptions revolve around the audience, not the writer.

In many fundraising letters (depending, of course, on the signer and the cause) I might use such phrases as "No way!" or "Guess again" to underline the informality of the appeal. Such examples of colloquial speech and even slang are more than just acceptable; they're sometimes essential. Like a chatty personal letter, a masterpiece of copywriting will read much more like a conversation at the supermarket than an article in the *Harvard Business Review.*

2. *Clichés.* Most people think, speak, and write in clichés. That, I believe, is *not* a good thing, but it's important for the copywriter to take it into account. Clichés, after all, are only one step removed from garden-variety colloquialisms; precisely because of their familiarity, they offer an easy way to communicate thoughts rapidly. For the same reason, many readers also find clichés boring, so a tired and overused turn of speech shouldn't be your first line of defense against the difficulty of explaining a complex set of circumstances or making a subtle argument. But sometimes when writing for results, an old chestnut can help you fill the understanding gap.

Consider, for example, that old cliché, the "pot of gold at the end of the rainbow." I wouldn't be caught dead using this phrase in everyday speech, even in a defenseless moment. But I can think of no other phrase that more readily communicates the concept of fabulous wealth and could better provide an appropriate image for a sweepstakes featuring large cash prizes. (Naturally it's been used—time and time again.)

3. *Figures of speech.* You'll probably remember from high school English that similes and metaphors are among the earmarks of fine literature. A simile is one of those hard-working figures of speech that crawls up the hillside "like a train trailing a hundred cars." By contrast, a metaphor forces the reader to do much of the work, taking it on faith that an abstraction such as a figure of speech might be a train, a Bengal tiger, or a pot of gold.

I have a simple rule about the use of similes and metaphors in writing for results: *Don't use them.* Metaphors require thought; even similes can slow the reader down, or worse. These figures of speech help communicate complex thoughts and feelings, but only by indirection; any complexities in your message need to be spelled out more directly, or you may lose your readers.

4. *Humor and irony.* Creative advertising copywriters notwithstanding, humor is rarely advisable in writing for results. And entirely avoid irony, that wry, sophisticated form of humor. It's not just that some people have no discernible sense of humor, or even that what's humorous to one person might seem tragic to another. The fundamental problem, I believe, is that the written word is an imperfect medium to convey good humor.

In speaking to an audience, you might get a laugh for even a poorly told joke by communicating the humor through tone of voice, gestures, facial expressions, and even the use of props, aided by the natural tendency for most people to feel sympathy for you when you're standing right there. You have none of those advantages when writing to that same audience. I suggest you keep the jokes to yourself, or tack them up on your refrigerator or the office bulletin board.

5. *Sentence structure.* I'll call her Miss Forsythe because, truth to tell, I can't remember her name. Forty-five years ago, she taught me in ninth-grade English that every sentence must contain a subject and a predicate. Among a great many other rules, all of them delivered in commanding tones and in language that inhibited questions, Miss Forsythe also insisted that a sentence *must never* begin with "and" or "but" and *must never* end with a preposition.

In some forms of writing, those rules are as true today as they were in the 1950s. But not in writing for results. To convey meaning simply and clearly—to respect the informal practices of natural, spoken language and place emphasis where it's needed—Miss Forsythe's rules sometimes need to be ignored. The result may be writing that fails all the tests of conventional sentence structure, punctuation and grammar—but yields the results you want.

Try these rules instead of Miss Forsythe's:

- A sentence expresses a single thought. Sometimes a thought can be expressed in just one word. One. And one's enough.
- Don't worry about ending sentences with prepositions. Sometimes a preposition is the very best word to end a sentence with.

- And it's okay to start a sentence with a conjunction. (But don't overdo it. Two sentences in a row that start with "but" are likely to confuse the reader.)
- If at first you're not convinced by these three rules, reread them carefully. You might change your mind.

6. *Punctuation.* We'll look at three specific forms of punctuation here.

Semicolons. I despise semicolons. My thoughts tend to break up into little pieces that don't quite justify sentences of their own, but I still refuse to follow the grammarian's rulebook and set one apart from another with a semicolon. Much better, I think, just to pretend I've written a sentence. Miss Forsythe would disapprove with her customary hauteur. But no matter: I get no complaints from my latter-day readers. And when I'm seeking results with my writing—when I want my readers to take action—I am especially zealous to root out all the semicolons.

Why? Because sentences are easier to read without semicolons. The eyes glaze over at the sight of long sentences. Periods provide rest and comfort. The capital letters that begin new sentences heighten interest. Besides, Miss Forsythe isn't here to kick me around anymore.

Dashes. In writing for results, it's often wise to use a dash—what typesetters call an "em dash" (about twice the width of a hyphen—technically, the width of a capital M). I use a lot of dashes when writing fundraising letters—and I don't feel guilty in the least, no matter what Miss Forsythe might say. Dashes lend emphasis to your thoughts by setting them apart and increasing the white space that surrounds them. (The German professor you met in Chapter Two insists that dashes arrest the reader's eye and make writing *less* readable, but I choose to ignore his advice on this highly personal matter of style.)

Ellipses. Miss Forsythe would cringe . . . but I don't care. Ellipsis points (". . .") have much the same effect as a dash, particularly if they are set off by blank spaces before and after the points. Both help convey meaning by splitting complex or urgent thoughts into their component pieces.

7. *Contractions.* Lawyers, top business executives, and even some journalists advocate the sparing use of contractions. Don't pay any attention to them if you want your readers to take action.

Purists would rather you spell out every word, erring on the side of precision, so there can be absolutely no confusion in the minds of your readers. I'd rather you use fewer words, favoring informality and natural speech patterns, so your readers won't feel that you're talking down to them.

Contractions such as *I'm, you've, don't,* and *can't* are usually preferable in copywriting to the longer expressions they're derived from: *I am, you have, do not,* and *cannot.* The shorter form is more easily taken in by the ear, and the eye quickly comprehends the meaning of contractions. Also, negatives catch the reader's attention, sometimes conveying precisely the wrong impression. The word *not* may lodge in the reader's eye like a cinder, causing him to misread the following sentence—or the point of the whole letter.

8. *Repetition.* Grammarians are often repelled by writing intended to persuade, because it's likely to be riddled with repetition. The repetition is not accidental. Just as a journalist leads an article with the most important piece of news, the copywriter is likely to emphasize the points of greatest potential interest to the reader by repeating them.

The English language possesses almost unmatched variety, so a writer can describe any benefit or make any offer in a hundred or a thousand different ways. The demands of writing a letter intended to sell products or secure contributions may force the writer to use precisely the same words over and over again.

9. *Underlining and italics.* Miss Forsythe told us never to italicize words unless they're book titles or come from a foreign language. In the days when handwriting and typewriters were the writer's only options, she meant not to underline words. Today some editors follow the same rule: I sometimes find my articles or columns appearing shorn of all their carefully chosen italicized emphasis. I keep submitting articles peppered with italics anyway, in hopes my editors will wake up and see what's obvious to me: *italics enhance the reader's understanding*—when used sparingly. Emphasizing important facts or thoughts makes it easier for the reader to grasp the writer's meaning and easier to review and remember key points. In writing typewriter style—as, for example, in most fundraising letters—I generally prefer underlining instead of italics, even though I might have hundreds of alternative typefaces at hand (and most of them available in italic as well as roman fonts). Often it's important to preserve the illusion that I'm really writing on a typewriter.

When Does the Fun Start?

Some writers can produce readable copy in a first, fluid draft. It seems as though the words just keep streaming out of their fingertips, all neatly arranged in precisely the right order. (God, I *hate* those people!) Within the ranks of the top freelance writers, stories abound about the geniuses who can sit down at the keyboard (a typewriter, often enough) at 9:00 in the morning and type without interruption for three hours. They knock off for an hour's lunch, return for four more hours of unruffled word processing in the afternoon—and end the day with five thousand salable words, or even ten thousand. But these are people who write hundreds of books, or thousands of stories or articles (or both). They've had a lot more practice than you're likely to get. And I don't mind admitting they've got a lot more innate talent for writing than I have.

So most of us have to revise, and rewrite, and revise again. Don't make the mistake of believing you've got it right the first time. Chances are that you don't. Whatever it is you're writing, set it aside for a day or two or a week after you've completed your first rough draft. Then take a fresh look at it. And don't forget to read your letter aloud. If you can't find something on every page that cries out for revision, you're either a far better writer than I am or you're kidding yourself.

Join me now in Part Three, "Customizing Your Appeal," where we'll review the seven common types of fundraising letters and the unique requirements each poses.

Part III

Customizing Your Appeal

In the following eight chapters, we'll take a walking tour through the thickets of fundraising, visiting, one at a time, each of the most common types of fundraising letters to examine their unique characteristics and the distinctive demands they impose on a writer. In the course of Part Three, we'll study letters designed to:

- Recruit new members or donors
- Welcome new donors
- Appeal for a special (additional) gift
- Request a year-end contribution
- Solicit larger, high-dollar gifts
- Persuade a donor to send bigger gifts
- Seek annual gifts
- Thank donors

10

Recruiting New Donors
Starting Intimate Conversations with Strangers

The term *direct mail* is most commonly associated with the letters that nonprofits mail, often in extremely large quantities, to enlist new members or donors from among a broad population of prospects. In reality, the other types of fundraising letters covered in the following chapters are in many ways (such as the substantial net revenue they generate) far more important to the financial health of nonprofit organizations than the "acquisition" or "prospect" packages that bring in new donors. Still, it's the acquisition letters that make the rest of the process possible by supplying a steady stream of new, first-time donors.

The reply device in Exhibit 10.1 is typical of those used to accompany acquisition letters mailed to prospective donors. How do you know the form comes from an acquisition (or prospect) package? Because the statement in large type—in the first complete sentence at the top—reads in part, "I've enclosed my membership contribution to support Bread for the World." This form is typical of acquisition packages in several other ways as well:

- The language used. The language on this response device makes clear that Bread for the World is dedicated not just to the specific, top-priority campaign that is the subject of this appeal (debt relief) but to a broader array of "issues affecting poor and hungry people," and the

Lift the burden of debt from the world's poorest countries

I've signed the Citizen Pledge below, and I've enclosed my membership contribution to support Bread for the World's efforts to persuade Congress to fully fund debt relief that benefits poor and hungry people.

☐ **$25**   ☐ **$50**   ☐ **$100**   ☐ **$** _____

Bread for the World
Seeking Justice. Ending Hunger.

50 F Street NW, Suite 500
Washington, DC 20001
800-82-BREAD
www.bread.org

See other side for important information. ▶

CITIZEN PLEDGE

SINCE 33 very poor countries in Africa, Latin America, and Asia face unpayable debts — and spend more in debt repayment than in health care, education, and nutrition;

SINCE Mozambique, Nicaragua, and some of the other poor countries weighed down by debt are also struggling to recover from natural disasters;

AND SINCE Archbishop Desmond Tutu and Pope John Paul II have called for a Jubilee Year of debt relief to begin in this new millennium,

I THEREFORE pledge to become actively involved in Bread for the World's historic campaign to lift the burden of debt from the world's poorest countries.

AND I PLEDGE to write my senators and representative in Congress to urge them to provide full funding for our country's share of the international debt-relief initiative.

Signed _____ Date _____

☐ I'm unable to become a member of Bread for the World at this time, but I'd like to receive the free packet of resource materials so I can communicate with our nation's leaders about debt relief and other issues affecting hungry people.

RECYCLED & RECYCLABLE / PRINTED WITH SOY INK   60172A

We use your contributions wisely and effectively

You are welcome to request a copy of our latest financial report by contacting: Bread for the World, 50 F Street NW, Suite 500, Washington, DC 20001-1565, (301) 608-2400 or 1-800-82-BREAD. Gifts to Bread for the World are not tax-deductible since our members lobby Congress on behalf of poor and hungry people. If you prefer to make a tax-deductible contribution to support research and education efforts, please make out your check to Bread for the World Institute.

If you are a resident of one of the states below, you may obtain financial information directly from the state agency: **FLORIDA** — A COPY OF THE OFFICIAL REGISTRATION AND FINANCIAL INFORMATION MAY BE OBTAINED FROM THE DIVISION OF CONSUMER SERVICES BY CALLING TOLL-FREE, (800) 435-7352 WITHIN THE STATE. REGISTRATION DOES NOT IMPLY ENDORSEMENT, APPROVAL OR RECOMMENDATION BY THE STATE. **MARYLAND** — For the cost of copies and postage: Office of the Secretary of State, State House, Annapolis, MD 21401. **MISSISSIPPI** — The official registration and financial information of Bread for the World may be obtained from the Mississippi Secretary of State's office by calling 1-888-236-6167. Registration by the Secretary of State does not imply endorsement. **NEW JERSEY** — INFORMATION FILED WITH THE ATTORNEY GENERAL CONCERNING THIS CHARITABLE SOLICITATION MAY BE OBTAINED FROM THE ATTORNEY GENERAL OF THE STATE OF NEW JERSEY BY CALLING (973) 504-6215. REGISTRATION WITH THE ATTORNEY GENERAL DOES NOT IMPLY ENDORSEMENT. **NEW YORK** — Office of the Attorney General, Department of Law, Charities Bureau, 120 Broadway, New York, NY 10271. **NORTH CAROLINA** — **Financial information about this organization and a copy of its license are available from the State Solicitation Licensing Branch at (919) 807-2214. The license is not an endorsement by the state.** **PENNSYLVANIA** — The official registration and financial information of Bread for the World may be obtained from the Pennsylvania Department of State by calling toll-free, within Pennsylvania, (800) 732-0999. Registration does not imply endorsement. **VIRGINIA** — State Division of Consumer Affairs, Department of Agricultural and Consumer Services, P.O. Box 1163, Richmond, VA 23218. **WASHINGTON** — Charities Division, Office of the Secretary of State, State of Washington, Olympia, WA 98504-0422; 1-800-332-4483. **WEST VIRGINIA** — Residents may obtain a summary from: Secretary of State, State Capitol, Charleston, WV 25305.

Registration with any of these states does not imply endorsement, approval or recommendation by the state.

To contact your members of Congress: Capitol Switchboard: 202/224-3121

To contact a U.S. Senator:
The Honorable _____
U.S. Senate
Washington, DC 20510

To contact a Representative:
The Honorable _____
U.S. House of Representatives
Washington, DC 20515

Bread for the World's 24 hour Legislature update: 800-82-BREAD

EXHIBIT 10.1 New Donor Response Device, Bread for the World

accompanying letter (not illustrated) makes that even clearer. Note, too, the organization's tagline next to the logo: "Seeking Justice. Ending Hunger." Although this appeal focuses on one leading issue, as a whole it asks the recipient to buy into the organization's mission and goals. That's what "joining" means. This is not an appeal to support a specific project.

• Suggested gift amounts. You'll note that these amounts are typeset, so the amounts are probably the same for all recipients of this letter. The amounts are comparatively small, affording an easy entry level for new members. But there are three gift choices, covering a fairly wide range, because little is known about those to whom the letter was mailed: they're strangers.

• Reader involvement. Note that the "Citizen Pledge" form at the bottom of the front of this appeal provides an opportunity for the prospect to become directly and immediately involved in Bread for the World's current lobbying campaign. Involvement devices of this sort aren't unique to acquisition letters, but they're more commonly found in that context. Involvement typically boosts response. It's a way to get strangers to pay attention.

How Donor Acquisition Letters Differ from Other Fundraising Appeals

Successful letters written to recruit new donors or new members come in all sizes, shapes, and flavors. They may be fat or thin, colorful or drab, up-to-the-minute or timeless. They're sometimes mailed using third-class bulk postage, sometimes (though less often) with first-class stamps. But there are five characteristics that the majority of donor acquisition letters share:

1. They are often long and occasionally contain lots of additional material too: brochures or folders, fliers, lift letters, buckslips, and premiums. Many charities fare better without using any of this stuff. Some well-known groups can get away with short letters too. Chances are, though, that a letter you write to prospective donors will need to be at least a little longer than the letters you usually write to previous donors. Otherwise prospects may not have enough information about your organization to decide whether they'll make a gift.

2. They typically appeal to prospects to support a charity's larger agenda: its goals, the full range of its programs (though one project or aspect of the work may get the lion's share of the attention in the letter). If prospective donors send gifts in response to such a letter, they're more likely to respond favorably when later asked for additional support.

3. References to "you" (the reader) are normally vague and general. Although you as the writer may know a great deal about the people on one of your prospect lists, you'll probably know next to nothing about those on other lists. With them, there isn't much to hang a relationship on. Chances are that the demands of economy will require that you mail the same letter, unchanged, to all your prospect lists.

4. Typically acquisition letters are undated and make few references to time or the calendar. That's because you'll probably want to use it over and over. Not just because of the need to economize, but because it normally takes repeated trial and error to write a really successful acquisition letter.

5. The minimum suggested gift amount tends to be low. Most charities seek to maximize the number of new donors: asking for less at the outset may serve that purpose.

Case Study: Western Pennsylvania Conservancy

The Western Pennsylvania Conservancy (Pittsburgh) asked me to edit this new-donor acquisition package (Exhibits 10.2 and 10.3).

As you can see, I made a number of changes:

- The most important change was to include an explicit ask for money, citing specific dollar amounts. (I had no way of knowing what those amounts might be in practice. They would depend on the "string" or range of gifts that had traditionally worked well for the Conservancy.) With only the rarest exceptions, a fundraising letter must cite at least one specific suggested gift amount.

- I also made significant changes in the Johnson's Box—the boldfaced copy that precedes the salutation. I dropped the language proposed in the draft. The parallelism of the wording worked fine, but "We need you" is a weak case for giving. Instead, I selected donor benefits to highlight there.

- Similarly, I overhauled the lead to emphasize benefits even more. Writing fundraising letters is, ultimately, all about spotlighting the benefits to the donor. Few people care about needs. As a result, I moved the "good neighbor" theme down a couple of pegs. But that was a good theme, so I fleshed it out a little.

- A four-page letter requires page numbers. Sometimes I like to dress them up a bit, as I did here, by adding a header consistent with the letter's theme.

- The copy called out for boldfacing and italics to emphasize key points, which was lacking in the draft. I focused on the major donor benefits and the most intriguing thoughts. Please note that I limited emphasis to two or three instances on each page—and that all of them are short.

- Generally, the executive director (or the equivalent) is the best signer. But if the statements made in the letter were more true of the director of membership or of someone else associated with the Conservancy, then that person could sign the appeal instead. With notable exceptions, the selection of a letter-signer is not that big a deal.

- I rarely write a direct mail letter without a P.S. Studies show that this copy receives very high readership, as I've noted earlier. That's why I placed the ask here.

We need you . . .

And, once you consider what we are doing to keep Pennsylvania's wild places wild and to make Pennsylvania's communities vibrant—I hope you'll say that you need us, too!

Dear Friend,

My message is simple. I need you to help us to save the places we all care about. We need you to join with us at Western Pennsylvania Conservancy.

Here's why. *We're **your neighbors,** and just like any good neighbor, we want to work with you, to save the places we care about.*

If you're like me, you probably don't know every one of your neighbors. So, in case you don't know us, let me tell you a few things about us. We've been your neighbor for more than 60 years, working to protect the most important wild places in Pennsylvania . . . from the shores of Lake Erie to the hills and valleys in our southernmost counties . . . from wildflowers along the Ohio border to Cherry Run, in the center of the state.

We're also the organization that maintains and operates Fallingwater, the world-famous house that Frank Lloyd Wright built in Mill Run. And we work with over five thousand volunteers' help to create some of the most beautiful community gardens in the eastern United States.

In the time since we opened the doors to Western Pennsylvania Conservancy, in 1932, we have purchased more than 204,500 acres of land in Pennsylvania. *These 204,500 acres remain open to the public—you and I—to visit and enjoy.*

You've probably been to some of the areas we've purchased and helped to preserve. Have you rafted the Youghiogheny River, through Ohiopyle State Park? Walked the Laurel Highlands Trail, in Laurel Ridge State Park? Did you ever take a boat on Lake Arthur in Moraine State Park? Have you hunted on the State Game Lands in Fulton County? Has your family fished at McConnell's Mills?

In the last six decades, we purchased the bulk of the lands at all these public spots, and then sold them to one of the state or federal public agencies (often far below costs, by the way) to create these great havens.

I've spent some time in many other parts of the country, and I have to tell you that our region is fortunate to have the amount of open space we have here. There aren't many areas where the public has our kind of access to such beautiful places.

EXHIBIT 10.2 Western Pennsylvania Conservancy Acquisition Letter, Before Edit

We, at Western Pennsylvania Conservancy, keep adding to the tally. Right now, we're working to protect another corridor of continuous open space—along the Clarion River. Starting more than 20 years ago, we have purchased more than 12,600 acres along a 41-mile stretch of this recreation corridor. We've already conveyed more than 8,000 of those acres to state and federal agencies, which protects them and gives you public access.

As I said in the beginning of the letter, we do more than protect these undeveloped lands. You might know us at Western Pennsylvania Conservancy as the neighbor who helps your community with a garden project. We have more than 400 separate garden projects all over western Pennsylvania.

We're proud of the success of our "community conservation" efforts in this region. We have a philosophy here that "communities make gardens grow, and gardens can help communities grow."

We bring together volunteers, corporate and foundation sponsors, and our understanding of how to produce a garden project in some of the most unlikely places. Working side-by-side, these partnerships have transformed some concrete flatland spaces into breathtaking displays of color, cultivated by the pride of every partner.

Through the generosity of partnerships, we facilitated garden projects in schoolyards, neighborhoods, at senior citizen complexes, and along highways. *We believe in the power of these garden projects to promote healthy and attractive communities.*

I know sprawl's a big word in conservation these days. Actually, I do believe that helping make existing communities more attractive helps reduce development pressures on undeveloped countrysides. It's a practical matter. *And we believe in practicality at Western Pennsylvania Conservancy.* We don't just talk about how to "protect land," or "improve urban living spaces." We don't think it's practical to just talk about it. We do it.

That brings me to Fallingwater, the house that Edgar J. Kaufmann entrusted to Western Pennsylvania Conservancy in 1963. It was his home; but he always knew it was more than that. "The union of powerful art and powerful nature into something beyond the sum of their separate powers deserves to be kept living," he said. He knew the house was an international treasure. *He thoughtfully pondered his choice for the organization to best protect this reverent location, and Mr. Kaufmann chose us—Western Pennsylvania Conservancy.*

We know why he entrusted Fallingwater to Western Pennsylvania Conservancy. *He knew that we understand the connection between man and nature.* It's in *why* we protect as much land as we do. It's in *why* we facilitate the growing number of garden projects we

EXHIBIT 10.2 Continued

choose every year. It's in *how* we preserve Fallingwater. And frankly, it's in how this staff approaches every work day here.

To give you a sense of what I mean, here's just a sample of what's on our organizational plate now.

—We must protect Fallingwater structurally. The famous "house on the waterfall" is more than 60 years old, and its signature cantilevers, which seem to hang in mid-air, have sagged, or deflected, past an acceptable point. We shored them up as a temporary measure. But we intend to strengthen the house internally without permanently impacting the visual integrity of this historic home.

—We intend to expand our traditional land protection through purchase by adding a community-based approach to conservation. Our field scientists have an amazing wealth of knowledge about the wildest places and their living resources of western Pennsylvania, and we know there are many more ways to use that information to create real progress in land protection without jeopardizing or diminishing in any way the human values.

Someone recently shared with me, "I don't know much about biodiversity, but I know it includes people!"

—It's always been our commitment to "include people," and here's how we intend to "do," not just "talk." We haven't uncovered every opportunity yet, but we are finding ways to link ecological health to local livelihoods, such as in agriculture, forestry and tourism, the top three economic forces in Pennsylvania today. In French Creek, we've already begun, with our partnership to form the French Creek Project, which works with landowners to protect this important and biologically rich watershed.

—As part of our mission to help connect people with nature, we are continuing to expand our members activities. In 2000, members will have a full year's worth of events to choose from—starting with our popular Valentine Day Hike at Bear Run; highlighting Earth Day, in the spring; and concluding the year with guided canoe floats and interpretive hikes all over western Pennsylvania.

—We aren't militant, by any means, but we do believe we are considered a reasonable voice for conservation. We are selective about the advocacy issues that we'll take on in Harrisburg or Washington, D.C. For instance, we delivered testimony to encourage the Pa. Fish and Boat Commissioners to approve changes to their list of Endangered and Threatened Species. After all, our scientists helped collect the data that led to some of the decisions about the list. We choose our involvements carefully, to save our most critical resources and to have the widest impact for the greatest good.

EXHIBIT 10.2 Continued

And that brings me back to the Clarion River. As I canoed it recently, I reflected on the notion that this was the crossroads of Conservancy's past, our present and our future. You see, 90 years ago, the Clarion was the most polluted waterway in the Commonwealth. Through the great efforts of a lot of people in the region, and beyond, the river was cleaned up. The river-side tannery industry was in decline, the paper industry changed their discharge habits, and community groups worked on abandoned mine drainage and other protection efforts. Then, 20 years ago, Western Pennsylvania Conservancy bought its first acre along the river. As I mentioned earlier, we've bought more than 12,000 acres in that watershed. Our goal is to see the Clarion River corridor connect with Cook Forest and Clear Creek State Park to form the largest State Park. With your help, we can make it happen.

To me, the future for Western Pennsylvania Conservancy is in continuing to work alongside the residents of the community as they cultivate the growing tourism as part of a sustainable economy while they maintain the serenity that attracts visitors in the first place! That's what we mean when we say we're "saving the places we care about!"

The way I look at it, *it's all part of being a good neighbor.*

So, neighbor, I hope you'll join us. Because, I need you! Please, join today.

You'll receive . . . .

EXHIBIT 10.2 Continued

Have you rafted the Youghiogheny River through Ohiopyle State Park? Walked the Laurel Highlands Trail in Laurel Ridge State Park? Has your family fished at McConnell's Mills?

If so, the Western Pennsylvania Conservancy has directly benefited you.

Dear Neighbor,

If you've ever taken a boat on Lake Arthur in Moraine State Park, or hunted on the State Game Lands in Fulton County, you've been to some of the land we've purchased and helped to preserve.

In the last six decades, the Western Pennsylvania Conservancy has purchased the bulk of the lands at all the public spots I've named. Then we turned right around and sold them to a state or federal agency—often far below cost—to create these priceless havens.

So, you might not know me, but I'm your neighbor—and like any good neighbor, _I want to help you enjoy the highest possible quality of life._

If you're like me, you probably don't know every one of your neighbors. So, just in case you don't know me or the organization I'm so proud to lead, let me tell you a few things about the Western Pennsylvania Conservancy.

For more than 60 years, the Conservancy has been working to protect the most important wild places in Pennsylvania—from the shores of Lake Erie to the hills and valleys in our southernmost counties . . . from wildflowers along the Ohio border to Cherry Run, in the center of the state.

We're also the people who maintain and operate Fallingwater, the world-famous house that Frank Lloyd Wright built in Mill Run. And we work with over five thousand volunteers, helping to create some of the most beautiful community gardens in the eastern United States.

Since we opened the doors to Western Pennsylvania Conservancy in 1932, we have purchased more than 204,500 acres of land in Pennsylvania . . . and opened those acres to the public—to you and me and our children's children—to visit and enjoy . . . forever.

I've spent some time in many other parts of the country, and I have to tell you that our region is fortunate to have the amount of open space we have here. _There aren't many places in America where the public has our kind of access to such beautiful spots._

But we keep adding to the tally. Right now, the Western Pennsylvania Conservancy is working to protect another corridor of continuous open space—along the Clarion River. Starting more than 20 years ago, we have purchased more than 12,600 acres along a 41-mile stretch of

EXHIBIT 10.3 Western Pennsylvania Conservancy Acquisition Letter, After Edit

An Appeal from Neighbor to Neighbor, page 2

this recreation corridor. We've already conveyed more than 8,000 of those acres to state and federal agencies, which protects them and gives you public access.

Of course, you might also know us at **Western Pennsylvania Conservancy** as the neighbor who helps your community with a garden project. We have more than 400 separate garden projects all over western Pennsylvania.

We're proud of the success of our "community conservation" efforts in this region. We have a philosophy here that "_communities make gardens grow, and gardens can help communities grow._"

We bring our know-how about garden projects together with volunteers and with corporate and foundation sponsors in some of the most unlikely places. Working side by side, these partnerships have transformed some concrete flatland spaces into breathtaking displays of color, cultivated by the pride of every partner.

Through the generosity of partnerships, we facilitate garden projects in schoolyards, neighborhoods, at senior citizen complexes, and along highways. I firmly believe these garden projects don't just enhance the beauty of our communities. They also promote _healthier community life._

Consider that for a moment. I think you'll agree with me.

I also believe strongly that helping make existing communities more attractive helps reduce development pressures on undeveloped countryside. It's a practical matter. And we believe in practicality at Western Pennsylvania Conservancy.

We don't just talk about how to "protect land" or to "improve urban living spaces." We don't think it's practical to just talk about it. We do it.

The same was true at Fallingwater, the house that Edgar J. Kaufmann entrusted to Western Pennsylvania Conservancy in 1963. It was his home—but he always knew it was more than that.

"The union of powerful art and powerful nature into something beyond the sum of their separate powers deserves to be kept living," Mr. Kaufmann said. He knew the house was an international treasure. He thoughtfully pondered his choice for the organization to best protect this reverent location, and Mr. Kaufmann chose us—Western Pennsylvania Conservancy.

I know why Edgar Kaufmann entrusted Fallingwater to Western Pennsylvania Conservancy.

He knew that we understand the connection between man and nature.

EXHIBIT 10.3 Continued

An Appeal from Neighbor to Neighbor, page 3

That connection helps explain why we protect as much land as we do. It explains why we support a growing number of garden projects every year. It shapes how we preserve Fallingwater. And it profoundly affects how my staff and I approach our work every day of the year.

To give you a sense of what I mean, here are just a few examples of what's on our organizational plate right now:

- The Western Pennsylvania Conservancy is working to protect the structural integrity of Fallingwater. The famous "house on the waterfall" is more than 60 years old, and its signature cantilevers, which seem to hang in mid-air, have sagged over the years. We shored them up as a temporary measure. But we intend to strengthen the structure internally without permanently impacting the visual integrity of this historic home.

- Someone recently shared an intriguing thought with me: _**I don't know much about biodiversity, but I know it includes people!**_" Here at the Western Pennsylvania Conservancy, it's always been our commitment to "include people." We haven't uncovered every opportunity yet, but we are finding ways to link ecological health to local livelihoods, such as in agriculture, forestry, and tourism (the top three economic forces in Pennsylvania today). In French Creek, for instance, we and our partners have already begun to form the French Creek Project, which will work with landowners to protect this important and biologically rich watershed.

- As part of _**our mission to help connect people with nature,**_ we are continuing to expand our members' activities. In 2000, members will have a full year's worth of events to choose from, starting with our popular Valentine's Day Hike at Bear Run . . . highlighting Earth Day, in the spring . . . and concluding the year with guided canoe floats and interpretive hikes all over western Pennsylvania.

- The Western Pennsylvania Conservancy is widely considered a _reasonable_ voice for conservation. We're selective about the advocacy issues that we'll take on in Harrisburg or Washington, D.C. For instance, we delivered testimony to encourage the Pennsylvania Fish and Boat Commissioners to approve changes to their list of Endangered and Threatened Species. After all, our scientists helped collect the data that led to some of the decisions about the list! We choose our involvements carefully, to save our most critical resources and to have the widest impact for the greatest good.

And that brings me back to the recreation corridor we've been protecting along the Clarion River. As I canoed there recently, I reflected on the notion that this was the crossroads of the Conservancy's past, our present, and our future.

EXHIBIT 10.3 Continued

An Appeal from Neighbor to Neighbor, page 4

You see, 90 years ago, the Clarion was the most polluted waterway in the Commonwealth. Through the combined efforts of a lot of people in the region (and beyond), the river was cleaned up. The riverside tannery industry was in decline, the paper companies changed their discharge habits, and community groups worked on abandoned mine drainage and other protection efforts.

Then, 20 years ago, Western Pennsylvania Conservancy bought its first acre along the river—the first of more than 12,000 acres in that watershed so far. Our goal is to see the Clarion River corridor connect with Cook Forest and Clear Creek State Park to form the [STATE'S?] largest State Park. With your help, we can make it happen.

To me, the future for Western Pennsylvania Conservancy lies in continuing to work alongside the residents of our communities. We play a vital role in helping cultivate the growing tourism that sustains our economy—by helping maintain the serenity that attracts visitors in the first place! That's what we mean when we say we're "saving the places we care about!"

The way I look at it, *it's all part of being a good neighbor.*

So, neighbor, I hope you'll join me and our fellow neighbors here at the Western Pennsylvania Conservancy—today! You may enlist as a member for as little as $XX.

As a member of the Western Pennsylvania Conservancy, you'll receive a number of valuable benefits:

- [BENEFIT 1. Newsletter??]

- [BENEFIT 2. Discounts, free passes, maps???]

- Most important of all, however, you'll gain the satisfaction of knowing that you're a good neighbor. Your support of the Western Pennsylvania Conservancy will help your neighbors—and all our children and our children's children—to enjoy the bounties of nature throughout all time.

In hope and gratitude,

[signature]

Name of Executive Director
Executive Director

P.S.   Please take a moment right now to complete the enclosed membership enrollment form and attach your check for $XX, $YY, $ZZ or more. Then return both the check and the form to me in the attached pre-addressed envelope. *You'll be glad you did!*

EXHIBIT 10.3 Continued

11

Welcoming New Donors
Treating People Like Part of the Family

Fundraisers are quickly coming to understand that direct mail cannot be treated simply as a way to haul in gifts. The letters we send our donors or members are just as important for the contributions they make to the relationship-building process that lays the groundwork for more and larger gifts over a long period of time. A welcome package for new donors or new members is the best example of this growing trend. These packages, mailed soon after the receipt of a donor or member's first check (in response to an acquisition or prospect package), are intended to open a dialogue between the individual and the organization by laying out, simply and clearly, all the benefits of supporting the organization and all the ways that a supporter may become directly involved.

The response device in Exhibit 11.1 comes from such a welcome package for new members. Its distinguishing characteristics are typical in many ways of welcome packages:

- The "Welcome!" message is impossible to miss.
- It contains a *bounce-back form,* which offers the new member the opportunity to obtain information about important Bread for the World programs.

Welcome!

Thank you for joining Bread for the World with your . . .

I'm pleased you've become Bread for the World's newest member. Your financial support and your active involvement make a real difference in this citizens' movement to end hunger in the U.S. and overseas.

PHOTO © BEN ZWEIG

David Beckmann

—David Beckmann, President

Tear off and keep this top portion. Please *return the bottom portion* to Bread for the World in the envelope provided. Thank you.

We'd like to hear from you . . .

☐ Bread for the World occasionally exchanges its mailing list with select organizations whose activities might be of interest to our members. Please check this box if you wish not to receive such mailings.

Please correct your name and address below if they aren't complete and accurate. The following information will help us provide you with improved membership services.

YOUR DENOMINATION OR CHURCH BODY

NUMBER OF MEMBERS AT THIS ADDRESS

Questions or concerns about your membership?

Call toll-free:
1-800-82-BREAD

Bread for the World
Seeking Justice. Ending Hunger.
1100 Wayne Avenue, Suite 1000
Silver Spring, MD 20910
800/82-BREAD

Want to be more involved?

☐ I'd like to be part of "Quickline" — Bread for the World's rapid response telephone and e-mail network — when urgent Congressional action is needed.

☐ I'd like to receive updates via e-mail — here's my e-mail address:

☐ Please let me know if there's a local Bread for the World group meeting in my area.

☐ I'd like more information about the Covenant Church program and other resources for churches and religious groups.

☐ Please send information about publications and other resources available from Bread for the World and Bread for the World Institute.

☐ I'm interested in joining the Baker's Dozen and having my membership renewed automatically — by having my bank send monthly gifts electronically. Please send me details.

Visit our web site:

www.bread.org.

RECYCLED & RECYCLABLE / PRINTED WITH SOY INK   0-60982W

Please see reverse side for important information

EXHIBIT 11.1 New Donor Welcome Package, Bread for the World

Hunger is one problem we can actually solve

But churches and charities can't do it all. Government must do its part. So *please contact your senators and representative in the U.S. Congress.* Urge them to increase the minimum wage by at least $1 over the next two years — and ask for their support of the Hunger Relief Act, which will reinstate food stamps for legal immigrants and provide fair access to food stamps for working families who still live in poverty.

Bread for the World

Seeking Justice. Ending Hunger.

1100 Wayne Avenue, Suite 1000
Silver Spring, MD 20910
800/82-BREAD

You may visit our web site (www.bread.org) or call the 24-hour Legislative Hotline (1-800-822-7323, ext. 5) for the latest legislative developments.

How to contact your member of Congress:

U.S. House of Representatives
Washington, D.C. 20515

U.S. Senate
Washington, D.C. 20510

Phone for both House and Senate:

202/224-3121

You are welcome to request a copy of our latest financial report by contacting: Bread for the World, 1100 Wayne Avenue, Suite 1000, Silver Spring, MD 20910; (301) 608-2400.

Contributions to **Bread for the World** are *not* tax-deductible since its members lobby Congress on behalf of poor and hungry people. If you wish to make a *tax-deductible gift,* please make out your check to **Bread for the World Institute** and your gift will support the Institute's work of research and education.

EXHIBIT 11.1 Continued

- There's space on the bounce-back form to supply information that will be useful to Bread for the World in targeting future requests for help, including the new member's e-mail address, which may be used in the organization's future on-line fundraising program.
- On the reverse of the bounce-back form is information the new member may use when participating in future Bread for the World grassroots lobbying campaigns.
- "Donor options" on the bounce-back form include opportunities to opt out of mailing list rentals and exchanges, enlist in the Baker's Dozen monthly giving program, and sign up for Bread for the World's rapid-response program of grassroots lobbying.

How New Donor Welcome Packages Are Different from Other Fundraising Appeals

In nonprofits' continuing search for heightened donor loyalty and higher renewal rates, welcome packages for new donors are becoming increasingly common. These packets of information mailed to newly recruited members or donors may be fat or thin, elaborate or simple. Typically, however, they share five attributes:

1. They strive to be warm, emphasizing the organization's appreciation rather than its needs and offering additional information. Short copy is common. The welcome letter's purpose is usually to inform the new donor about the organization's programs and its donor benefits and services.

2. Any copy that refers to the new member personally is likely to be vague and general; usually the charity knows too little to personalize the letter in any meaningful way. One important exception is the amount of the initial gift, which may be inserted in the cover letter if it's personalized or noted on a gift receipt.

3. Some charities use the opportunity to request a second gift or even to suggest that a new donor join a giving club, such as a monthly sustainer program. But it's more common—and, I think, more advisable—*not* to seek a gift with this package. For example, if you've decided that the best time to invite members to join a monthly pledge program is immediately after they join,

I suggest you *first* mail them a welcome package and *then,* perhaps a week or ten days later, send the pledge invitation.

4. To introduce new donors to the organization's work, a recent issue of its magazine or newsletter is often enclosed. Sometimes brochures about its programs and services are included. Welcome packages are often heavy and expensive. They're an investment in future fundraising efforts.

5. Welcome packages frequently offer new donors multiple opportunities to respond—through surveys, requests for additional information, "member-get-a-member" programs, donor options, or other involvement devices.

Six Reasons You Should Mail Welcome Packages

Let's take a look first at the many roles that a welcome package is created to play. Then we can review several possible elements you might consider including in your own welcome package or adding to your existing new donor acknowledgment.

It seems to me there are six reasons to go to the expense and trouble of sending new members a special, initial package that's more than a simple gift receipt or thank-you note.

1. All donors expect to be thanked for their support. A simple receipt is probably not enough to make them think you're being nice. And treating members well increases the chances they'll renew their annual support. This is especially important if (like most other charities these days) your first-year renewal rate is very low.

2. Donors are most receptive to your message immediately after making their first gifts. This is the best time to approach them about such fundraising options as monthly sustainer programs or "friend-get-a-friend" efforts. (However, it's not *necessarily* the best time to ask for a second gift.) If you can move a new member to take action right after joining—almost any action, in fact—you'll be well on your way to building a strong, mutually beneficial, long-term relationship. But timing is important here;

receptivity fades fast, and donors can all too easily forget having contributed to a charity that's new to them.

3. Donors' first impression of your organization is likely to affect their views of all subsequent communications. A cheap thank-you, such as a postcard or an impersonal letter, may impress a few donors with its frugality, but far more donors are likely to be flattered by a carefully prepared, well-thought-out introductory package that underscores how very important their financial support is. I'm convinced most donors secretly think you're wasting money on fancy packages to *other* people but not when you spend money on *them*.

4. Donors are too often skeptical about how their contributions are put to use. They sometimes need to be persuaded that their gifts accomplish more than raise additional money. By describing your work in detail and offering opportunities for members to contribute more than money, a welcome package can drive home the message that your organization is lean, hard working, and cost-effective. This is true even if any individual member has no interest at all in contributing volunteer time. The offer and the opportunities communicate an important message.

5. Donors probably won't understand your organization and its programs unless yours is a local group that provides a single, direct, easily grasped service. Any nonprofit that's engaged in multiple projects—especially if it's a large, decentralized, complex nonprofit—will need a well-organized welcome package so donors will understand your work and the role they can play in it. If they do understand you well, they're much more likely to respond favorably when you ask for additional support.

6. Not all donors are created equal. Some may be delighted to send a small monthly contribution. Others may want to contribute only once per year. Still others might be interested in joining a high-dollar giving club. The welcome package is an excellent opportunity to test their preferences on these and other fundraising questions by giving them a questionnaire, or at least by clearly offering several different fundraising options and an easy way to request more information about them.

If your organization mails new donors more than a simple tax receipt or thank-you note, you may already be addressing some of the six opportunities I've just listed. But there may be a number of other ways you can accomplish a whole lot more. You might consider adding some enclosures to your thank-you letter or a full-fledged new donor welcome package:

- A small brochure or folder that catalogues membership services and benefits
- An involvement device that includes a *brief* new member survey
- An explanation of how the organization works, either in a brochure or flier or in copy in the cover letter
- A membership card, with an abbreviated listing of membership benefits on the reverse
- A brochure about your monthly sustainer program
- A brochure about your bequest and planned giving programs, if any
- A flier that includes an order form for merchandise you sell, featuring a discount offer for new members

Case Study: Co-op America "Welcome Aboard" Package

Co-op America asked my help to overhaul the "Welcome Aboard Kit" it sends to new members. On the telephone and in two face-to-face discussions, we reviewed in detail my recommendations for upgrading the welcome process. Our shared hope, of course, was that new members exposed to a more intensive welcoming process would be more generous and more loyal in the future. My recommendations, in fact, were for a *process* for welcoming new members that fills at least 210 days, or seven months. Exhibit 11.2 shows how the process was intended to work. Here's how to read the chart:

- Days elapsed: This first column shows the approximate number of days elapsed since receipt of a new member's first gift. For example, about ninety days, or three months, after joining, a member would be invited to join Co-op America's monthly sustainer program.
- Segment: The second column specifies the "segment" or group of new donors to be included at that stage of the process. For example, I recommended that Co-op America test a thank-you telephone call to new members whose initial gift was $25 or larger 45 days after receipt of the first gift.

- Nature of contact: The third column describes the nature of the contact: a letter, telephone call, magazine, or something else.

Most of Co-op America's previous "Welcome Aboard Kit" is shown in Exhibits 11.3 through 11.6. The revised version, incorporating the changes I specified, is a two-part mailing shown in Exhibits 11.7 through 11.16. The initial welcome package was mailed first class, and the follow-up welcome package was mailed nonprofit bulk rate.

Co-op America was starting at a point that few other nonprofits have yet reached: it was already mailing a new member welcome package. The most meaningful changes I introduced were to fit the welcome package into a year-long *process* and to emphasize two-way communications between Co-op America and its new members.

Each of the two parts of the revised package includes an involvement device. There's a new member survey in part one and a feedback form in part two. This is all part of the process of sustaining a dialogue between Co-op America and its members—a continuation of the dialogue opened up by the acquisition package.

Days Elapsed	Segment	Nature of Contact	Notes
None	All new members	Thank-you letter (welcome package, part one)	Ideally, a lasered one-page letter with closed-face outer and first-class stamp—revealing a special telephone number and staff contact for member inquiries; new member priorities survey; business reply envelope
Up to 15 days	All new members	Benefits package, mailed bulk (welcome package, part two)	Generic thank-you letter; folder or brochures on member services; copies of publications promised in acquisition package; information on donor programs
As available (15–30 days)	All new members	Quarterly magazine	
As available (15–90 days)	All new members	Merchandise catalogue	
45 days	Test new members with initial gift of $25 or more	Thank-you call	An opportunity to test different approaches: pure thank-you versus soliciting interest in member services versus offering information about donor programs
90 days	Initial gift less than $50	Monthly sustainer program invitation	Fully personalized package; phone follow-up after 3–4 weeks
135–150 days	Current special appeal (whatever appeal is being sent to other, older members)		
180 days	All	Early-renewal letter (beginning of the membership dues renewal series)	
210+ days	All	Return to membership mailstream (no more special new-member treatment!)	

EXHIBIT 11.2 Proposed Welcome Process for New Members, Co-op America

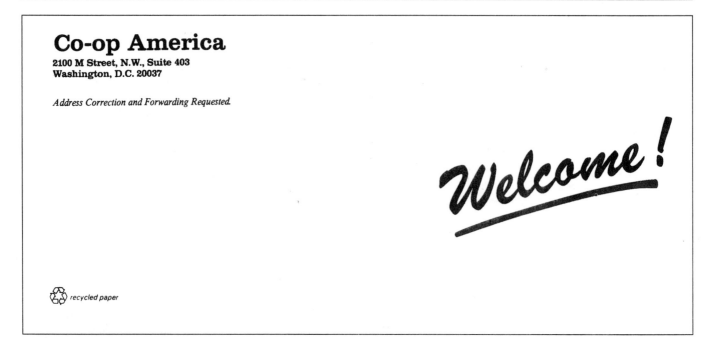

EXHIBIT 11.3 Original Outer Envelope, New Member Welcome, Co-op America

Dear Member,

Welcome to Co-op America!

Thank you for joining. We're pleased to be working with you to build a sustainable economy based on peace, justice, cooperation and environmental responsibility.

Through your new membership you are supporting your commitment to positive social change. As a member of Co-op America, you are an economic activist -- helping to transform the economic system to one that values the earth and all its people.

Our commitment to you is to provide you with the **information, socially responsible products and services, and action programs** you need to make a difference.

As a member, you will receive practical **information** on economic strategies for creating social change through these publications, which are yours as member benefits:

*   The <u>Co-op America Quarterly</u>, our magazine, covers the emerging ideas, institutions and strategies required by the sustainable economy. It offers you ideas, references and resources you can use to create positive social change. Your regular subscription will start with the next published issue (Spring, Summer, Fall or Winter). During the year of your membership, you will receive four issues.

*   <u>Boycott Action News</u>, published within the <u>Quarterly</u>, gives you the background, news, status and "where to write and what to do" for social change boycotts.

*   <u>Co-op America's Socially Responsible Financial Planning Handbook</u>, provides you with information about social investment strategies and the ABCs of social investing. Watch for it in the mail next quarter.

*   Our <u>National Directory of Green Businesses</u> gives you instant access to all the businesses on the cutting edge of social and environmental responsibility.

Part of our mission is to provide you with <u>socially responsible products and services</u> that you can use to channel your money to building economic alternatives when you buy the things you need and when you invest. We're proud to offer you access to these socially responsible products and services as a benefit of membership:

*   The <u>Co-op America Catalog -- your marketplace for peace, cooperation and a healthy planet</u> -- showcases socially and environmentally responsible organizations from around the world. You will get at least two catalogs a year. Your first catalog will be in the mail to you in either March or September, whichever is closer to the date you joined Co-op America.

*   <u>Socially Responsible financial planning services</u> through First Affirmative Financial Network. Turn to First Affirmative to help you meet your financial and social change goals when you invest. Learn how to invest in socially and environmentally

(over, please)

2100 M Street, N.W. • Suite 403 • Washington, D.C. 20037 • (202) 872-5307   ♻ Printed on recycled paper

EXHIBIT 11.4 Original Letter, New Member Welcome, Co-op America

responsible mutual funds, IRAs, CDs, stocks, bonds, low-income housing partnerships, and community projects.

* Travel-Links, our full service travel agency, will help you meet all your travel needs and assist you with a comprehensive range of culturally and environmentally sensitive travel options.

* The Co-op America VISA Card gives you a way to support the sustainable economy by channelling a percentage of your monthly charges into Co-op America's programs. A postage paid application is enclosed.

* Alternative Long Distance through Working Assets gives you monthly free calls to key decisionmakers on critical social and environmental issues, while offering top quality service and competitive rates.

* Alternative Health and Life Insurance plans give you access to innovative coverage. Provided by Consumers United, a worker-owned insurance company, our plans offer non-discriminatory rates, allow you to choose your own practitioner, and invest your premiums responsibly.

We've enclosed a folder for you with brochures about each of these socially responsible products and services. Please send in the coupons for more information on those you're interested in now -- and save the folder for others you may need later on.

Here at Co-op America, we also launch **action programs** to create economic change on specific aspects of our economy. Your dues will help support -- and we hope you'll become actively involved in -- programs like these:

* Rainforest Recovery -- We work with citizens in rainforest areas to find products that will sustain the rainforests, and help local farmers plant trees to reforest parts of Costa Rica -- we planted over 20,000 trees last year!

* The Valdez Principles of Corporate Environmental Responsibility -- We encourage U.S. corporations to make a commitment to ecological stewardship by signing the principles.

Please write or call any time you have any ideas, suggestions -- or a problem with any of our products or services. Part of social responsibility is responsiveness to you.

Once again, thank you for your support. We look forward to working with you to help bring about a just, cooperative, sustainable economy.

In cooperation,

Alisa Gravitz

Alisa Gravitz
Executive Director

P.S. Enclosed you will find a dual-purpose postcard. Use it to tell us about friends to whom you'd like us to send information about Co-op America and/or to tell us to take your name off the mailing list we share with like-minded organizations.

EXHIBIT 11.4 Continued

CO-OP AMERICA
2100 M Street, N.W., #403
Washington, D.C. 20037

Welcome!

"BUILDING AN ALTERNATIVE MARKETPLACE"

Thank you for joining Co-op America. This handy member card has the numbers for Co-op America services listed on the back. Carry it with you for quick reference to socially and environmentally responsible products and services.

CO-OP AMERICA
Membership Card
2100 M Street, N.W., #403
Washington, D.C. 20037
1-800-424-2667   202-872-5307

Member Number

Member

Signature _____

Welcome Aboard! We value you as a member. Together, we are building a more co-operative, humane and sustainable economy. Along with being part of this crucial work, we hope you enjoy the benefits of Co-op America membership:

Keep These Numbers Handy
- Co-op America — 1-800-424-2667 or 202-872-5307
- Co-op America Catalog — 202-223-1881
-
-
- Travel-Links — 1-800-648-2667
- Co-op America's VISA® with Vermont National Bank - 1-800-367-8862
- Working Assets Long Distance Phone Service - 1-800-788-8588 ext. 840
This is not an insurance card

1) Your subscription to *The Co-op America Quarterly*. Your subscription will start next quarter — and you'll get four issues of this information-packed publication in your membership year.

2) Your annual Co-op America Catalogs.

3) Your copy of Co-op America's Personal Guide to Socially Responsible Financial Planning — on its way to you next quarter.

4) Access to Co-op America's socially responsible services — financial, insurance, VISA®, Working Assets Long Distance Phone Service, and travel. Refer to the back of your member card for the phone numbers, and review the enclosed brochures describing these services in detail, and look in *The Co-op America Quarterly* for new information on these and other Co-op America programs. Thanks for joining!

PLEASE NOTE: Send us your address change along with your member number when you move.

EXHIBIT 11.5 Original Membership Card, New Member Welcome, Co-op America

Co-op America's Socially and Environmentally Responsible Services

In this folder, you will find a wide range of services that can help meet your needs. When you use these services, you will help reallocate money to businesses that share your vision of a just, cooperative, sustainable economy. These companies are working hard to change the way America does business.

We offer these services to you in the spirit of expanding your choices. Our program of providing socially and environmentally responsible services is only a small part of our work. The center of our mission is providing education and action programs to help create a just and sustainable society. As a member supporting our work, you will receive our magazine, the *Co-op America Quarterly* which includes *Boycott Action News*, our directory of Green Businesses, our biannual catalog and our *Socially Responsible Financial Planning Handbook*.

Thank you for joining.
We look forward to working with you!

Co-op America is a member-controlled and worker-managed non-profit organization promoting a sustainable economy and educating consumers and businesses about how to align their buying and investing habits with values of peace, cooperation and environmental protection. By using our collective economic power, we can begin to change the American economic system to one that is just and sustainable.

We at Co-op America have an ongoing commitment to serve as a model for social responsibility. Should you experience a problem with any of the goods, services or programs we provide, or if you are not receiving all of your Co-op America publications, we urge you to call our Member Services Department at (800) 424-2667 or (202) 872-5307. Please call or write us — any time — if you have a suggestion or idea.

Please keep this folder as a handy reference.

Your Name _____   Your Member # _____

SHARE THE MESSAGE

❑ **Yes,** I would like to share the Co-op America message with my friends. Please send the following people more information about Co-op America.

Friend's Name _____

Address _____

_____

Friend's Name _____

Address _____

_____

OFF THE MAILING LIST

❑ Co-op America occasionally lets other like-minded organizations mail their literature to Co-op America members. If you do <u>not</u> want to receive additional mailings from organizations working on issues related to Co-op America's mission, check this box, and be sure to write down your name and member # above.

EXHIBIT 11.6 Original Membership Services Brochure, New Member Welcome, Co-op America

Welcome aboard!

Your new member kit enclosed! Open immediately.

To:

EXHIBIT 11.7 Outer Envelope for Revised New Member Welcome Package, Part One, Co-op America

CO-OP AMERICA

Dear New Member:

<u>Welcome to Co-op America</u>!

Thank you for joining us in the movement for a just and sustainable economy!

As a member of Co-op America, you are already helping change the way America does business. Your membership support makes it possible for us to encourage corporate responsibility ... help socially responsible businesses emerge and thrive ... build sustainable communities ... and provide people with the information they need to use their economic power to maximum effect.

Your complimentary copy of the <u>National Green Pages</u> and your <u>Socially Responsible Financial Planning Handbook</u> will be mailed to you within two or three weeks. You'll also enjoy many other valuable publications, including:

» Our quarterly magazine, the <u>Co-op America Quarterly</u>, packed with practical, down-to-earth economic ideas and information. Your regular subscription will start with the next published issue.

» <u>Boycott Action News</u>, published within the <u>Quarterly</u>, gives you background, news, "where to write and what to do" for social change boycotts.

» <u>The Co-op America Catalog</u> -- a showcase of socially and environmentally responsible businesses. Members receive the catalog every Spring and Fall.

Please write or call any time you have an idea or suggestion -- or if you have a problem with any of our products or services.

For Co-op America, being socially responsible means being responsive to <u>you</u>.

Once again, thank you for your support! I look forward to working with you to create a just and sustainable economy.

In cooperation,

Alisa Gravitz

Alisa Gravitz
Executive Director

P.S. You and your views are important to all of us here at Co-op America. To get to know you and your needs, I'm enclosing your <u>New Member Survey</u>. Please take a few minutes right now to complete and return it to me. Thank you!

1850 M Street NW, Suite 700 ■ Washington, DC 20036 ■ 800-424-2667

printed on non-chlorine bleached, 100% recycled paper

EXHIBIT 11.8 **Letter for Revised New Member Welcome Package, Part One, Co-op America**

CO-OP AMERICA • 1850 M Street NW, Suite 700 • Washington, DC 20036

Thank you for joining Co-op America. This handy membership card has the numbers for Co-op America's services listed on the back. Carry it with you for quick reference to socially and environmentally responsible products and services.

Welcome!

"creating a just and sustainable society"

printed with
soy-based inks

CO-OP AMERICA
MEMBERSHIP CARD

Member No.
Member

Signature _____

1850 M Street NW, #700 • Washington, DC 20036
800-424-2667 • 202-872-5307

Welcome aboard!

We value you as a member. Together, we are building a more socially just and environmentally sustainable society. Along with participating in our crucial work, we hope you enjoy your benefits as a Co-op America Member:

1 Your subscriptions to the **Co-op America Quarterly** and **Boycott Action News**

2 The **Co-op America Catalog**

3 Socially Responsible Services:

The Co-op America VISA® Card — get your credit card services from Vermont National Bank; **Working Assets Long Distance** — telephone service that lets you make free calls to government and corporate leaders; **Travel-Links** — a socially responsible travel service.

You will receive more information about these services in a separate package in 2-3 weeks.

Thanks for joining.

Please note: *Send us your address change along with your membership number when you move.*

KEEP THESE NUMBERS HANDY

Co-op America 800-424-2667 or 202-872-5307 in DC

Co-op America Catalog 202-223-1881

Travel-Links 800-648-2667 or 617-497-8163 in MA

Co-op America VISA with Vermont National Bank
800-367-8862

Working Assets Long Distance Phone Service
800-788-8588 ext. 840

EXHIBIT 11.9 Membership Card for Revised New Member Welcome Package, Part One, Co-op America

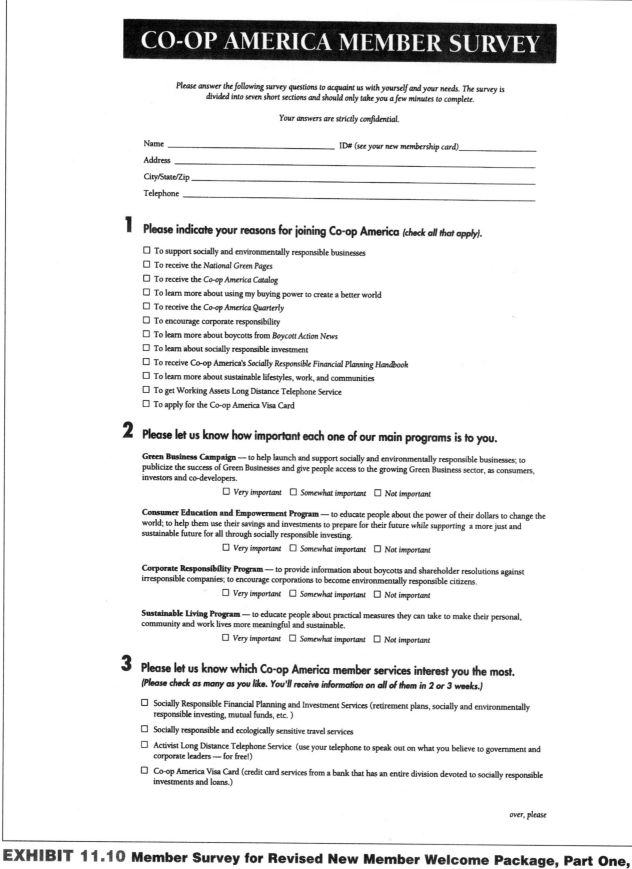

CO-OP AMERICA MEMBER SURVEY

Please answer the following survey questions to acquaint us with yourself and your needs. The survey is divided into seven short sections and should only take you a few minutes to complete.

Your answers are strictly confidential.

Name _____ ID# *(see your new membership card)* _____

Address _____

City/State/Zip _____

Telephone _____

1 Please indicate your reasons for joining Co-op America *(check all that apply)*.

☐ To support socially and environmentally responsible businesses
☐ To receive the *National Green Pages*
☐ To receive the *Co-op America Catalog*
☐ To learn more about using my buying power to create a better world
☐ To receive the *Co-op America Quarterly*
☐ To encourage corporate responsibility
☐ To learn more about boycotts from *Boycott Action News*
☐ To learn about socially responsible investment
☐ To receive Co-op America's *Socially Responsible Financial Planning Handbook*
☐ To learn more about sustainable lifestyles, work, and communities
☐ To get Working Assets Long Distance Telephone Service
☐ To apply for the Co-op America Visa Card

2 Please let us know how important each one of our main programs is to you.

Green Business Campaign — to help launch and support socially and environmentally responsible businesses; to publicize the success of Green Businesses and give people access to the growing Green Business sector, as consumers, investors and co-developers.

☐ *Very important*　☐ *Somewhat important*　☐ *Not important*

Consumer Education and Empowerment Program — to educate people about the power of their dollars to change the world; to help them use their savings and investments to prepare for their future *while supporting* a more just and sustainable future for all through socially responsible investing.

☐ *Very important*　☐ *Somewhat important*　☐ *Not important*

Corporate Responsibility Program — to provide information about boycotts and shareholder resolutions against irresponsible companies; to encourage corporations to become environmentally responsible citizens.

☐ *Very important*　☐ *Somewhat important*　☐ *Not important*

Sustainable Living Program — to educate people about practical measures they can take to make their personal, community and work lives more meaningful and sustainable.

☐ *Very important*　☐ *Somewhat important*　☐ *Not important*

3 Please let us know which Co-op America member services interest you the most.

(Please check as many as you like. You'll receive information on all of them in 2 or 3 weeks.)

☐ Socially Responsible Financial Planning and Investment Services (retirement plans, socially and environmentally responsible investing, mutual funds, etc.)
☐ Socially responsible and ecologically sensitive travel services
☐ Activist Long Distance Telephone Service (use your telephone to speak out on what you believe to government and corporate leaders — for free!)
☐ Co-op America Visa Card (credit card services from a bank that has an entire division devoted to socially responsible investments and loans.)

over, please

EXHIBIT 11.10 Member Survey for Revised New Member Welcome Package, Part One, Co-op America

4 Please let us know if you would be interested in any of the following ways to support the work of Co-op America *(check as many as you like).*

☐ *monthly sustainer program:* members lower our fundraising costs and assure us of reliable operating funds by giving $10 or more per month

☐ *Partners in Cooperation:* help Co-op America expand key programs by pledging $150 or more per year

☐ *Sponsors of specific publications* such as *Co-op America's National Green Pages*

☐ *Planned Giving:* members ensure the perpetuation of their values — and gain tax benefits — by making long-term gifts

☐ *Corporate Matching Gifts:* eligible members double the value of their gifts with employers' matching funds

5 More About You *(This section is optional. Your answers will help us decide which services to offer you.)*

- **Birthdate** _____ – _____ – _____
- **Gender** ☐ Male ☐ Female
- **Occupation** *(please check one only)*
  ☐ Professional/Technical/Managerial
  ☐ Sales/Clerical
  ☐ Teacher/Professor
  ☐ Craftsperson/Foreman/Other Worker
  ☐ Farmer
  ☐ Home Manager
  ☐ Retired
  ☐ Unemployed
  ☐ Other_____

- **Education** *(please check one only)*
  ☐ Elementary and/or some high school
  ☐ High school graduate
  ☐ Some college
  ☐ College graduate
  ☐ Graduate or professional degree
  ☐ Post-college without degree

- **Number of adults in household**
  ☐ 0 ☐ 1 ☐ 2 ☐ 3 ☐ 4 or more
- **Number of children in household**
  ☐ 0 ☐ 1 ☐ 2 ☐ 3 ☐ 4 or more
- **Have you bought anything from a mail-order catalog in the last 6 months?** ☐ Yes ☐ No
- **Do you have a computer in your home?**
  ☐ Yes ☐ No
- **Is your computer equiped with a modem?**
  ☐ Yes ☐ No
- **Do you have a fax machine in your home?**
  ☐ Yes ☐ No
- **Do you have a VCR in your home?** ☐ Yes ☐ No

- **Household Income**
  ☐ under $10,000
  ☐ $10,000 – 19,999
  ☐ $20,000 – 29,999
  ☐ $30,000 – 49,999
  ☐ $50,000 – 74,999
  ☐ $75,000 – 99,999
  ☐ $100,000 or more

6 Mailing List

Sometimes we share our mailing list with other like-minded organizations. If you would like us to take your name off the list we share with other groups check the box below.

☐ Please take my name off the mailing list you share with other organizations (***Important:*** *be sure to include your ID# at the beginning of this survey*)

7 Suggestions and Ideas

Please let us know if you have any comments about our work in the space below.

_____

_____

_____

_____

_____

☐ check this box if you would like us to get back to you.

Thank you for completing this survey!

Co-op America • 1850 M Street NW, Suite 700 • Washington, DC 20036

non-chlorine bleached, 100% recycled paper (10% post-consumer)

EXHIBIT 11.10 Continued

EXHIBIT 11.11 Outer Envelope and Survey Return Envelope for Revised New Member Welcome Package, Part One, Co-op America

CO-OP AMERICA

Dear Co-op America Member,

Thank you again for joining Co-op America! Enclosed you'll find your complimentary copies of <u>Co-op America's National Green Pages</u> and our <u>Financial Planning Handbook</u>. These are both essential tools for creating a just and sustainable economy. They're yours to keep. Use them well!

You'll also find a folder that contains introductory brochures on our membership services. Please look these over carefully to see which you would like to participate in. Each brochure has an easy-to-use reply device that you can send back to us or to the companies we work with.

Also included in this package is a Feedback Form you can send back to us if you have any comments, questions or concerns about your Co-op America Membership. You may also use the form to list the name of friends to whom you'd like us to send more information about Co-op America. Or, if it's more convenient for you to call, please don't hesitate to use our toll-free membership number, 1-800-424-2667.

We hope you enjoy all of these publications, products and services. These and all of our programs are designed to be used to transform the way business is done in America.

Thanks again for joining. It's good to be working with you to create a just and sustainable society.

In cooperation,

Alisa Gravitz
Executive Director

1850 M Street NW, Suite 700 ■ Washington, DC 20036 ■ 800-424-2667

printed on 100% recycled paper (10% post-consumer) with soy-based ink

---

EXHIBIT 11.12 Letter for Revised New Member Welcome Package, Part Two, Co-op America

FEEDBACK FORM

If you have any questions, comments or suggestions please use the space below or call our toll-free membership number, 800-424-2667.

_____

_____

_____

_____

_____

_____

_____

_____

_____

If you think any of your friends would be interested in learning more about Co-op America, please list up to three names and addresses below.

If you'd like to give _gift memberships_ to any of those you list below, please check the appropriate boxes. The first gift membership is $20. Each subsequent gift membership is $15. If you'd like you may also include any additional contributions in the enclosed reply envelope.

Your Name _____

Address _____

City/State/Zip _____

Your Membership No. _____
(on your membership card)

1 Please send more information to:

Name _____

Address _____

City/State/Zip _____

☐ Please send a gift membership in my name — $20

2 Please send more information to:

Name _____

Address _____

City/State/Zip _____

☐ Please send a gift membership in my name — $15

☐ _I'm enclosing an additional contribution of $_____._

Total amount enclosed $_____.

3 Please send more information to:

Name _____

Address _____

City/State/Zip _____

☐ Please send a gift membership in my name — $15

**Thanks again for joining Co-op America!**

Co-op America • 1850 M Street NW, Suite 700 • Washington, DC 20036

non-chlorine bleached, 100% recycled paper (10% post-consumer) • soy-based inks

EXHIBIT 11.13 Feedback Form for Revised New Member Welcome Package, Part Two, Co-op America

EXHIBIT 11.14 Membership Benefits Brochures for Revised New Member Welcome Package, Part Two, Co-op America

EXHIBIT 11.14 Continued

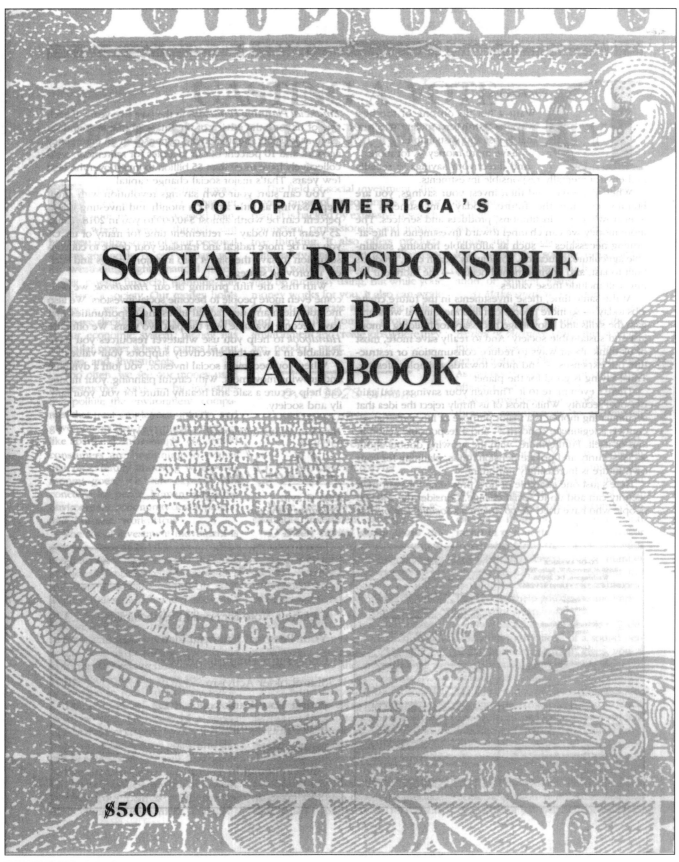

EXHIBIT 11.15 *Socially Responsible Financial Planning Handbook* **for Revised New Member Welcome Package, Part Two, Co-op America**

Co-op America's
National Green Pages

1993 Premiere Issue

The Directory of Socially & Environmentally Responsible Companies & Organizations

Workers

Consumers

FOOD CO-OP

The planet does not need saving. It's got another 2-3 billion good years left. What needs saving is ourselves, and the ecosystems we depend on. Presumably we've got about 10 years to do it. We're going to need everybody's help. And there is one human institution powerful and innovative enough to pull this off. Business. A new kind of business that cares about all stakeholders...

Communities

Environment

THIS IS NOT A DUMP!!

Let your conscience do the walking...™

EXHIBIT 11.16 *National Green Pages* **for Revised New Member Welcome Package, Part Two, Co-op America**

Appealing for Special Gifts

Bringing Your Case Down to Earth

Aspecial appeal urges donors or members to focus on one of the organization's individual programs, a specific issue, a season of the year, or a particular need or opportunity. Normally the letter makes clear that funds contributed in response to a special appeal are undesignated—in other words, that they provide general operating support—even though the letter may heavily emphasize a single issue or project.

Exhibit 12.1 shows a response device representative of the thousands of special appeals mailed every year by nonprofit organizations to their previous donors. It could hardly be more obvious, with its request for "an extra measure of support during the critical summer months."

The distinguishing characteristics of this response device are typical of special appeals:

- Bread for the World was seeking support for a specific purpose: to support the organization during the summer. So, unlike an acquisition letter, this appeal could not be continuously remailed. Special appeals are typically one-time (or annual) propositions.
- The ask amounts ($1,000, $500, $250) are appropriate for donors who have already established relationships with Bread for the

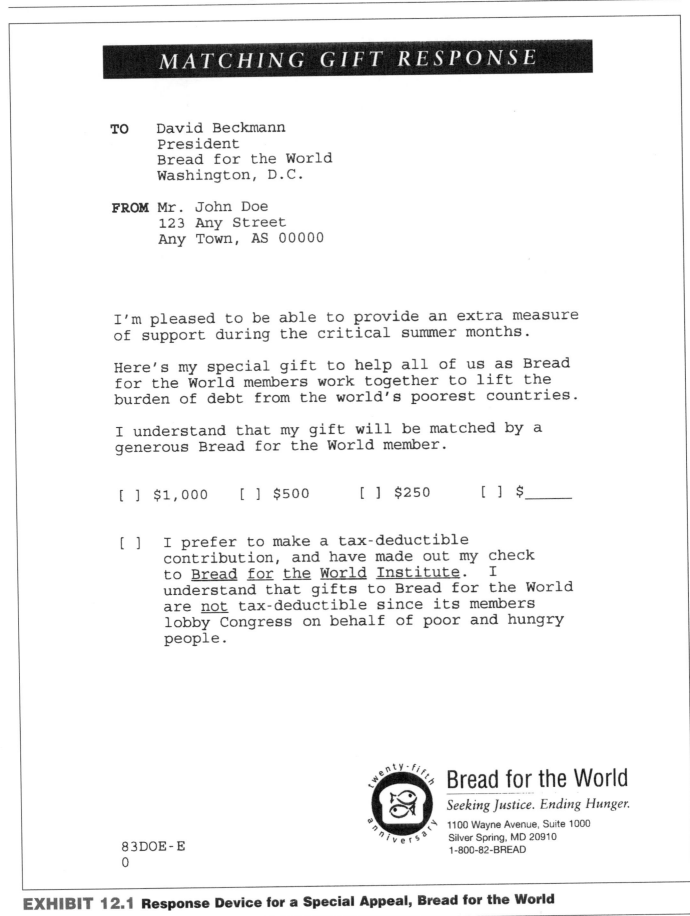

MATCHING GIFT RESPONSE

TO   David Beckmann
President
Bread for the World
Washington, D.C.

FROM Mr. John Doe
123 Any Street
Any Town, AS 00000

I'm pleased to be able to provide an extra measure of support during the critical summer months.

Here's my special gift to help all of us as Bread for the World members work together to lift the burden of debt from the world's poorest countries.

I understand that my gift will be matched by a generous Bread for the World member.

[ ] $1,000   [ ] $500   [ ] $250   [ ] $_____

[ ]   I prefer to make a tax-deductible contribution, and have made out my check to <u>Bread</u> <u>for</u> <u>the</u> <u>World</u> <u>Institute</u>. I understand that gifts to Bread for the World are <u>not</u> tax-deductible since its members lobby Congress on behalf of poor and hungry people.

Bread for the World
Seeking Justice. Ending Hunger.
1100 Wayne Avenue, Suite 1000
Silver Spring, MD 20910
1-800-82-BREAD

83DOE-E
0

EXHIBIT 12.1 Response Device for a Special Appeal, Bread for the World

You are welcome to request a copy of our latest financial report by contacting:
Bread for the World, 1100 Wayne Avenue, Suite 1000, Silver Spring, MD 20910,
(301) 608-2400.

If you are a resident of one of the states below, you may obtain financial information directly from the state agency: **FLORIDA** — A COPY OF THE OFFICIAL REGISTRATION AND FINANCIAL INFORMATION MAY BE OBTAINED FROM THE DIVISION OF CONSUMER SERVICES BY CALLING TOLL-FREE, (800) 435-7352 WITHIN THE STATE. REGISTRATION DOES NOT IMPLY ENDORSEMENT, APPROVAL OR RECOMMENDATION BY THE STATE. **MARYLAND** — For the cost of copies and postage: Office of the Secretary of State, State House, Annapolis, MD 21401. **NEW JERSEY** — Information filed with the Attorney General concerning this charitable solicitation may be obtained from the Attorney General of the State of New Jersey by calling (201) 504-6215. Registration with the Attorney General does not imply endorsement. **NEW YORK** — Office of the Attorney General, Department of Law, Charities Bureau, 120 Broadway, New York, NY 10271. **NORTH CAROLINA** — FINANCIAL INFORMATION ABOUT THIS ORGANIZATION AND A COPY OF ITS LICENSE ARE AVAILABLE FROM THE STATE SOLICITATION LICENSING BRANCH AT (919) 733-4510. THE LICENSE IS NOT AN ENDORSEMENT BY THE STATE. **PENNSYLVANIA** — The official registration and financial information of Bread for the World may be obtained from the Pennsylvania Department of State by calling toll-free, within Pennsylvania, (800) 732-0999. Registration does not imply endorsement. **VIRGINIA** — State Division of Consumer Affairs, Department of Agricultural and Consumer Services, P.O. Box 1163, Richmond, VA 23209. **WASHINGTON** — Charities Division, Office of the Secretary of State, State of Washington, Olympia, WA 98504-0422; 1-800-332-4483. **WEST VIRGINIA** — Residents may obtain a summary from: Secretary of State, State Capitol, Charleston, WV 25305.

Registration with any of these states does not imply endorsement, approval or recommendation by the state.

EXHIBIT 12.1 Continued

World. Few nondonors would consider making such large gifts the first time they donated to an organization.

- The only truly general description of Bread for the World's mission is to be found in the tagline in the lower right corner ("Seeking Justice. Ending Hunger."), although the letter expands on that point with more general references to the organization's work. In any case, it's assumed that most readers of this appeal are familiar with the organization's purpose.

How Special Appeals Are Different from Other Fundraising Letters

Most special appeals share six characteristics:

1. They contain specific time references because special appeals are usually mailed only once, through a narrow window on the calendar. To emphasize urgency and underline how different they are from other solicitations from the same charity, most special appeals refer to passing conditions or one-time opportunities or circumstances.

2. The ask amount is variable. Usually a special appeal is segmented; that is, different versions of the appeal are sent to distinct groups of donors. For example, those who've never contributed more than $50 at any one time might be asked for $75, and previous donors of between $200 and $499 would be urged to send a minimum of $500.

3. There are specific program references. These are, after all, *special* appeals. More often than not, the funds requested are to support one particular project or program.

4. Special appeal letters are frequently short—just one or two pages. Many low-budget organizations, as well as some that are well heeled, include few inserts. The assumption is that proven donors are well acquainted with the charity's work and need few reminders about its value. This assumption is questionable, but it's common nonetheless. Also, inserts such as brochures or fliers may make a mailing seem less personal, blunting its effect. (There are many exceptional circumstances that justify such inserts, however. The dreamcatcher package from St. Joseph's

Indian School in Chapter Two is a good example. But even that letter is a short one.)

5. A special appeal is far more likely to be personalized than a donor acquisition mailing. It's also more likely to include "live postage" (stamps) and use high-quality paper. The extra expense is often considerable, and it's magnified by the lower volume that's also typical of mailings to proven donors. But the resulting higher cost per unit tends to be justified by the response, which is customarily about five to seven times as great as that from a donor acquisition mailing.

6. The copy is likely to be warm and personal. It's built on individual donor histories. A charity knows a few things about its donors, such as when they started giving, the sizes of their largest gifts, and the number of gifts they've sent. In a well-run fundraising program, those things are reflected in the frequent special appeals mailed in search of additional support.

Case Study: Human Service Agency Special Appeal

Human Service Agency (not its actual name) is typical of many other local human service providers all across America in its dependence on government contracts (60 percent of its $3.6 million budget) and the relatively modest scope of its efforts to raise funds from individuals (accounting for just 12 to 15 percent of the budget).

The agency's one-person development shop consists of a development director, a simple, off-the-shelf database management program, and a laser printer. The database hovers around three thousand, with about seven hundred donors annually. Appeals are produced in-house, allowing the agency to print donors' names and addresses directly on the envelope rather than use labels.

The relatively simple database program doesn't let the director refer to past giving in his letters. In any case, he's reluctant to write separate letters for renewals and prospects because it's so time-consuming.

In a typical appeal, the agency uses one letter for the entire database, although all letters are personalized ("Dear Mr. and Mrs. Jones"). Board members send the letter over their signature to personal friends and business contacts with a hand-written postscript. About nine hundred names of the database are linked to a board member. Of the remaining unlinked solicitation pieces, all but five hundred have received at least one mailing in the past. Unlinked letters go out over the board chairman's signature without a postscript. All signatures are handwritten. Linked letters go out first class with commemorative postage stamps. Unlinked letters are mailed nonprofit bulk rate in envelopes with a preprinted indicia square. A six-page agency newsletter is sent out at some point before the appeal.

In other words, each package the agency mails is intended to serve double duty: as both a special appeal (to proven donors) and an acquisition letter (to prospective donors). In fact, one letter usually can't adequately meet both types of letters, presenting the *general* case for making a first gift and the *special* case for additional support. Nonetheless, many nonprofits feel forced by limitations in their budgets or the size of their mailings to send a single version of a fundraising letter to both donors and prospects. This is one of those cases.

The text of the letter I was sent to edit is reproduced as Exhibit 12.2. My edited version is shown in Exhibit 12.3. In the original, the names of the agency's board members were listed on the left side of the letterhead. The full package also contained a laser-addressed, closed-face outside envelope; a preprinted wallet-flap remittance envelope; and copies of two editorials on a two-sided sheet.

Critique of the Original Letter

The Human Service Agency did an outstanding job of wordsmithing; the letter required few changes in wording. The agency's staff told an engaging story and made a strong case for supporting their work. The lead was involving, and the closing tied the case and the story together. All good.

The only significant problem in the body of the letter was that it didn't directly ask for *money*. It's very important that a fundraising letter come clean on the subject of money—the earlier and the more straightforward, the better.

Ideally, of course, they'd insert a specific, appropriate ask amount in each individual letter. (That amount might be 15 percent or 20 percent higher than the donor's gift last year, for example.) Unfortunately, that wasn't feasible in this project: it was prohibitively costly to insert a specific amount of money tied to the donor's previous support. But a second-best alternative comes to mind: to ask for gifts within a certain range (say, $150, $400, $1,000 or more). There's a pitfall in that approach, though: you've got to be sure not to send the same letter to everyone. You don't want to ask donors for *less* money than they've given before.

A third-best alternative is to ask for "a generous gift" or something else nonspecific. But make sure there's no question you're asking for money.

A lesser problem, occasioned by the shortness of the letter, perhaps, was that there was no P.S. With only the rarest of exceptions, I include one in every fundraising letter. Typically that involves singling out some aspect of the appeal with high reader interest. So I added a P.S., and transferred one of the strongest elements of the agency's case to that location. In the case of the linked letters, board members could easily add either a P.P.S. or an unlabeled personal note.

Date

Name

Address

City/zip

Dear xxxxx,

<u>Jeffrey is going to see his dad today and he is terrified.</u>

Jeffrey is seven and hasn't seen his dad in three years. His parents were divorced four years ago in a bitter fight. First Jeffrey lived with his mom, and his dad visited him every week. Then his dad stopped coming because "seeing his ex-wife was too difficult." Now Jeffrey has a new stepfather and a new last name. And his dad wants to see him again.

If Jeffrey is lucky, the court will order supervised visits at the Human Service Agency visitors' facility. It's a cheerful, home-like place where Jeffrey can feel safe as he and his dad get to know each other again.

Many families turn to Human Service Agency—for supervised visits in custody cases or treatment for sexually abused children. For hot meals for frail seniors or safe child care when parents work. And for counseling when lives are devastated by conflict and abuse.

That's why I'm asking you to help Human Service Agency now. During these difficult economic times, the demand for services has exploded. In the last six months, for example, the number

EXHIBIT 12.2 Original Combination Special Appeal and Acquisition Letter, Human Services Agency

of people in counseling has increased 40% over the previous six months. And 89 cents out of every dollar contributed directly benefits the families who need a helping hand.

I know that if you could help just one child like Jeffrey, you would. You and I agree that families are the backbone of our society and that successful families build a healthy and strong community. Won't you join me in making sure that no family is turned away for lack of funds? Jeffrey and his dad are counting on us to give them a second chance.

Sincerely,

Avery I. Person

Board Chairman

EXHIBIT 12.2 Continued

Date

Name

Address

City/zip

Dear xxxxx,

Jeffrey is going to see his Dad today—and he's <u>terrified</u>.

Jeffrey is seven and hasn't seen his Dad in three years. His parents were divorced four years ago in a bitter fight.

First Jeffrey lived with his Mom, and his Dad visited him every week. Then his Dad stopped coming because "seeing his ex-wife was too difficult."

Now Jeffrey has a new stepfather and a new last name. And his Dad wants to see him again.

If Jeffrey is lucky, the court will order supervised visits at the Human Service Agency visitors' facility. It's <u>a cheerful, homey place</u> where Jeffrey can feel safe while he and his Dad get to know each other again.

Many families turn to Human Service Agency —for supervised visits in custody cases or treatment for sexually abused children. For hot meals for frail seniors, safe child care when parents work, or counseling when lives are devastated by conflict and abuse.

Ironically, despite the current boom, the <u>demand for our services has exploded</u>. In the last six months, for example, the

EXHIBIT 12.3 Revised Combination Special Appeal and Acquisition Letter, Human Services Agency

number of people in counseling has increased 40% over the previous six months.

That's why I'm asking you to help Human Service Agency today with a tax-deductible gift of $XXX or more.

<u>I know that if you could help just one child like Jeffrey, you would.</u> You and I agree that families are the backbone of our society and that successful families build a healthy and strong community.

Will you join me in making sure that no family is turned away for lack of funds? Jeffrey and his Dad are counting on us to give them a second chance.

With high hopes,

Avery I. Person

Board Chairman

P.S. Your support for the Human Service Agency will make a big difference here in [name of town]. <u>89 cents out of every dollar</u> contributed directly benefits the families who need a helping hand.

EXHIBIT 12.3 Continued

The original writer seems to have struggled to squeeze this letter onto a single page. To me, it's far more important to tell the story—and use the space necessary to do so—than to hold to some arbitrary length limit. In this case, that resulted in a two-page letter, with slightly broader margins. (Incidentally, since I know letter length is often a controversial question among people unfamiliar with fundraising practice, I sliced up my own edited version and reduced the letter to a single page again when I did the original work.)

Format Changes

I'm going to repeat here what I said to the Human Service Agency at the time. It's what I say to almost every other local and regional nonprofit organization that gives me the opportunity: listing the members of the board of directors on the side of a fundraising letter is a distraction. And unless your agency is very different from most others, the directors are not nearly so well known as you—or they themselves—might think they are. (I'm supremely confident about this statement because I reviewed mounds of public opinion polling data firsthand quite a number of times during years of full-time involvement in local politics.)

So if you don't have a closetful of letterhead and a high wall of political resistance to moving the listings off the letterhead (for fundraising letters only), you could list them on the back of a reply device or—in some other appeal—on a brochure. A fallback position is to place the listings more unobtrusively at the *bottom* of the first page of the letter, in the smallest type you can get away with.

As for the format of the text, you'll note in my edited version that I eliminated italics, using a limited amount of underlining instead, indented every paragraph, and broke up the text into smaller paragraphs. I made all of these changes to enhance the readability of the copy and make the letter seem a little more personal and less institutional.

Outer Envelope

I very much liked the use of laser addressing on a closed-face envelope, as the agency had planned to do. But I thought that using a postal indicia would detract from the personalized character of the envelope. I strongly recommend either first-class stamps or a postage meter (at least for prospects who aren't linked to board members but are past donors nonetheless). Another alternative, which I don't favor highly but think superior to an indicia, is to use precanceled nonprofit bulk mail stamps.

Remittance Envelope

I'm not a big fan of *bang-tail or wallet flap remittance envelopes* like the one the Human Service Agency was planning to use. Those are envelopes with long, rectangular flaps on the back, usually printed both inside and out. Results are usually better with a detached, personalized reply device (so the donor doesn't have to write out all the information) and a business reply envelope that's big enough to hold the reply device without folding.

The best reply devices are involving. They affirm the donor's eagerness to help (usually by using the word *YES!*) and repeat and underline the principal reason or reasons given in the letter for supporting the agency *at this time*. You can't achieve that with preprinted remittance envelopes.

The agency talked about a "partnership level" on the remittance envelope but mentioned the concept nowhere else. Perhaps they had explained it in an earlier letter but left the copy on the envelope (another reason not to preprint remittance envelopes).

13

Asking for Year-End Contributions
Making the Most of the Holiday Spirit

For the overwhelming majority of Americans, the final weeks of the calendar year are a time for giving. It's no accident that a hugely disproportional share of the funds that nonprofit organizations raise each year are realized in the several weeks before New Year's. Nor is it coincidental that virtually every nonprofit organization that has its fundraising act together mails a year-end appeal to its donors or members.

The business end of most year-end appeals resembles the Bread for the World response device reproduced in Exhibit 13.1. At least five elements show that this is obviously a year-end appeal to donors:

- It says so. You can't mistake the words "special year-end gift." No subtlety here (and none called for).
- The reference to the "new year" implies that gifts will continue efforts the donor has (presumably) supported in the past.
- The ask amounts are high enough to suggest that the people to whom this letter was mailed have a history of support for Bread for the World. Few nondonors would seriously consider gifts so generous.
- The offer of a tax-deductible option is likely to be of special interest because the end of the tax year is approaching.

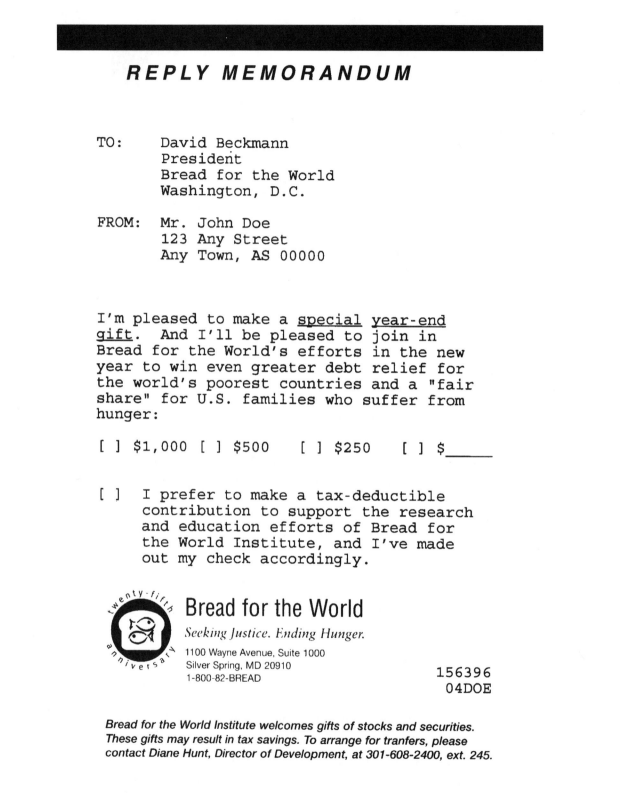

REPLY MEMORANDUM

TO: David Beckmann
        President
        Bread for the World
        Washington, D.C.

FROM: Mr. John Doe
        123 Any Street
        Any Town, AS 00000

I'm pleased to make a <u>special</u> <u>year-end</u> <u>gift</u>. And I'll be pleased to join in Bread for the World's efforts in the new year to win even greater debt relief for the world's poorest countries and a "fair share" for U.S. families who suffer from hunger:

[ ] $1,000   [ ] $500   [ ] $250   [ ] $_____

[ ]   I prefer to make a tax-deductible contribution to support the research and education efforts of Bread for the World Institute, and I've made out my check accordingly.

Bread for the World
Seeking Justice. Ending Hunger.
1100 Wayne Avenue, Suite 1000
Silver Spring, MD 20910
1-800-82-BREAD

156396
04DOE

Bread for the World Institute welcomes gifts of stocks and securities. These gifts may result in tax savings. To arrange for tranfers, please contact Diane Hunt, Director of Development, at 301-608-2400, ext. 245.

RECYCLED & RECYCLABLE / PRINTED WITH SOY INK   60042

EXHIBIT 13.1 Response Device for a Year-End Appeal, Bread for the World

*Contributions to **Bread for the World** are not tax-deductible since its members lobby Congress on behalf of hungry people. Tax-deductible gifts may be made to **Bread for the World Institute** to support research and education.*

You are welcome to request a copy of our latest financial report by contacting: Bread for the World, 1100 Wayne Avenue, Suite 1000, Silver Spring, MD 20910, (301) 608-2400.

If you are a resident of one of the states below, you may obtain financial information directly from the state agency: **FLORIDA** — A COPY OF THE OFFICIAL REGISTRATION AND FINANCIAL INFORMATION MAY BE OBTAINED FROM THE DIVISION OF CONSUMER SERVICES BY CALLING TOLL-FREE, (800) 435-7352 WITHIN THE STATE. REGISTRATION DOES NOT IMPLY ENDORSEMENT, APPROVAL OR RECOMMENDATION BY THE STATE. **MARYLAND** — For the cost of copies and postage: Office of the Secretary of State, State House, Annapolis, MD 21401. **NEW JERSEY** — Information filed with the Attorney General concerning this charitable solicitation may be obtained from the Attorney General of the State of New Jersey by calling (201) 504-6215. Registration with the Attorney General does not imply endorsement. **NEW YORK** — Office of the Attorney General, Department of Law, Charities Bureau, 120 Broadway, New York, NY 10271. **NORTH CAROLINA** — FINANCIAL INFORMATION ABOUT THIS ORGANIZATION AND A COPY OF ITS LICENSE ARE AVAILABLE FROM THE STATE SOLICITATION LICENSING BRANCH AT (919) 733-4510. THE LICENSE IS NOT AN ENDORSEMENT BY THE STATE. **PENNSYLVANIA** — The official registration and financial information of Bread for the World may be obtained from the Pennsylvania Department of State by calling toll-free, within Pennsylvania, (800) 732-0999. Registration does not imply endorsement. **VIRGINIA** — State Division of Consumer Affairs, Department of Agricultural and Consumer Services, P.O. Box 1163, Richmond, VA 23209. **WASHINGTON** — Charities Division, Office of the Secretary of State, State of Washington, Olympia, WA 98504-0422; 1-800-332-4483. **WEST VIRGINIA** — Residents may obtain a summary from: Secretary of State, State Capitol, Charleston, WV 25305.

Registration with any of these states does not imply endorsement, approval or recommendation by the state.

EXHIBIT 13.1 Continued

- The appeal is personalized. This package cost Bread for the World a significant amount of money for data processing. It's unlikely the group would spend as much on fundraising letters to nondonors.

How Year-End Appeals Are Different from Other Fundraising Letters

The end of the year is a special time for most U.S. nonprofit organizations. A spirit of generosity holds sway, and donors turn to thoughts of tax deductions, including charitable giving. In fact, many of the donor motivations described in Chapter One—loneliness, to cite just one example—are felt most strongly during the year-end holidays.

Year-end appeals are a major source of support for the nation's nonprofit organizations, because an estimated 40 percent of all charitable giving takes place during the final three months of the year. They can be either annual (or membership) renewal mailings or special appeals (seeking gifts for earmarked purposes). But the fundraising letters that charities mail during this time tend to exhibit most of the following six characteristics:

1. There are usually references to the season (particularly by religious organizations). The benefits of year-end tax deductions are commonly mentioned too. Often the two are connected.

2. Ask amounts are usually variable. The generosity of year-end giving makes it possible for most groups to invest a little more in personalizing their appeals.

3. For the same reasons, many charities spend more on producing their year-end appeals than they do on fundraising letters mailed at other times of the year—not just on personalization but also on paper stock, ink colors, and premiums such as holiday greeting cards.

4. A favored theme is "looking back, looking forward." The widespread tendency in the United States to think about New Year's resolutions lends itself to this Janus-like approach.

5. More often than at other times of the year, charities may launch multipart appeals, consisting of a series of two or three letters, perhaps even combined with a telephone call.

6. Year-end appeals are often mailed to large proportions of the donor file.

Case Study: Hebrew Women's League End-of-Year Appeal

The draft text of this straightforward year-end appeal is shown in Exhibits 13.2 and 13.3. My edited version follows in Exhibits 13.4 and 13.5. Look at both versions, and you'll grasp the essence of what I did to strengthen this appeal:

- Changed the emphasis from *we* to *you*.
- Altered the look of the letter, adding subheads, underlining sparingly, and switching typefaces from Times Roman to Courier.
- Dropped the credit card payment option. At the time I edited this letter, I was not recommending that clients include such an option. While results varied from one organization to another, tests often showed that a credit card option lowered response. I now believe that is no longer so likely to be the case.

I also reinforced the seasonal connections. In the first paragraph of the revised reply device in Exhibit 13.5, above the string of ask amounts, note the words used there: "2001," "tax-deductible," "year-end." With these few straightforward words and a few relatively subtle changes in the letter itself, what was originally a generic special appeal became a year-end appeal.

"It's like a house of cards. Right now it is standing, but I feel like the slightest breath of wind, the merest breeze could knock down a wall, a room or the whole structure."

A mother of two young boys talking about balancing her work and family responsibilities.

December _____

Dear HWL Member:

Every day more and more American families juggle the demands of work and family commitments. And, in family after family, it is women who bear the major burden of this task. In one out of _____ families, women are the only adult parent in the home. In one out of _____ families they care for children and aging relatives. In one out of _____ families they have children and hold down a job. In one out of _____ families, they work and care for a frail elderly relative.

When I think of these American families, I think about all the talk we hear these days about strengthening the family, about how much of it is just talk. And, I know the difference, because our organization—the Hebrew Women's League—knows the difference between talk and action for American families. After all, come _____, we will have been acting on behalf of families for 100 years.

We help. We help parents of young children give those children the gift of the joy of learning. HWL's Learning Is for Kiddies (LIKE) Program has become a national force in the arena of preparing children to succeed in school. We are now serving 9,000 families in 17 states and new requests for LIKE are dramatically increasing. Children and their families, educators, legislators and HWL members are forming an educational partnership that has become a force for the future.

We care. We know how parents feel when they leave their little children in child care and go off to work. Our American Family Project and the projects it nurtured are trying to make sure that affordable, quality day care is there for families.

EXHIBIT 13.2 Original Letter for Year-End Appeal, Hebrew Women's League

We lead by stimulating community action. It mobilizes communities to help employers assist their employees with their child and elder care needs.

We stand up for what American families need. On January 15, _____, in every HWL community across the country, you will take part in a coordinated advocacy event for American families. On HWL's Women at Work Day, mayors and governors across America will be presented with "Food for Thought" lunchboxes filled with action information to help families care for their young and oldest members.

As _____ draws to a close and you consider the charitable contributions you want to make, please make a tax-deductible contribution . . . To support HWL's work for families. (Use the enclosed card to tell us where you want your money to go).

This letter also brings you my best wishes for 2001 . . . our Centennial year.

With my warmest regards,

Marsha

P.S.

EXHIBIT 13.2 Continued

Hebrew Women's League, 255 East Lexington Avenue, New York, NY 10001

Dear Marsha,

☐ Yes, you may have my vote to support HWL's Family Agenda

      $100 $75 $50   Other $

I want you to use my donation to increase HWL's work with:

    ☐   LIKE (Learning Is for Kids) Program

    ☐   Work/Family Project—Putting family values on America's Corporate Agenda.

    ☐   Women at Work Day . . . January 15, _____, when we draw national attention to the dependent care needs of working parents.

    ☐   HWL's Advocacy on behalf of legislation such as the Family and Medical Leave Act, the Violence Against Women Act, Women's Apprenticeship Bill and the Comprehensive Children's Initiative.

    ☐   You decide where it's most needed for HWL's Family Agenda.

Card # _____

Visa ☐   MasterCard ☐   Expiration Date _____

Signature _____

Please make checks payable to Hebrew Women's League. Contributions may be charged to credit cards. Fill in your card number, expiration date and signature above. All contributions are tax-deductible to the extent allowed by law. Your canceled check is your receipt.

EXHIBIT 13.3 **Original Reply Device for Year-End Appeal, Hebrew Women's League**

"It's like a house of cards. Right now it is standing, but I feel like the slightest breath of wind, the merest breeze could knock down a wall, a room or the whole structure."

> — A mother of two young boys, talking about balancing her work and family responsibilities

December ———

Dear Friend of American Families:

As a member of the Hebrew Women's League, you know the difference between talk and action when it comes to family values. Because you're already taking action.

** <u>You help.</u> **

Your membership support for HWL helps parents give their young children the joy of learning through the Learning Is for Kiddies Program (LIKE).

This model program has become a national force in the arena of preparing children to succeed in school. With your generous help, we're now serving over 9,000 families in 17 states—and new requests for LIKE are increasing dramatically.

Children and their families, educators, legislators and HWL members are forming an educational partnership that has become a force for a more hopeful future.

** <u>You care.</u> **

You know how parents feel when they leave their little children in inadequate child care arrangements and go off to work. Your American Family Project and the projects it nurtured are trying to make sure that affordable, quality care is there for families.

** <u>You lead.</u> **

As an HWL member, you're taking the lead by stimulating community action. Your Women at Work Project helps employers assist their employees with their child and elder care needs.

** <u>You're standing up for American families.</u> **

On January 15, ———, HWL members across the country will take part in a coordinated advocacy event for American families.

On HWL's Women at Work Day, mayors and governors across America will be presented with "Food for Thought" lunchboxes filled with action information to help families care for their young and oldest members.

EXHIBIT 13.4 *Revised Letter for Year-End Appeal, Hebrew Women's League*

As ——— draws to a close and you consider how you'll direct your year-end charitable giving, please consider how much more you can do to help American families by sending a special, tax-deductible year-end gift to the Hebrew Women's League.

As you consider the size of your year-end gift, please think about the magnitude and the importance of the challenge you and I are facing:

Every day, more and more American families must juggle the demands of work and family commitments. And, in family after family, it is women who bear the major burden of this task.

In one out of xx families, a woman is the only adult parent in the home.

Women in one out of every xx families care for children and aging relatives, in one out of xx they have children and hold down jobs.

Please take a moment right now to write as generous a check as you can—and return it to me today in the enclosed self-addressed envelope.

As I look ahead to our Family Agenda for ———, I have to calculate how much funding will be available for each of our urgent and critical action programs. It will help so very much if I can have your year-end gift in hand by the 31st of December!

You may use the enclosed card to tell us which of the League's most urgent programs you want your gift to support.

With my warmest regards, and my best wishes for your health and happiness in ———,

[sign "Marsha"]

Marsha [Lastname]

P.S. Come ——— the Hebrew Women's League will have been acting on behalf of American families for 100 years! To commemorate the beginning of our Centennial year, and give an extra boost to our Family Agenda for 2001, will you consider a special, tax-deductible year-end gift of $100 or more?

EXHIBIT 13.4 Continued

To Marsha [Lastname], Hebrew Women's League

Dear Marsha,

Yes, you have my support for the Hebrew Women's League's Family Agenda for _____! To help meet the most urgent needs, I'm rushing you my special, tax-deductible year-end gift in the amount of:

☐ $100   ☐ $75   ☐ $50   ☐ Other $_____

Please use my gift to give an extra boost to your work on behalf of American families in the following area:

☐ Learning Is for Kiddies Program (LIKE)

☐ American Family Project (putting family values on America's corporate agenda)

☐ Women at Work Day, January 15, ____

☐ Advocacy (for legislation such as the Family and Medical Leave Act and the Violence Against Women Act)

☐ Please put my gift to work where it's most urgently needed.

Please complete and return this form with your check by December 31st

Please make your check payable to HWL and mail in the enclosed self-addressed envelope to: Hebrew Women's League, 255 East Lexington Avenue, New York, NY 10001. All contributions are tax-deductible to the extent allowed by law. Your cancelled check is your receipt. Thank you very much!

EXHIBIT 13.5 Revised Reply Device for Year-End Appeal, Hebrew Women's League

14

Soliciting High-Dollar Gifts
Framing the Case for Major Contributions

Direct mail fundraising typically attracts modest gifts, usually of less than $100. Within the last couple of decades, however, direct mail fundraisers have come to understand that similar techniques, carefully honed for greater impact on more upscale donors, can generate gifts by mail of $500, $1,000, or more. The so-called high-dollar appeals that seek (and, increasingly, yield) such gifts are fast becoming a fixture in the pantheon of nonprofit fundraising.

Bread for the World used the reply device in Exhibit 14.1 in a high-dollar appeal that's typical of the genre in many ways:

- Clearly this is a leadership appeal—a request that's far out of the ordinary, if only because it asks for an unusually large sum of money. It even uses the phrase "leadership level." Bread for the World is asking John Doe to enroll in its Founder's Society by raising the total of his gifts for the year to $2,500.
- This appeal requests a gift of $1,000 or more—obviously untypical of direct mail fundraising letters.
- The importance of the $1,000 ask amount is highlighted by the final laser-printed line, which makes clear that gifts at this "leadership level" are recognized in the Bread for the World Annual Report.

REPLY MEMORANDUM

FROM: Mr. John Doe
        123 Any Street
        Any Town, AS 00000

TO: Diane Hunt
        Director of Development
        BREAD FOR THE WORLD
        Washington, D.C.

I'm pleased to renew my annual support of Bread for the World at a leadership level.

[ ]   I wish to be a member of the Founder's Society, and I've enclosed a gift of $1,500 so that my total 1999 contributions are $2,500.

[ ]   At this time I prefer to make a special gift:

      [ ] $250   [ ] $100   [ ] $_____

[ ]   I wish to make a <u>tax-deductible</u> <u>gift</u> to support the research and education efforts of Bread for the World Institute, and I've made out my check accordingly.

[ ]   I prefer that my gift remain anonymous and not be recognized in the Annual Report.

Bread for the World
Seeking Justice. Ending Hunger.

1100 Wayne Avenue, Suite 1000
Silver Spring, MD 20910
1-800-82-BREAD

                                              0
                                           01DOE

RECYCLED & RECYCLABLE / PRINTED WITH SOY INK   60012

EXHIBIT 14.1 Reply Device for a High-Dollar Appeal, Bread for the World

You are welcome to request a copy of our latest financial report by contacting:
Bread for the World, 1100 Wayne Avenue, Suite 1000, Silver Spring, MD 20910,
(301) 608-2400.

If you are a resident of one of the states below, you may obtain financial information directly from the state agency: **FLORIDA** — A COPY OF THE OFFICIAL REGISTRATION AND FINANCIAL INFORMATION MAY BE OBTAINED FROM THE DIVISION OF CONSUMER SERVICES BY CALLING TOLL-FREE, (800) 435-7352 WITHIN THE STATE. REGISTRATION DOES NOT IMPLY ENDORSEMENT, APPROVAL OR RECOMMENDATION BY THE STATE. **MARYLAND** — For the cost of copies and postage: Office of the Secretary of State, State House, Annapolis, MD 21401. **NEW JERSEY** — Information filed with the Attorney General concerning this charitable solicitation may be obtained from the Attorney General of the State of New Jersey by calling (201) 504-6215. Registration with the Attorney General does not imply endorsement. **NEW YORK** — Office of the Attorney General, Department of Law, Charities Bureau, 120 Broadway, New York, NY 10271. **NORTH CAROLINA** — FINANCIAL INFORMATION ABOUT THIS ORGANIZATION AND A COPY OF ITS LICENSE ARE AVAILABLE FROM THE STATE SOLICITATION LICENSING BRANCH AT (919) 733-4510. THE LICENSE IS NOT AN ENDORSEMENT BY THE STATE. **PENNSYLVANIA** — The official registration and financial information of Bread for the World may be obtained from the Pennsylvania Department of State by calling toll-free, within Pennsylvania, (800) 732-0999. Registration does not imply endorsement. **VIRGINIA** — State Division of Consumer Affairs, Department of Agricultural and Consumer Services, P.O. Box 1163, Richmond, VA 23209. **WASHINGTON** — Charities Division, Office of the Secretary of State, State of Washington, Olympia, WA 98504-0422; 1-800-332-4483. **WEST VIRGINIA** — Residents may obtain a summary from: Secretary of State, State Capitol, Charleston, WV 25305.

Registration with any of these states does not imply endorsement, approval or recommendation by the state.

Questions or concerns about your membership?
Call 1-800-82-BREAD (1-800-822-7323)

EXHIBIT 14.1 Continued

- There are two donor options, which are infrequent in appeals to small donors because they may cause confusion (and thus delay). This is a special case, however. The Internal Revenue Service requires the disclosure that most gifts to Bread for the World are not tax deductible, because the group engages in *lobbying* on behalf of poor and hungry people. Gifts are tax-deductible only if made payable to the Bread for the World Education Fund. The organization offers this option, knowing that the distinction is important to some donors.

How High-Dollar Appeals Are Different from Other Fundraising Letters

A high-dollar package may be used in the service of a great many fundraising purposes, even recruiting new donors. More typically, however, these high-cost efforts are directed at a nonprofit's most generous and responsive supporters—as special appeals or upgrade efforts, for example. But whether used in mailings to the "housefile" (the list of previous donors) or in acquisition, high-dollar fundraising letters usually share at least five characteristics:

1. The ask amount is high. And that amount isn't just the highest in a string of suggested amounts that would let a donor off easy. If there's a choice of gift levels, *every* choice is a big number.

2. The packaging is often very expensive. These are upscale appeals, designed to communicate a feeling of exclusivity. High-dollar packages accomplish this aim by looking and feeling different from most other direct mail fundraising letters. Sometimes they're different in size, shape, texture, and color as well as elegant design. High-dollar appeals embody what Hollywood calls "high production values."

3. Almost always, high-dollar appeals are personalized, and often extensively so. Your chances of obtaining a $1,000 gift are slim with a letter beginning "Dear Friend."

4. The copy is often upscale in tone and approach. Many high-dollar fundraising letters are built around snob appeal or exclusivity (for example, through invitations to "exclusive" or "intimate" events or societies).

5. Most important, a strong high-dollar appeal features a uniquely appropriate marketing concept: an offer to match the high-level ask. In other words, a genuine high-dollar letter doesn't just ask for a larger sum of money than other fundraising letters do; it supplies the donor with a special and credible reason to send the amount of money asked for. In other words, a high-dollar letter has a marketing concept all its own. (See Chapter Nine for a detailed discussion of this concept.) And to reinforce the marketing concept, there may be only a *single* specified gift level. Often the offer involves a "gift club" or "giving society" that entails unique benefits or privileges.

Case Study: San Francisco AIDS Foundation High-Dollar Renewal and Upgrade Letters

I'm going to depart from the format I've established for the case study sections, which is otherwise devoted to before and after case studies. I want to share the full text of one high-dollar fundraising appeal that worked exceptionally well.

The appeal consisted of two high-dollar packages mailed at an interval of four weeks. These mailings represented the work of my colleagues Bill Rehm and Susie Fought for our client, the San Francisco AIDS Foundation. The two packages are reproduced in full, the first in Exhibits 14.2 through 14.5 and the second in Exhibit 14.6.

Package One consisted of the following elements:

- A 6- by 9½-inch closed-faced outer envelope on high-quality, textured cream stock, laser-addressed, and bearing first-class stamps (including a commemorative) (Exhibit 14.2)
- A one-page, 8½- by 11-inch personalized and dated letter on matching paper, hand signed in dark blue ink (Exhibit 14.3)
- A four-panel, two-color folder measuring 4 by 8 inches when folded (Exhibit 14.4)
- A 4¼- by 5½-inch one-color response card.
- A 5½- by 8½-inch two-color personalized response device—the Memorandum of Acceptance (Exhibit 14.5b).
- A 4¾- by 6½-inch preaddressed reply envelope bearing a first-class postage stamp (Exhibit 14.5c)

Package Two, mailed about four weeks later, contained the following components:

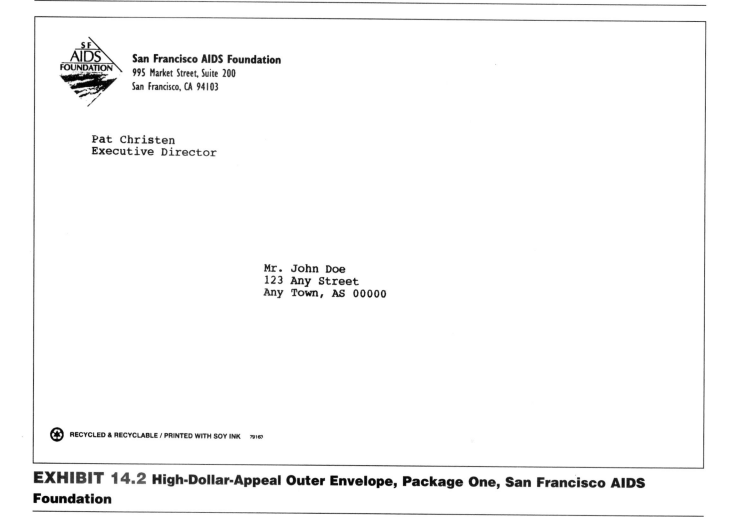

San Francisco AIDS Foundation
995 Market Street, Suite 200
San Francisco, CA 94103

Pat Christen
Executive Director

Mr. John Doe
123 Any Street
Any Town, AS 00000

RECYCLED & RECYCLABLE / PRINTED WITH SOY INK   79163

EXHIBIT 14.2 High-Dollar-Appeal Outer Envelope, Package One, San Francisco AIDS Foundation

- A plain white outer envelope, 4⅜ by 5½ inches, on laid finish stock, hand-addressed but otherwise devoid of printed markings, with a first-class stamp (Exhibit 14.6a)
- A 4¼ by 5½ inch note card, printed in two colors on heavy white stock, with a personalized note in the same handwriting as that on the outer envelope (Exhibit 14.6b)
- A laser-personalized response device measuring 4¼ by 5½ inches (Exhibit 14.6c)
- A plain white reply envelope, printed in two colors, 6½ by 3⅜ inches, featuring live first-class postage consisting of five stamps (Exhibit 14.6d)

These packages certainly had an upscale look and feel, but they also emphasized the leadership role that donors played by consistently contributing generous sums on an annual basis. That's an *upscale offer*, entirely consistent with the high production values, the $1,000-and-up ask of

San Francisco AIDS Foundation
995 Market Street, Suite 200
San Francisco, CA 94103

Pat Christen
Executive Director

October 15, 1999

Mr. John Doe
123 Any Street
Any Town, AS 00000

Dear Mr. Doe,

I want to thank you for your continuing commitment and your generosity as a member of our Leadership Circle.

Your leadership support has played an important part in helping to reduce the number of deaths due to AIDS in San Francisco. At the San Francisco AIDS Foundation, we're providing services and information for more than 1,200 people each month. But there is still so much more to do. Today, there are more people than ever before living with HIV and AIDS in San Francisco. And we continue to see individuals newly diagnosed with HIV disease.

I'm writing today to ask you to renew your support as a member of the Leadership Circle of the San Francisco AIDS Foundation.

Your renewed support will help make sure people affected by HIV and AIDS in San Francisco have the information, support, and basic services they need to live longer, healthier lives.

Your gift of $1,000 in March of last year shows a real commitment to our work, and I hope you'll match that contribution today. Your gift of $1,000 will qualify you for membership in the Cornerstone Circle -- and we'll be pleased to recognize your support by including your name in our next "Year in Review" Annual Report.

Once again, I thank you for your support and look forward to our continuing partnership.

Sincerely,

Pat Christen

Pat Christen
Executive Director

P.S. Please let me know if you'll be able to join us at our annual Leadership Circle Reception. Hawthorne Lane Restaurant, in downtown San Francisco, will host the reception on World AIDS Day, Wednesday, December 1. I'd be pleased to welcome you as our guest.

RECYCLED & RECYCLABLE / PRINTED WITH SOY INK   79341

EXHIBIT 14.3 High-Dollar-Appeal Letter, Package One, San Francisco AIDS Foundation

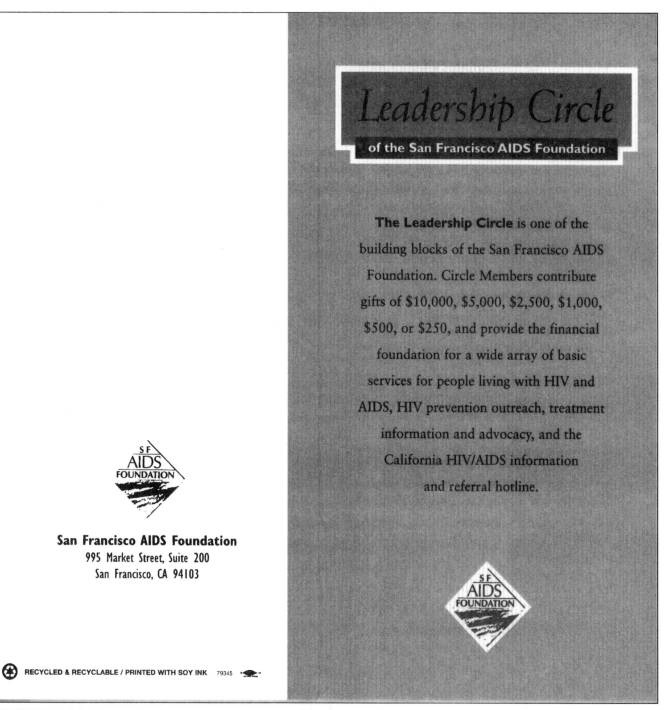

EXHIBIT 14.4 High-Dollar-Appeal Folder, Package One, San Francisco AIDS Foundation

◆ Members of the **President's Gold Circle** who contribute $10,000 or more will be invited to special briefings hosted by Executive Director Pat Christen and the Board of Directors. Members will also receive invitations to all Leadership Circle receptions and events, and receive grateful recognition in the Foundation's Annual Report. Additional benefits include complimentary subscriptions to the donor newsletter, to the highly acclaimed treatment journal *BETA*, and to San Francisco AIDS Foundation public policy reports. Gold Circle members also receive a special quarterly update from the Executive Director, an invitation to a Leadership tour of the new *Action Point* offices, and a special invitation to attend the Board of Directors' annual strategic plan meeting.

◆ Members of the **President's Silver Circle** who contribute $5,000 will be invited to special briefings hosted by Executive Director Pat Christen and the Board of Directors, and will receive invitations to Leadership Circle receptions and events. Members of the Silver Circle also receive recognition in the Annual Report, and free subscriptions to the donor newsletter, and to *BETA*, the acclaimed treatment journal. Additional benefits include a quarterly update from the Executive Director, and an invitation to tour the new *Action Point* offices.

◆ Members of the **President's Bronze Circle** who contribute $2,500 will be invited to briefings hosted by Executive Director Pat Christen and the Board of Directors, and to Leadership Circle receptions and events. Members of the Bronze Circle receive recognition in the Annual Report and free subscriptions to the donor newsletter and to *BETA*, the treatment journal. Additional benefits include a quarterly update from the Executive Director.

◆ Members of the **Cornerstone Circle** who contribute $1,000 will receive invitations to two Leadership Circle receptions, recognition in the Annual Report, a free subscription to the donor newsletter, and a quarterly update from the Executive Director.

◆ Members of the **Founder's Circle** who contribute $500 receive an invitation to a Leadership Circle reception, recognition in the Annual Report, a free subscription to the donor newsletter, and a quarterly update from the Executive Director.

◆ Members of the **Partner's Circle** who contribute $250 receive recognition in the Annual Report, an invitation to a Leadership Circle reception, and a free subscription to the donor newsletter.

EXHIBIT 14.4 Continued

r s v p

You are cordially invited to attend our annual reception *for Leadership Circle members* of the San Francisco AIDS Foundation. Hawthorne Lane Restaurant, in downtown San Francisco, will host the reception on World AIDS Day, Wednesday, December 1.

Senior staff of the AIDS Foundation will give you an update on advances and challenges in AIDS treatment, services, and prevention activities. You'll also get a chance to meet other members of the *Leadership Circle*.

Please return this card in the enclosed envelope to the San Francisco AIDS Foundation. We look forward to seeing you at our World AIDS Day reception.

Name(s) _____

Address _____

City, State, Zip _____

Phone _____

San Francisco AIDS Foundation
995 Market Street, Suite 200
San Francisco, CA 94103
415-487-3000

RECYCLED PAPER / SOY INK 79340

a

MEMORANDUM OF ACCEPTANCE

0
34DOE-B

TO: Pat Christen
        Executive Director
        San Francisco AIDS Foundation

FROM: Mr. John Doe
        123 Any Street
        Any Town, AS 00000

RE: <u>My Commitment to ending the AIDS pandemic</u>

I'm pleased to continue my partnership with the San Francisco AIDS Foundation. Enclosed is my gift of:

[ ] $1,000 — to renew my commitment to ending the AIDS pandemic as a member of the **Cornerstone Circle**.

[ ] $2,500 — to increase my commitment to ending the AIDS pandemic as a member of the **President's Bronze Circle**.

[ ] I prefer to make an additional gift of $_____.

I'd like to make this gift

[ ] in memory of: [ ] in honor of:

_____

Your contribution to the San Francisco AIDS Foundation is fully tax-deductible. Thank you.

San Francisco AIDS Foundation
995 Market Street Suite 200
San Francisco, CA 94103

RECYCLED PAPER / SOY INK 79342

b

San Francisco AIDS Foundation
995 Market Street, Suite 200
San Francisco, CA 94103

<u>Attn</u>: Pat Christen
      Executive Director

San Francisco AIDS Foundation
File 72635, P.O. Box 60000
San Francisco, CA 94160-2635

RECYCLED & RECYCLABLE / PRINTED WITH SOY INK 79346

c

EXHIBIT 14.5 **High-Dollar-Appeal Reply Devices, Package One: (a) One-Color Response Card, (b) Two-Color Personalized Response Device, (c) Reply Envelope**

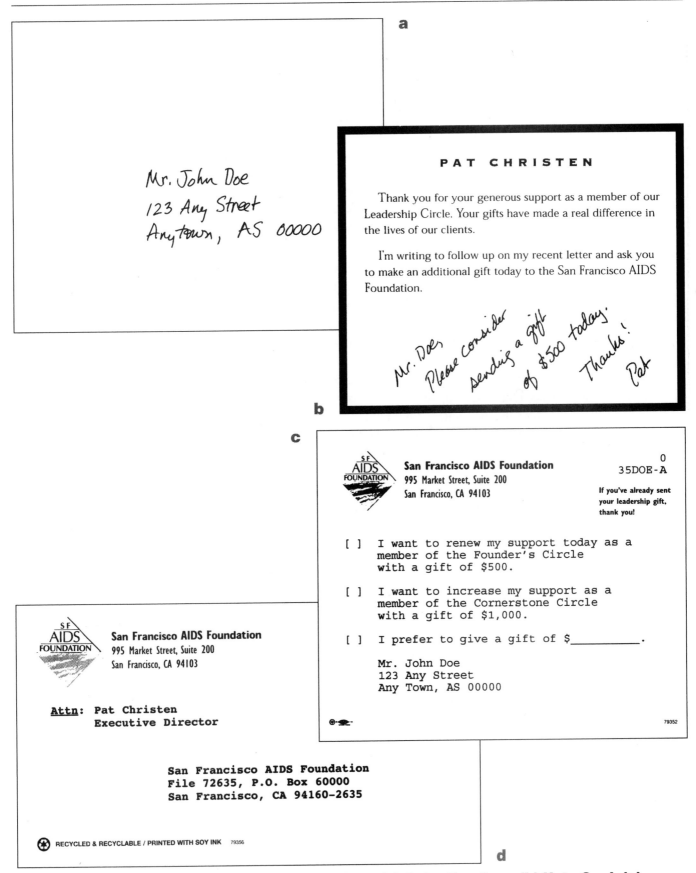

a

Mr. John Doe
123 Any Street
Anytown, AS 00000

b

PAT CHRISTEN

Thank you for your generous support as a member of our Leadership Circle. Your gifts have made a real difference in the lives of our clients.

I'm writing to follow up on my recent letter and ask you to make an additional gift today to the San Francisco AIDS Foundation.

*Mr. Doe,
Please consider
sending a gift
of $500 today.
Thanks!
Pat*

c

San Francisco AIDS Foundation
995 Market Street, Suite 200
San Francisco, CA 94103

0
35DOE-A

If you've already sent
your leadership gift,
thank you!

[ ] I want to renew my support today as a member of the Founder's Circle with a gift of $500.

[ ] I want to increase my support as a member of the Cornerstone Circle with a gift of $1,000.

[ ] I prefer to give a gift of $_____.

Mr. John Doe
123 Any Street
Any Town, AS 00000

79352

d

San Francisco AIDS Foundation
995 Market Street, Suite 200
San Francisco, CA 94103

Attn: Pat Christen
Executive Director

San Francisco AIDS Foundation
File 72635, P.O. Box 60000
San Francisco, CA 94160-2635

RECYCLED & RECYCLABLE / PRINTED WITH SOY INK 79356

EXHIBIT 14.6 High-Dollar Appeal, Package Two: (a) Outer Envelope, (b) Note Card, (c) Response Device, (d) Reply Envelope

the first letter and the $500 request in the second. (In practice, the ask was consistent between the two appeals. The two packages in the exhibits were mailed to different individuals.) The same copy wouldn't work well with a $25 ask in a more cheaply produced package. That wouldn't be credible.

But the writing style in this letter is not fundamentally different from that in other strong fundraising appeals. It's involving, liberally using the word *you*. It's personal, even chatty. It uses short sentences, short paragraphs, an indented paragraph for emphasis, and broad margins. There's no effort to impress the reader with obscure information or fancy language. In other words, these are well-crafted high-dollar appeals because they frame an appropriate offer in a setting that enhances its credibility.

If you're accustomed to receiving lots of solicitations in the mail, you may have begun tuning out years ago. Chances are that you go through a routine a lot like the one I described in Chapter Two, when I reviewed Siegfried Vögele's research findings. Certainly most of your donors go through routines like that.

Ask yourself this: if you come across a letter like one of the San Francisco AIDS Foundation appeals, would you toss it into the wastebasket along with all that unwanted "junk mail" or would you open it, just to find out what all the excitement's about? And what would your donors do?

Packages like this are not suitable in most circumstances. They're rarely cost-effective using run-of-the-mill mailing lists. But with carefully selected lists of donors or prospects, high-dollar letters like this outstanding example may help your organization raise far more money than would otherwise be possible.

Going for Bigger Gifts
Persuading Donors to Make an Extra Commitment

Most nonprofit organizations slyly imply in their appeals to donors or members that a gift that's larger than the donor's previous gifts would be . . . well, better. They do this by suggesting gift amounts that are larger than the donors' earlier gifts by some prescribed amount—say, 25 percent or 50 percent or just $10 more.

However, there is a special class of fundraising appeal specifically designed to solicit an increased gift. These donor upgrade letters—sometimes special appeals or year-end appeals, sometimes membership or annual giving "renewal" letters—go out of their way to supply reasons how a donor's increased level of support will bring additional benefits. The Bread for the World response device reproduced in Exhibit 15.1 illustrates three of the elements commonly encountered in donor upgrade efforts:

- You can tell at a glance that its purpose is to upgrade John Doe's support. The appeal requests a gift of $100 or more—clearly a larger amount than Doe has ever contributed in the past—and offers him a special premium (a free copy of an important report) in exchange. This is a standard membership renewal notice to Bread for the World members, but its stated and obvious purpose is to persuade already generous members to contribute even larger sums.

Please renew your 1999 membership

Yes, I want to renew my annual membership -- and help sustain Bread for the World for the next 25 years. Here's my anniversary membership gift:

| YOUR MEMBER NUMBER: 99999 |
| DATE OF LAST GIFT: 01/01/1998 |

[ ] $250   [ ] $100   [ ] $50   [ ] $_____

Mr. John Doe
123 Any Street
Any City AS 12345

☐ I've contributed $100 or more. Please send me a free copy of the *1999 Hunger Report: The Changing Politics of Hunger.*

R99DOE-A   99999

☐ I'm making a membership gift of $250 — and I'd also like to receive the special 25th anniversary lapel pin.

◄ *See reverse side for important information*

Mr. Doe —

Each year, at this time, we ask *all* Bread for the World members to renew their annual support -- to help provide the financial resources we need to launch our new Offering of Letters campaign.

Please consider renewing your membership with a gift of $50 -- to celebrate Bread for the World's 25th Anniversary and to lay the foundation for the *next* 25 years.

If you renew with a gift of $100 or more, you may request a free copy of the 1999 Hunger Report--*The Changing Politics of Hunger.* And with a membership renewal of $250 or more, you'll also receive the attractive Bread for the World 25th Anniversary lapel pin.

Whatever your renewal level, please send your gift today -- and save the time and expense of additional reminders. Thank you!

To contact Bread for the World:

- David Beckmann, President
- Carole Southam, Vice President
- Dick Hoehn, Bread for the World Institute
- Barbara Howell, Government Relations
- Diane Hunt, Development and Membership
- Kathy Pomroy, Organizing
- Joel Underwood, Church Relations
- Lynora Williams, Communications

Questions about your membership?
Comments or concerns?
Call toll-free: 1-800-82-BREAD (1-800-822-7323).

9-60972A

Your *25th Anniversary*
Membership Card

Bread for the World
1100 Wayne Avenue, Suite 1000
Silver Spring, MD 20910
Phone: 800/82-BREAD

Mr. John Doe

IS A MEMBER IN GOOD STANDING

David Beckmann

DAVID BECKMANN, PRESIDENT OF BREAD FOR THE WORLD

EXHIBIT 15.1 Response Device for Donor Upgrade, Bread for the World

You are welcome to request a copy of our latest financial report by contacting:
Bread for the World, 1100 Wayne Avenue, Suite 1000, Silver Spring, MD 20910; (301) 608-2400.

If you are a resident of one of the states below, you may obtain financial information directly from the state agency:
FLORIDA — A copy of the official registration and financial information may be obtained from the Division of Consumer Services by calling toll-free, (800) 435-7352 within the state. REGISTRATION DOES NOT IMPLY ENDORSEMENT, APPROVAL OR RECOMMENDATION BY THE STATE. **MARYLAND** — For the cost of copies and postage: Office of the Secretary of State, State House, Annapolis, MD 21401. **NEW JERSEY** — Information filed with the Attorney General concerning this charitable solicitation may be obtained from the Attorney General of the State of New Jersey by calling (201) 504-6215. Registration with the Attorney General does not imply endorsement. **NEW YORK** — Office of the Attorney General, Department of Law, Charities Bureau, 120 Broadway, New York, NY 10271. **NORTH CAROLINA** — Financial information about this organization and a copy of its license are available from the State Solicitation Licensing Branch at (919) 733-4510. The license is not an endorsement by the state. **PENNSYLVANIA** — The official registration and financial information of Bread for the World may be obtained from the Pennsylvania Department of State by calling toll-free, within Pennsylvania, (800) 732-0999. Registration does not imply endorsement. **VIRGINIA** — State Division of Consumer Affairs, Department of Agricultural and Consumer Services, P.O. Box 1163, Richmond, VA 23209. **WASHINGTON** — Charities Division, Office of the Secretary of State, State of Washington, Olympia, WA 98504-0422; 1-800-332-4483.
WEST VIRGINIA — Residents may obtain a summary from: Secretary of State, State Capitol, Charleston, WV 25305.

Registration with any of these states does not imply endorsement, approval or recommendation by the state.

Contributions to **Bread for the World** are not tax-deductible since its members lobby Congress on behalf of poor and hungry people. If you wish to make a tax-deductible gift, please make out your check to **Bread for the World Institute** and your gift will support the Institute's work of research and education.

Please write or call your senators and representative in Washington, D.C. Urge your members of Congress to pass legislation that will lift the burden of debt from the world's 40 poorest countries — and make sure that debt relief benefits poor and hungry people in those countries. Please check your Bread newsletter, phone the Legislative Update, or visit our web site for specific actions you can take.

Please sign and detach your membership card—and keep the information to the right with your calendar or telephone directory. Thank you. ▶

▶

▼

To contact a Representative:
The Honorable _____
U.S. House of Representatives, Washington, DC 20515
To contact a U.S. Senator:
The Honorable _____
U.S. Senate Office Building, Washington, DC 20510
Congressional phone: 202/224-3121
To contact the President:
President Bill Clinton
The White House, Washington, DC 20500
White House Comments: 202/456-1111
Bread for the World's 24-hour Legislative Update:
301/588-7439
http://www.bread.org

How to be most effective

Urge your senators and representative in Washington to support aid to Africa that supports agricultural development which is vital to Africa's rural poor. When you contact your members of Congress, remember to ...

- Write your own letter and personally sign it.
- Put your return address on the letter as well as on the envelope (envelopes get thrown away).
- Be brief and courteous.
- Be specific. Identify the specific legislation you're writing about. Explain your reasons for supporting or opposing a particular measure.
- Time your letter or phone call for the greatest impact. For legislative updates, call 301/588-7439 or visit our web site at http://www.bread.org.

RECYCLED & RECYCLABLE / PRINTED WITH SOY INK

EXHIBIT 15.1 Continued

- Several gift amounts are suggested, allowing Doe the opportunity to set the level most comfortable for him.
- Two upgrade levels are featured—$250 and $100—each with its own distinctive premium.

How Donor Upgrade Appeals Are Different from Other Fundraising Letters

Fundraising letters of many types—including special appeals, renewals, and high-dollar appeals—frequently feature donor upgrade options, but those options are rarely emphasized. A true upgrade letter lays out a set of reasons that the donor should give more—and the argument to give more is a central theme in the copy, not an afterthought. This is the primary characteristic of an upgrade letter.

For example, a special appeal might seek gifts equal to or greater than the donor's highest previous contribution (HPC) to the charity. The reply device might even offer three alternative giving levels: the HPC, the HPC plus 25 percent, and the HPC plus 50 percent. But that alone wouldn't make the letter an upgrade appeal. To qualify for that characterization, the letter would need to build a case for the *increase* in support. In inflationary times, that case might be to help the organization cope with steadily rising costs, and the letter might illustrate just how quickly costs were rising by giving concrete examples. Or the letter might spell out how much more the charity can accomplish if the donor sends a gift that's 25 percent or 50 percent larger than in the past. More commonly, however, an upgrade appeal is distinguished from a special appeal because it invites the donor to join a special group or giving category that requires significantly higher gifts. (That's the case with all the examples in this chapter.)

Three additional traits are shared by most upgrading efforts:

1. Upgrade letters customarily spotlight opportunities to join giving clubs or otherwise feature special benefits, premiums, or incentives for making the larger gifts requested. (Keep in mind that some or all of those benefits or incentives may be intangible.) In other words, there's a marketing concept appropriate to the request for a larger gift.

2. Upgrade efforts frequently offer two, three, or more alternative levels of support. Although this approach isn't universally used in upgrading efforts, it's common, because the purpose of such efforts is usually to secure the largest possible gift—and the writer rarely knows how much that's likely to be.

3. Personalization and high-quality paper stock are often used in upgrade appeals—to match the ambitious request.

Case Study: People for the Environment Monthly Sustainer Invitation

Once again I'm going to depart from form with an illustration that's not a before-and-after case study. The letter and reply device appearing in Exhibits 15.2 and 15.3 were parts of a monthly sustainer invitation package I wrote for an organization I'm calling People for the Environment (PFE). This package depicts what I believe is the single most important way to persuade donors to give more money: launching a monthly giving program.

Almost every nonprofit can benefit from a monthly giving program. For many charities that depend on small gifts from donors recruited through the mail, monthly giving or sustainer programs can bring in as much as *one-third* of their contributed income. But take care about using this letter as an example. Launching and managing such a program entails significant investment and continuing attention. It's not an effort to be undertaken lightly—certainly not as a short-term excuse to ask donors for larger gifts.

This package was conceived as an invitation from PFE's executive director to more than half of the organization's 80,000 members. Its purpose was to ask them to become charter members in the new Friends of the Environment, a monthly sustainer program featuring six categories or levels of support, from $10 per month to $50 per month. Those who "cannot join at this time" were to have the option of making one-time gifts.

Eventually every level of membership in the program would offer unique benefits or services. Initially the concrete benefits of Charter Membership at any level were to consist of just four items:

- A personalized certificate
- An "insider's newsletter" compiled by PFE staff and tentatively titled *PFE in Perspective,* which would be published at least six times per year
- Listing as a charter member in *PFE in Perspective*
- Automatic renewal of PFE membership—with freedom from regular and frequent fundraising letters (except the year-end appeal and any emergency package)

DAY OF WEEK, DATE

NAME1
NAME2
ADDRESS 1
ADDRESS 2
ADDRESS 3

Dear SALU:

I get lots of questions from committed PFE members like you.

I'm often asked whether there's any way a PFE member can do <u>more</u> to help heal the earth. Something that a busy person without a whole lot of money can do--without changing jobs, or flying to Brazil, or going into debt.

Something that will really make a <u>difference</u>.

Concerned members like you also frequently ask me what we can do to reduce PFE's fundraising costs. Our fundraising program is already one of the most efficient, but I share your concern to make it even <u>more</u> efficient. So I, too, have asked whether there isn't some way to send fewer fundraising letters--and still raise enough money to meet PFE's growing budget.

These are questions we wrestle with all the time at PFE.

Now, finally, we've come up with an answer to both these important questions. It's a way for you to <u>multiply the impact</u> of your PFE membership-- and help us save substantially on fundraising costs.

I'm writing you today because I want you to be among the first to know about this exciting opportunity.

The new program is called the PFE <u>Friends of the Environment</u>. I invite you to get in on the ground floor.

As a Charter Member of the Friends of the Environment, you'll receive special, <u>additional</u> membership benefits and privileges.

More important, though, your participation in this important new program will help sustain PFE's worldwide <u>leadership role</u> in protecting wildlife and the environment.

Here's what the Friends of the Environment is all about:

EXHIBIT 15.2 Monthly Sustainer Invitation, People for the Environment

Whenever I need to raise money to support a crucial PFE program like saving the rainforests or countering threats to endangered species, I know I can count on you. PFE members are extremely generous. You've always come through in the past.

But raising money by mail takes time, so it's tough to assemble the necessary funds to respond quickly to a sudden, unexpected crisis.

For example, when [INSERT EXAMPLE OF EMERGENCY HERE], there wasn't time for me to send you a letter to ask for your financial support.

But there was no choice. I simply had to take action. I know you would've <u>insisted</u> I do!

Still, [THAT ACTION] took money. And, instead of taking your support for granted, I sure could've used a "ready-response" reserve fund.

Also, some PFE programs are long-term efforts, requiring <u>years and years</u> of dedicated work. But it's wasteful to write you when there's no new news.

Our work on the landmark [ENVIRONMENTAL LEGISLATION] is a perfect example. That bill included an innovative amendment--drafted by PFE--that will permanently [ACCOMPLISH SOMETHING VERY IMPRESSIVE].

But many <u>years</u> of work by PFE staff members preceded that crucial amendment. We had to fund their work, day in and day out, during times when public awareness of [THAT ISSUE] wasn't very high.

And that points to another important truth about our work: PFE programs sometimes just aren't very popular!

For instance, PFE played a leading role in [COMBATTING A MAJOR WORLD-WIDE ENVIRONMENTAL PROBLEM].

But when PFE scientists <u>began</u> their work on [THAT PROBLEM] years earlier, the issue was hardly known outside scientific circles. And few people--except a handful of dedicated environmentalists such as you--were ready to step forward with financial support.

As you can see, the crux of the matter is this: PFE needs a stable, <u>dependable</u> source of funds. Money we can count on, month after month, through good times and bad.

- Page 2 -

EXHIBIT 15.2 Continued

We need the resources to help us <u>meet emergencies</u> and continue our work on a <u>broad range</u> of environmental issues--without interruption.

That's why we've decided to launch the Friends of the Environment. And that's why I'm turning to you again.

To become a Charter Member in the Partnership, what I need from you today is a commitment to make a small, monthly gift to PFE--as little as $10 per month.

Here's how the program will work:

o   As soon as I receive your check in payment of your initial monthly gift, I'll see to it that your name is removed from the list of those PFE members who are sent regular, frequent fundraising appeals.

o   You'll continue to receive the PFE newsletter. But I'll <u>also</u> see to it that you're mailed the premier issue--and every suc-ceeding issue--of <u>PFE in Perspective</u>. This is a very special new "insiders-only" newsletter we'll be sending at least six times per year--exclusively to members of our Board of Trustees and a few others.

o   Your name will appear in the Charter Membership Roll published in <u>PFE in Perspective</u>.

o   And I'll inscribe and mail you a certificate of appreciation for enrolling as a Charter Member in the Friends of the Environ-ment.

o   Then, each month thereafter--unless you decide to cancel-- you'll receive a reminder from us with a remittance envelope enclosed.

As you can see at a glance, the Friends of the Environment answers <u>both</u> the challenges I mentioned at the beginning of this letter:

(1)   Your <u>reliable</u>, monthly support will help PFE continue--and expand--our worldwide leadership role in protecting the envi-ronment.

(2)   You'll substantially <u>lower our fundraising</u> costs--and reduce our consumption of paper--by enabling us to mail you fewer solicitations.

- Page 3 -

EXHIBIT 15.2 Continued

I hope you'll accept this opportunity today to become a Charter Member of the Friends of the Environment.

Your dependable monthly gift of $50, $25, $20, $15, $12, or even $10 will multiply the impact of your membership in PFE manyfold.

I urge you to consider those gifts an investment in your future--and the future of your children and your children's children. They're an investment in the future of our planet.

Thank you sincerely for hearing me out.

In high hopes,

Barton Snodgrass
Executive Director

P.S. If you accept Charter Membership in the Friends of the Environment at the level of $20 per month or more, I'll be pleased to send you a copy of xxxx as a token of my appreciation. This magnificent volume . . . .

- Page 4 -

EXHIBIT 15.2 Continued

CHARTER MEMBERSHIP ENROLLMENT FORM
People for the Environment
Friends for the Environment

Prepared expressly for PFE Member(s):

NAME1
NAME2
ADDRESS 1
ADDRESS 2
ADDRESS 3

YES, I am pleased to accept Barton Snodgrass's invitation to join PFE's exciting new Friends of the Environment as a Charter Member.

I want to play an active, ongoing part in helping PFE sustain its leadership role over the long haul—and rapidly respond to new threats to the environment as soon as they arise.

☐ I'm enclosing my check in payment of my first monthly contribution, and I pledge to send the same amount each month. Please bill me. I understand I may cancel this arrangement at any time.

☐ **$50** ☐ **$25** ☐ **$20** ☐ **$15** ☐ **$12** ☐ **$10** ☐ **$**_____

_____   _____

Signature: NAME 1   Date signed

☐ I cannot join the Friends of the Environment as a Charter Member. But here's my special contribution to PFE in the
amount of:

☐ **$HPC+50%** ☐ **$HPC** ☐ **$**_____

EXHIBIT 15.3 Monthly Sustainer Reply Device, People for the Environment

Friends of the Environment
Charter Membership Benefits

o Help PFE sustain its worldwide leadership role in protecting the environment.

o Help PFE reduce its fundraising costs.

o Complimentary subscription to *PFE in Perspective,* a newsletter published at least six times per year exclusively for PFE's most loyal and involved supporters.

o Your name removed from the list of those who are mailed regular and frequent fundraising letters.

o Listing in the Charter Membership Roll in *PFE in Perspective.*

o Automatic renewal of your PFE membership for as long as you remain a member of the Friends of the Environment.

o Special certificate acknowledging your Charter Membership.

o You may cancel your participation at any time.

And you'll continue to receive the PFE newsletter, and enjoy all the other benefits and privileges of your PFE membership.

Six Ways to join PFE's Friends of the Environment:

☐ Friend—$10 per month   ☐ Leader*—$20 per month

☐ Colleague—$12 per month   ☐ Patron*—$25 per month

☐ Associate—$15 month   ☐ Founder*—$50 per month

* If you accept Charter Membership in the Friends of the Environment at any of these levels, we will be pleased to send you as a token of our deep appreciation, a copy of xxxxxxxx. This magnificent, full-color volume is xxxxxx and retails for $xxxxx.

EXHIBIT 15.3 Continued

In addition, anyone who joined at the level of at least $20 per month would receive a complimentary copy of a highly prized coffee-table book.

This initial sustainer invitation package was to be followed up with telephone calls within a month of the mail date to at least the most promising segments of the file. It was also to be adapted into an invitation sent to every new member shortly after a welcome package was sent.

The welcome package would consist of four items:

1. Outer envelope. This was to be a #9 (slightly smaller than a standard business envelope), nonwindow ("closed-face") envelope addressed by laser printer. The paper stock would be off-white (obviously recycled). Letters sent to the most loyal and generous members would bear first-class stamps; others would receive their letters with bulk postage. In the upper left-hand corner, the PFE name, logo, and return address would be printed in color, with the executive director's name typed above it. Lower, on the left, there was to be a bold teaser: *New Opportunity for PFE Members.*

2. Letter. The letter would be four pages long, printed in the format of standard PFE letterhead, with page 1 laser-personalized if possible. Text was to be printed in black, with the PFE logo and the signature on page 4 printed in dark blue. To fit the #9 envelope, the paper stock would be 8 by 10 inches, and it was to match the color and weight of the paper in the envelope.

3. Reply device. This form, headed "Charter Membership Enrollment Form," was to be laser-personalized, measuring 8 by 10 inches and printed on tinted, recycled stock different from that of letter and carrier. (The form was to match the reply envelope.) It was to be printed in three colors: black text, plus the blue of the PFE logo with a green "Friends of the Environment" name and logo. The list of membership benefits would appear on a perforated, detachable panel (to reduce the size of reply device so that it would fit neatly into the reply envelope). Only three specific ask amounts were to be offered to any individual member. Amounts would be assigned based on giving history.

4. Reply envelope. This was to be addressed to "Personal Attention: Barton Snodgrass [the executive director]." In letters sent to all active donors, the reply envelope would bear live stamps (either two or three stamps or one commemorative); others would receive business reply envelopes instead. The reply envelope was to be a size #6¾ or #7, with the paper stock matching that of the reply device. In either case, the "Friends" name and logo was to be printed on the left side.

Seeking Annual Gifts
Building Long-Term Loyalty, One Year at a Time

The backbone of most direct mail fundraising programs is an annual membership or "Annual Fund" program. Most such programs use a technique borrowed from the magazine subscription business to maximize donor participation: they mail a series of letters (or "notices"), stopping only when a member's gift is finally received. Smaller nonprofits may limit their "renewal series" to three or four such notices. Larger organizations with huge donor databases may send out ten notices or more (just as do major national magazines).

The Bread for the World membership renewal device reproduced in Exhibit 16.1 contains four elements that are both important and typical of the renewal notices used by nonprofits:

- This is clearly about renewing annual membership.
- As the letter that is part of the reply device notes, a membership card is enclosed.
- The form offers several different membership levels, so that the recipient may upgrade voluntarily.
- The message is extremely brief and focused almost exclusively on the relationship between the individual member and the organization.

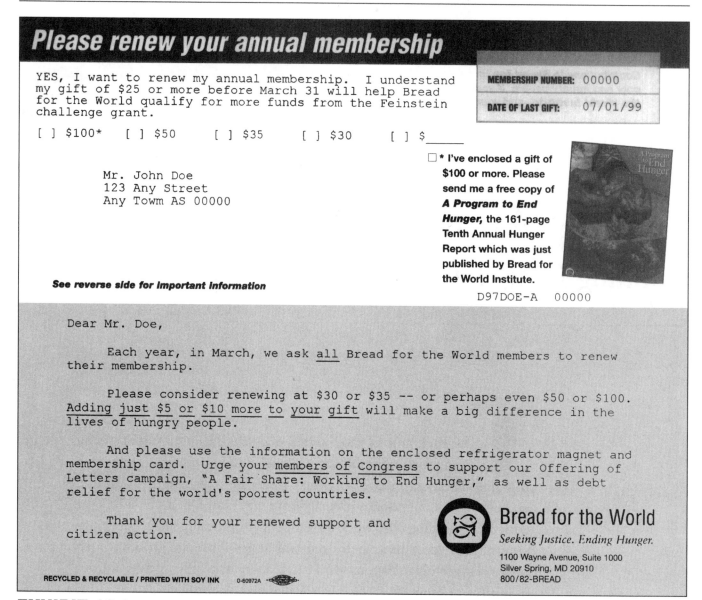

Please renew your annual membership

YES, I want to renew my annual membership. I understand my gift of $25 or more before March 31 will help Bread for the World qualify for more funds from the Feinstein challenge grant.

MEMBERSHIP NUMBER: 00000

DATE OF LAST GIFT: 07/01/99

[ ] $100*   [ ] $50   [ ] $35   [ ] $30   [ ] $_____

☐ * I've enclosed a gift of $100 or more. Please send me a free copy of *A Program to End Hunger,* the 161-page Tenth Annual Hunger Report which was just published by Bread for the World Institute.

Mr. John Doe
123 Any Street
Any Towm AS 00000

See reverse side for important information

D97DOE-A   00000

Dear Mr. Doe,

　　Each year, in March, we ask all Bread for the World members to renew their membership.

　　Please consider renewing at $30 or $35 -- or perhaps even $50 or $100. Adding just $5 or $10 more to your gift will make a big difference in the lives of hungry people.

　　And please use the information on the enclosed refrigerator magnet and membership card. Urge your members of Congress to support our Offering of Letters campaign, "A Fair Share: Working to End Hunger," as well as debt relief for the world's poorest countries.

　　Thank you for your renewed support and citizen action.

Bread for the World
Seeking Justice. Ending Hunger.

1100 Wayne Avenue, Suite 1000
Silver Spring, MD 20910
800/82-BREAD

RECYCLED & RECYCLABLE / PRINTED WITH SOY INK   0-60972A

EXHIBIT 16.1 **Annual Renewal Response Device, Bread for the World**

*Contributions to **Bread for the World** are not tax-deductible since its members lobby Congress on behalf of poor and hungry people. If you wish to make a tax-deductble gift, please make out your check to **Bread for the World Institute**, and your gift will support the Institute's work of research and education.*

You are welcome to request a copy of our latest financial report by contacting Bread for the World, 1100 Wayne Avenue, Suite 1000, Silver Spring, MD 20910; (301) 608-2400.

If you are a resident of one of the states below, you may obtain financial information directly from the state agency: **FLORIDA** — A copy of the official registration and financial information may be obtained from the Division of Consumer Services by calling toll-free, (800) 435-7352 within the state. REGISTRATION DOES NOT IMPLY ENDORSEMENT, APPROVAL OR RECOMMENDATION BY THE STATE. **MARYLAND** — For the cost of copies and postage: Office of the Secretary of State, State House, Annapolis, MD 21401. **NEW JERSEY** — Information filed with the Attorney General concerning this charitable solicitation may be obtained from the Attorney General of the State of New Jersey by calling (201) 504-6215. Registration with the Attorney General does not imply endorsement. **NEW YORK** — Office of the Attorney General, Department of Law, Charities Bureau, 120 Broadway, New York, NY 10271. **NORTH CAROLINA** — Financial information about this organization and a copy of its license are available from the State Solicitation Licensing Branch at (919) 733-4510. The license is not an endorsement by the state. **PENNSYLVANIA** — The official registration and financial information of Bread for the World may be obtained from the Pennsylvania Department of State by calling toll-free, within Pennsylvania, (800) 732-0999. Registration does not imply endorsement. **VIRGINIA** — State Division of Consumer Affairs, Department of Agricultural and Consumer Services, P.O. Box 1163, Richmond, VA 23209. **WASHINGTON** — Charities Division, Office of the Secretary of State, State of Washington, Olympia, WA 98504-0422; 1-800-332-4483. **WEST VIRGINIA** — Residents may obtain a summary from: Secretary of State, State Capitol, Charleston, WV 25305.

Registration with any of these states does not imply endorsement, approval or recommendation by the state.

Please contact your senators and representative in the U.S. Congress

Urge them to increase the minimum wage by at least $1 over the next two years — and ask for their support of the *Hunger Relief Act,* which will reinstate food stamps for legal immigrants and provide fair access to food stamps for working families who still live in poverty. Letters to Congress and the Administration are also needed to help complete the Jubilee of debt relief for the world's poorest countries. Visit our web site (www.bread.org) or call the 24-hour Legislative Hotline (1-800-822-7323, ext. 5) for the latest legislative developments.

EXHIBIT 16.1 Continued

How Renewal Letters Are Different from Other Fundraising Appeals

Annual renewal efforts are of two general types: annual fund appeals (most commonly found at schools and colleges) and membership renewal series (which aren't limited to organizations with formal membership structures but are most frequently used by them). Both types usually share the following five characteristics:

1. There are clear and explicit references to membership dues or the annual gift. In other words, it's unmistakably clear that the organization expects the donor's support, this year and every year.
2. The letter focuses on the process of renewal, repeating an action taken last year (and maybe for many years past).
3. The case is usually made in general and institutional terms rather than focusing on a particular program or special need. An annual gift, after all, represents support for the institution, not for some limited aspect of its work.
4. Renewal letters are typically short. The most important point to make in such letters is "please renew"—and that may be all you really need to say.
5. The element of time and its limits is always at least implicit: "this year's dues," "your expiration date," "the deadline for renewing."

Case Study: Peace Action Membership Renewal Series

Some years ago, Peace Action asked me to help fine-tune its membership renewal series. Exhibits 16.2 through 16.6 reproduce the draft text of the five-letter series in the form I received it. The final text of my edited five-letter series is reproduced in Exhibits 16.7 through 16.11. While the message in these letters is clearly out of date, I've elected to include this renewal series in this revised edition because it illustrates so many of the fundraising (and copywriting) challenges nonprofit organizations continue to face.

I'm reproducing the full draft series in sequence followed by the full final series in sequence to emphasize the importance of looking at a renewal series as a whole. These are not individual fundraising letters. They're components of a continuing program to elicit annual support from a member, year after year.

One very important point is brought to the light by the mere existence of this membership renewal series. Unlike so many other nonprofit organizations, Peace Action has taken one of the most critical steps available toward the long-term financial health of its direct response fundraising efforts: operating a genuine membership development program. It's also significant that Peace Action's renewal series had five notices. Most nonprofits stop (prematurely) with two or three, and a disturbing number mail only one.

With that said, my principal criticisms of the renewal series follow.

Renewals Versus Appeals

These letters read too much like special appeals and not enough like renewal notices. To serve well as renewal notices, they need to be more businesslike, devoting fewer words to the issues and values that dominate the draft copy and more to the business of the relationship between Peace Action and its individual members. The general model to follow is the subscription renewal notices sent by magazines. Many people will respond to a renewal series, particularly the first two notices, simply because you tell them it's time to renew. But that goal has to be downright obvious. It can't be buried in copy about issues or programs. Membership dues are the business at hand in these letters.

Benefits

There's far too little emphasis on membership benefits in the draft letters. Every direct response appeal should focus on benefits, even if they're all intangible, and this is doubly true of a renewal series.

Benefits are central to a membership development program and must be emphasized at every opportunity. If you're constructing a comprehensive list of benefits for members (or donors) of your organization, I suggest you include everything: newsletters, action alerts, networking, access to local affiliates, national or regional events, or whatever else there is. Forget about subtlety here, and label the list clearly—something like "Membership Benefits"—and include it as a stand-alone insert in effort 1.

In subsequent renewal efforts, you might consider including the benefits list on the response device—on the front in some cases, on the back in others. Don't hesitate to include it in every notice (although I'd suggest varying the typeface, size, color, and position on the response device, or some combination of these variations).

Format

The proposed format of this series was unvaried. I prefer to see renewal packages alternate envelope sizes and formats, because otherwise many members might think, "I've already gotten that letter," and throw it out. If production budgets allow, you might use, for example, a #10 envelope for the first effort, then a #9, then a Monarch (#7¾), then another #9, and finally a #10 again.

"Our world is a neighborhood. We must learn to live together as brothers (and sisters) or we will perish as fools. For I submit, nothing will be done until people put their bodies and souls into this."
Martin Luther King, Jr.
April 3, 1968

February 20, 1993

1—?
2—?
3—?
4—?

Dear 6—,

For the second time in three years, U.S. military forces spent this season of peace on foreign soil with their lives at risk.

I know you are concerned with news reports of violence and starvation at home and around the world. Please take a moment to consider the importance of a strong peace movement in the years ahead **and if what I have to say makes sense to you, renew your support to PEACE ACTION.***

In many ways our domestic ills are a mirror image of our foreign policies. We flood the world with weapons and suffer a flood of weapons at home . . . we are quick to employ the use of force to solve international problems and suffer an increasingly violent culture . . . we spend billions of our tax dollars on all the security weapons can buy and suffer an insecure future.

President Clinton has begun the first hundred days of his presidency. He ushers in a new era and it begins with great hope.

But it will take hard work and not hope alone to solve these problems. You are part of the solution.

If this is to be a time of healing and rebuilding the place to start is reordering our priorities as a society. Let our priorities reflect our values. Let our priorities mirror the kind of future we hope for.

Your membership in PEACE ACTION is one step you have taken in this direction. I'm sure there are other groups you belong to and actions you take in your community. That is why there is hope.

*formerly SANE/FREEZE: Campaign for Global Security

EXHIBIT 16.2 Draft Membership Renewal Letter, First in Series, Peace Action

With your support we will:

* reduce the use of our tax dollars for funding the defense of western Europe and Japan and see that money is directed instead to rebuilding our economy

* support efforts to strengthen non-proliferation of weapons of mass destruction

* work to end the international arms trade

* end the B-2 bomber and Star Wars programs

We know the time is ripe for change. Through your membership in PEACE ACTION you have become an agent of hope for the future.

Please renew today. The momentum is with us. But we have yet to win the race. **Your membership can make a difference, both for the financial support you give and the moral support it represents.**

Yours in Peace,

Peter Deccy
Membership Director

P.S. The Cold War is over, but peace has not been won. We need your continued support. If you can renew at the 9—level this year, it will be a great help. **Thank you!**

EXHIBIT 16.2 Continued

February 20, 1993

Dear Member,

Your membership is about to expire and we need you!

President Clinton has begun the first hundred days of his presidency. He has inherited a staggering debt, millions unemployed and both this country and the world riddled with violence and war.

But a powerful movement has formed to promote solutions to these challenges. And you are a part of the solution! You continued support for PEACE ACTION* puts you on record as supporting global cooperation and a peace economy.

Your membership in PEACE ACTION amplifies the voice for sanity in the nuclear age, sanity in the way we spend our tax dollars and sanity in the way we relate to the rest of the world.

The military industrial complex is launching an all out effort to keep military spending levels at Cold War levels. At the same time, they are working feverishly to increase the sale of arms overseas. More often than not, these weapons are sent to the world's most troubled regions.

In fact the United States transferred over $300 million in weapons to Somalia during the 1980s. The practice of arms transfers continues, creating tomorrow's excuse for continued Cold War levels of military spending.

Military contractors can spend millions lobbying for your tax dollars now and pass on the expense of that lobbying to the Pentagon later. We pay at both ends.

They need to be challenged, or they will stand in the way of our efforts to curb the international arms trade and stop nuclear weapons proliferation.

They need to be challenged, or they will block our country's efforts to make the transition from Cold War levels of military spending and increased investment in our economic future.

The work we do is instrumental in building a movement that is strong enough to effect change. Your membership is essential to keeping that work going.

* formerly SANE/FREEZE: Campaign for Global Security

EXHIBIT 16.3 Draft Membership Renewal Letter, Second in Series, Peace Action

With your support we will:
• reduce the use of our tax dollars for funding the defense of western Europe and Japan and see that money is directed instead to rebuilding our economy
• support efforts to strengthen non-proliferation of weapons of mass destruction
• work to end the international arms trade
• end the B-2 bomber and Star Wars programs
We know the time is ripe for change. Through your membership in PEACE ACTION you have become an agent of hope for the future.

Please renew today. The momentum is with us. But we have yet to win the race. **Your membership can make a difference, both for the financial support you give and the moral support it represents.**

Yours in Peace,

Peter Deccy
Membership Director

P.S. The Cold War is over, but peace has not been won. We need your continued support. If you can renew at the 9~ level this year, it will be a great help. **Thank you!**

EXHIBIT 16.3 Continued

February 20, 1993

Dear Member,

You are part of the solution!

We can solve the problems of a staggering national debt, millions unemployed and both this country and the world riddled with violence and war.

Your membership is very important to PEACE ACTION* and we need you to renew your membership today! Being a member of PEACE ACTION amplifies the voice for sanity in the nuclear age, sanity in the way we spend our tax dollars and sanity in the way we relate to the rest of the world.

Think about it!

• While nuclear war looks less likely today than it did five years ago, more and more nations are on the threshold of developing nuclear weapons.
• While the Warsaw Pact has vanished, we still spend more money defending Germany than they spend defending themselves.
• While our education, health care systems and our environment are in crisis, we are spending more on Star Wars than ever before.
• War and famine fueled by the international arms trade rages around the world.

PEACE ACTION has become the largest grassroots peace organization in American history. It is your support that got us to this point.

So please renew your membership today. Working for peace is as important today as it ever was.

In Peace

Peter Deccy
Membership Director

*formerly SANE/FREEZE: Campaign for Global Security

EXHIBIT 16.4 Draft Membership Renewal Letter, Third in Series, Peace Action

February 20, 1993

Dear Friend,

PEACE ACTION* is working to make real our hope for the future. An effective peace movement is essential if we are to counteract the influence of those who profit from the status quo. They have brought us the problem of staggering national debt, millions unemployed and a world riddled with violence and war. **You are part of the solution!**

Your continued support is critical during the first hundred days of the Clinton Administration. What happens in the next few months will set the pace for the next four years.

The membership of PEACE ACTION is the source of our strength. Every member is important. So please renew your membership today!

We are closer than ever to winning substantial legislation that will:

* reduce the number of nuclear weapons in the world
* reduce the military budget and increase investment in domestic needs
* give job training to workers in defense plants and provide businesses with funds to help them convert to civilian production
* provide funds for the clean-up of the thousands of toxic dump sites the military has left all over country
* work to curb the global arms trade and nuclear weapons proliferation

Membership is the engine of our organization. Many of our members are very active in their local communities. Others write their senators and congresspersons several times a year at our request. Others lend only financial support. **Every member is important.**

We need you in the struggles ahead. Please renew your membership today.

In Peace,

Peter Deccy
Membership Director

*formerly SANE/FREEZE: Campaign for Global Security

EXHIBIT 16.5 Draft Membership Renewal Letter, Fourth in Series, Peace Action

February 20, 1993

Dear Friend,

Your past support to PEACE ACTION* has made us the largest grassroots peace organization in American history.

I want to ask you again to renew your membership. Your membership is important to us, both for the financial support you give and the moral support it represents.

For over five years now we have been building a powerful movement to win a shift in government spending away from expensive and unnecessary military spending to increased investment in our economic future. And that message has been well received by President Clinton and many members of Congress.

But the military/industrial complex has been busy too. They have launched a major campaign to keep military spending at Cold War levels and to offset any losses in lucrative contracts with the sale of arms to other nations. We cannot allow their greed to shatter the hope we all feel.

During the 1980s we transferred over $300 million in weapons to Somalia. Weapons sold during the Cold War are causing havoc around world. Yet, the practice of weapons transfers continues, creating tomorrow's excuse for Cold War levels of military spending.

In many ways our domestic ills are the mirror image of our foreign policies. We flood the world with weapons and suffer from a flood of weapons at home. We are quick to employ the use of force and suffer from an increasingly violent culture. We spend billions of our tax dollars on all the security weapons can buy and suffer an insecure future.

A strong, effective peace movement is necessary to hold the Clinton Administration to remain true to the promise of increased investment in our future and global cooperation.

Please renew your membership today. Our strength comes from you.

In Peace

Peter Deccy
Membership Director

*formerly SANE/FREEZE: Campaign for Global Security

EXHIBIT 16.6 Draft Membership Renewal Letter, Fifth in Series, Peace Action

February 20, 1993

1~?
2~?
3~?
4~?
5~?

Dear 6~,

Are you part of the *solution*? Or are you part of the *problem*?

All our lives, you and I have resisted the mindless oversimplifications of the Radical Right. But *one* question isn't very complicated at all:

For the second time in three years, U.S. military forces spent the past season of peace on foreign soil. The question is, do you *support* the policy that placed our troops at risk—or do you *oppose* it?

If you question the dangerous, interventionist policies of the Pentagon, as I do, then there's an easy and important step for you to take right now:

<u>RENEW YOUR PEACE ACTION MEMBERSHIP TODAY.</u>

Your membership is due to expire very soon—but I invite you to be part of the solution by renewing *BEFORE* the [DATE HERE] deadline.

The organization you and I called SANE/Freeze has a new name now: PEACE ACTION. But the issues that led you and me to give so much of our heart and soul to PEACE ACTION have *not* changed.

And if you renew before [DATE HERE], you'll be helping in four different ways:

(1) You'll save money for PEACE ACTION by lowering our fundraising costs.

(2) You'll allow us to put your membership dues to work right away—without delay.

(3) You'll help conserve resources by saving precious paper.

(4) And you'll be saving yourself the time and trouble of responding to additional appeals by mail.

EXHIBIT 16.7 **Edited Membership Renewal Letter, First in Series, Peace Action**

Like me, you may look to the new Clinton Administration with great hope. But it will take a lot of <u>hard work</u>—not hope alone—to solve the age-old problem of war and peace.

And I'm betting that you're part of the solution. I know how generous you've been in the past, and I'm very grateful to you.

With your generous support, PEACE ACTION has already taken giant strides—despite the hostility we encountered in the White House for 12 long years:

** We've built substantial grassroots support for <u>reductions in military spending</u> with increased funding for education, job creation and other domestic needs.

** PEACE ACTION has taken a leadership role in forging a <u>strong coalition</u> working to stop the global arms trade and nuclear proliferation.

** We've continued to be the nation's <u>strongest voice</u> for disarmament.

Now, with a more favorably disposed administration, our hopes have grown. But you and I will have to challenge the Clinton Administration to be as thoughtful and forward-looking on peace issues as it is on health care reform and civil rights.

And that's why we need an effective peace movement.

As you know, perhaps better than I, PEACE ACTION is effective because we are <u>the</u> grassroots peace organization.

We are the voices for peace in every community in the land . . . in every Congressional District . . . in all 50 States.

For the sake of our nation, and the future of our children and our children's children, our voice for peace must not be stilled.

Please continue to be a part of this vital work. Renew your membership <u>today</u>.

- Page 2 -

EXHIBIT 16.7 Continued

In Peace,

Peter Deccy
Membership Director

P.S.   Last year, according to our records, you contributed $xx to SANE/Freeze. Will you consider renewing your membership in PEACE ACTION by increasing your gift to $xxxx? Please indicate the level of your dues support on the enclosed Membership Renewal Confirmation Form and return it to me before the [DATE HERE] Due Date. Thank you!

- Page 3 -

EXHIBIT 16.7 Continued

February 20, 1993

1—?
2—?
3—?
4—?
5—?

Dear 6—,

Your membership in PEACE ACTION (formerly SANE/FREEZE: Campaign for Global Security) will expire on [DATE HERE].

I'm writing you because I want to give you eight reasons why it's so very important that you <u>renew your membership before [DATE HERE]:</u>

(1)   President Clinton has inherited a staggering debt, millions unemployed and a world riddled with violence and war. Your continued support for PEACE ACTION puts you on record as supporting <u>global cooperation</u> and a peace economy.

(2)   The military industrial complex is launching an all-out effort to keep <u>military spending</u> levels at Cold War levels. Your membership in PEACE ACTION amplifies the voice for sanity in the nuclear age.

(3)   <u>Military contractors</u> are spending millions lobbying for your tax dollars now. They need to be challenged, or they'll stand in the way of PEACE ACTION's efforts to curb the international arms trade and stop nuclear weapons proliferation.

(4)   Without your help to challenge the military contractors, they'll block our country's efforts to make the transition from Cold War levels of military spending and increased investment in our <u>economic future</u>.

(5)   PEACE ACTION needs your continued membership support to push for cuts in spending for the defense of <u>western Europe and Japan</u>. Your membership dues help us lobby to direct that money instead to rebuilding the U.S. economy.

EXHIBIT 16.8 Edited Membership Renewal Letter, Second in Series, Peace Action

(6)   Your dues help underwrite PEACE ACTION's efforts to strengthen <u>non-proliferation</u> of weapons of mass destruction.

(7)   Your membership support helps our work to end the international <u>arms trade</u>.

(8)   You can help PEACE ACTION put an end to the <u>B-2 bomber and Star Wars</u> programs.

        Through your membership in PEACE ACTION, you've become an agent of hope for the future, and I'm very grateful to you.

        Please renew before [DATE TODAY]. To be sure you don't set this notice aside, write and mail your check <u>today</u>.

        Your membership can make a difference, both for the financial support you give and the moral support it represents.

                                        Yours in Peace,

                                        Peter Deccy
                                        Membership Director

P.S.   I'm enclosing an important "Peace Action Membership Priorities Survey." Please take a moment right now to complete it—and return it <u>today</u> along with your check. Thank you!

EXHIBIT 16.8 Continued

February 20, 1993

Dear PEACE ACTION Member,

In less than one week, your membership in PEACE ACTION will expire.

Unless you act **today,** you'll no longer be an active member of the largest grassroots peace organization in American history.

Remember, it's **you** that got PEACE ACTION to this point. Your support for SANE/FREEZE: Campaign for Global Security (our former name) was generous—and I, for one, am very grateful to you.

As a member of PEACE ACTION, you amplify the voice for sanity in the nuclear age—sanity in the way we spend our tax dollars, and sanity in the way we relate to the rest of the world.

- While nuclear war looks less likely today than it did five years ago, more and more nations are developing **nuclear** weapons.

- While the Warsaw Pact has vanished, the U.S. government still spends **more** money defending Germany than Germany spends defending itself!

- While our education and healthcare systems and our environment are in crisis, our government is spending **more** on Star Wars than ever before!

Please renew your PEACE ACTION membership today. Working for peace is **more** important today than ever!

In Peace,

Peter Deccy
Membership Director

P.S.   There's still time to renew your PEACE ACTION membership without interruption. Just drop the enclosed Membership Renewal Form in the mail along with your check **today**. Thank you!

EXHIBIT 16.9 **Edited Membership Renewal Letter, Third in Series, Peace Action**

February 20, 1993

Dear Soon-to-be Ex-Member of PEACE ACTION,

This is your *last chance* to renew your membership in PEACE ACTION.

Because you've been such a loyal member in the past, with your generous support for SANE/FREEZE: Campaign for Global Security, I'm sure it's an oversight that you haven't renewed before now.

As an active member, you help us wield great strength. PEACE ACTION is the largest grassroots peace group in our nation's history. With your renewed support, PEACE ACTION will redouble its effort for legislation that will:

o   Reduce the number of nuclear weapons in the world.

o   Lower the military budget—and increase investment in meeting domestic needs.

o   Offer job training to workers in defense plants, and provide businesses with funds to help them convert to civilian production.

o   Fund the clean-up of thousands of toxic dump sites the military has left all over country.

o   Curb the global arms trade and nuclear weapons proliferation.

As a member of PEACE ACTION, you are the sole source of our strength. Your support *matters*.

Please renew your membership *today*. Thank you!

In Peace,

Peter Deccy
Membership Director

EXHIBIT 16.10 Edited Membership Renewal Letter, Fourth in Series, Peace Action

February 20, 1993

Dear Former PEACE ACTION Member,

Your past support helped make PEACE ACTION the largest grassroots peace organization in American history.

Because you were so steadfast in your backing for SANE/FREEZE: Campaign for Global Security (our former name), I want to ask you one more time to renew your membership.

Your PEACE ACTION membership may be far more important than you think—for three reasons.

(1)   Your dues provide <u>financial support</u> for the peace movement--doubly important these days, when so many funders have gone on to more glamorous and higher-profile issues.

(2)   Our <u>strength in numbers</u> gives us clout on Capitol Hill when key military spending bills are on the table.

(3)   Your participation lends <u>moral support</u> to PEACE ACTION staff and other activists all across the country.

Your support for PEACE ACTION during the past five years has enabled us to build a powerful movement for new priorities. Now we're on the verge of winning a shift in government spending--<u>away</u> from expensive and unnecessary military spending and *toward* increased investment in our country's economic future.

But the military-industrial complex has been busy, too. They've launched a major campaign to keep military spending at Cold War levels.

Please don't let their greed shatter the hope we all feel!

Weapons sold during the Cold War are causing havoc around the world. (During the 1980s, the U.S. transferred over $300 million in weapons to Somalia alone!) Yet, the practice of weapons transfers continues, creating tomorrow's excuse for Cold War levels of military spending.

Only a strong, effective peace movement can hold the Clinton Administration to remain true to the promise of global cooperation and increased investment in our future.

    <u>Please restore your membership today.</u> You are our strength!

In Peace,

Peter Deccy
Membership Director

EXHIBIT 16.11 Edited Membership Renewal Letter, Fifth in Series, Peace Action

In cases like these, the letters could be printed simultaneously with a special appeal. This would achieve economies of scale, particularly for the envelopes, which are the most expensive elements in most direct mail packages. This approach should make it possible to keep production costs low enough to make varied envelope sizes practical. If that proves impractical, then choose two different sizes to alternate, one after another. But also be sure to use bold colors on the envelopes to help distinguish one effort from the next.

Teasers

I favor bold envelope teasers on most renewal notices. In this case, I suggested the following, in the order shown here:

> MEMBERSHIP RENEWAL NOTICE
> It's Time to Renew Your Membership!
> Before it's too late . . .
> LAST CHANCE!
> Have You Forgotten?

These proposed teasers are consistent with the themes and approaches I've worked into each of the corresponding letters.

Survey

I like the idea of a poll or survey to help boost response, as the draft copy proposed. Writing the survey itself was not part of this project, so I can't show the one used. Instead, I'm including a similar device used by Co-op America in its year-end appeal (Exhibit 16.12).

Generally I include a survey of this sort in the third or a later notice of a renewal series, because I'm optimistic that the notice alone will do the trick with the first two notices. But that's a judgment call, and—barring test results to the contrary—not a significant one, so I've recommended leaving the poll in the second effort, thinking it's unnecessary in the first effort and not wanting to repeat the idea. It's important to make such devices as credible as possible by taking one or more of the following actions:

- Call it a "Membership Priorities Survey" or some such rather than a poll. *Polling* suggests bigger numbers than is the case here.
- Consider at least one substantive question to which the answer isn't an obvious yes or no (though not one that requires a lot of thought and thus poses potential delays).
- Use the laser printer on which these appeals will be printed to number and print the questions and spaces for answers, so the poll will look (and be) more up-to-the-minute.

1999 CO-OP AMERICA MEMBERSHIP CHALLENGE

Deadline: January 15, 2000

To: Alisa Gravitz, Executive Director

From: MEMBER NAME + ADDRESS

YES, Alisa, I want to help Co-op America make 2000 a turning point in the movement for a just and sustainable society! I'm rushing you my tax-deductible, year-end Membership Challenge gift to beat the deadline. I understand my gift will be doubled with a matching gift from the $50,000 Membership Challenge Fund:

(personalized ask)

Please make your check payable to Co-op America and return it with this entire form to: Co-op America, 1612 K Street NW, Suite 600, Washington, DC 20006. Thank you very much!

MEMBERSHIP PRIORITIES SURVEY

Please indicate which programs you want Co-op America to devote the most resources to in 1999. Circle "1" for your highest priority and "4" for your lowest priority.

ENCOURAGING CORPORATE RESPONSIBILITY   1   2   3   4

To pressure corporations to be more responsible—by exposing irresponsible activities and alerting the public about boycotts, and by continuing to work with our allies to bring an end to sweatshop labor.

ORGANIZING CONSUMERS AND INVESTORS   1   2   3   4

To give millions more consumers and investors the information and tools they need to vote with their dollars for a better world.

BUILDING THE GREEN BUSINESS SECTOR   1   2   3   4

To help build a sustainable economy by fostering the growth of new green businesses and supporting those that already exist through technical assistance, networking, conferences, and more.

BUILDING SUSTAINABLE COMMUNITIES   1   2   3   4

To bring more and more people into the movement for a sustainable future—to increase the visibility of our work and spread information to concerned citizens.

EXHIBIT 16.12 Draft Response Device Incorporating Membership Priorities Survey, Co-op America

Deadlines

Just as a laser printer can plug in a personalized name or ask amount, it can easily insert a different deadline every day. I urge making use of this capability in the first two, personalized efforts in a renewal series such as this. Deadlines are compelling, especially for that minority of members who'll be quick to renew. Certainly there needs to be planning to work out appropriate deadlines for efforts 1 through 3 (read Exhibits 16.2 through 16.4, and you'll see what I mean) but the effort involved will be worth it. Deadlines work in direct response.

Appreciation

In a couple of places, I've inserted thank-you language. It's almost always in order to express appreciation for past support when asking for another gift. Every solicitation ought to be a thank-you.

Name Change

I used several similar devices to make passing reference to Peace Action's name change in each of the letters. But I didn't think it is necessary (or desirable) to use the same language indefinitely. Such references could be dropped from the renewal series after three or four months. Presumably, by that time, each member would have gotten the same message at least three other times, through newsletters, appeals, and other materials. Three times should be enough. Nevertheless, even then, it would be worthwhile to include a tagline on the response device (and possibly even the letterhead, too—wherever the new name and logo are run) for six months or so, just to be certain. Keep in mind that this is advertising, and research demonstrates that just when advertisers get bored with the repetition of the message, most consumers are just starting to notice it.

Lead Quotation

The draft of effort 1 (Exhibit 16.2) begins with a quotation from Dr. Martin Luther King, Jr. Although it was powerful, I dropped it because it detracts from the impact of the personalization, since it's positioned on top, and the quotation isn't directly related to the line of argument in the letter. If the quotation is really needed to help set the right tone and establish the correct associations in the minds of members, then it could be put in big type, boxed, and placed on the reply device, preferably with a small photo of Dr. King.

Type and Formatting

In membership renewal letters, many of which don't pretend to be personal notes from one person to another, I often alternate between 12-point Courier and a proportional font like Palatino to achieve variety. I reformatted these five draft letters accordingly. (In special appeals, I almost never use proportional fonts, however. They are almost always "personal notes.") In a typeface like Palatino, devices such as boldfacing and italics are perfectly natural. But I generally avoid them in Courier, because that typeface suggests the fiction that the letter was typed, an impression that's undermined by italics or boldfacing, which can't be performed easily with typewriters. Admittedly, that fiction becomes more transparent with every passing year. Nevertheless, lots of people still assume the original copy at least was actually typed—and that assumption will persist for several more years at least.

17

Thanking Your Donors
Friend-Raising Before Fundraising

You probably figured this out a long time ago: writing fundraising letters is no way for your organization to make a quick buck. Raising money by mail, like fundraising conducted by any other means, is a long-term process. The fundraising letters you mail as that process unfolds may differ dramatically from one another, because your relationships with donors change over time. You know much more about your donors in the later stages of the process than you do at the earlier, and your letters will reflect that knowledge in ways that are both obvious and profound. But there's one element all effective fundraising letters share: they show appreciation.

Even when you're writing a prospective donor who's known to you only as a name on a list, it's sound practice to find a way to compliment her while you make your case for a gift—and then to thank her in advance for agreeing to help. It's the *polite* thing to do.

When you write to a proven donor to solicit additional support, it's important to reinforce her goodwill (and her memory) by thanking her for her past generosity. It's not only polite to do that; it's sure to make your letter work better.

And when you're asking a donor to make an extra special effort to upgrade her support—by joining a high-dollar club or a monthly sustainer program, for example—you'll get the best results when you include repeated, heartfelt thanks in your letter. After all, the donors you select to include in most upgrade campaigns are very special people who've already given you more money, or given more frequently, or for a longer period of time than all the rest of your supporters. It's polite, effective, and natural to thank them in an upgrade appeal.

In other words, every fundraising letter is a thank-you.

Even so, that's not enough. The savviest fundraisers learn early on that they need to mail special letters dedicated exclusively to thanking their donors.

The Bread for the World acknowledgment letter reproduced in Exhibit 17.1 is an excellent example. This letter displays five elements that clearly set it apart as a thank-you and nothing more:

- In five straightforward paragraphs and a postscript, the message here is consistently "thank you!"
- As the second paragraph makes abundantly clear, this letter was mailed only to long-time and frequent donors, the backbone of any fundraising program.
- The enclosed lapel pin was sent purely as a gesture of appreciation— unasked and unexpected.
- The third paragraph recognizes that membership in Bread for the World is much more than a checkbook relationship for the donor. The donor is actively engaged in concert with Bread for the World's staff in pursuing the organization's mission.
- The message is brief and to the point, so as not to muddy the thank-you theme. And there is no ask anywhere in the package.

Why You Need to Write Thank-Yous

Focus group research consistently turns up comments like the following:

> "I sent them some money over a year ago, but I never got a thank-you. Well, never again!"
>
> "I've been giving to them for years, twenty, twenty-five bucks at a time. They got a hundred bucks from me recently—and all they sent back was the same preprinted postcard they always send. How much do you think they're going to get the next time around?"

Bread for the World

Seeking Justice. Ending Hunger.

1100 Wayne Avenue, Suite 1000
Silver Spring, MD 20910
1-800-82-BREAD

Dear Friend,

I'm pleased to be sending you Bread for the World's 25th anniversary lapel pin. I hope this small gift expresses <u>our</u> <u>very</u> <u>big</u> <u>thanks</u> to you for your faithful and generous support.

With your repeated contributions over the years, you've demonstrated your deep commitment to our work together as Bread for the World members. Your citizen action and your financial support have played a key role in Bread for the World's success in seeking justice and ending hunger, both here in the United States and around the world.

The loyalty of members like you is truly inspiring to those of us who serve on Bread for the World's staff. It's an honor to assist you as you communicate with our nation's leaders about legislation such as our Debt Relief and Poverty Reduction Act now before Congress.

And I hope you join all of us in celebrating our 25th anniversary -- and the beginning of our next 25 years.

Sincerely,

David Beckmann

David Beckmann
President

P.S. If you'd like a second pin for another member of your household, please write or <u>call</u> <u>our</u> <u>Membership</u> <u>Services</u> <u>department</u> <u>at</u> <u>800-82-BREAD</u>. We'd be glad to send off another pin -- or to answer any questions or concerns you might have about your membership.

RECYCLED & RECYCLABLE / PRINTED WITH SOY INK   9-60981

EXHIBIT 17.1 Thank-You Letter, Bread for the World

"The thing that burns me up is getting a thank-you about two months after I send a check—after they've already asked me for more money! I won't give to a group that's that disorganized . . . or rude."

Why do comments like these so commonly turn up in focus group research? Because so many charities defy what I call the Golden Rule of Donor Acknowledgments: thank your donors promptly!

Consider what I call the Phantom Donor. This generous soul sends $15, $20, or $25 gifts once or twice a year to some of the nation's top nonprofit organizations—and studies the mail that comes in return.

Several years ago, the Phantom paid special attention to the donor acknowledgment practices or his (or her) favorite charities. The experience was sobering. The Phantom mailed a round of $15 checks to twenty organizations, all on the same day and accompanying the most recent reply device and reply envelope received from each of the mailers. Eight weeks later, the Phantom Donor had been thanked by only fifteen of the twenty groups. One of them, the American Red Cross, got out a thank-you (admittedly only a postcard) within less than one week. But few others arrived within the first month. The typical response time was five to seven weeks.

That performance was pathetic. And we're not talking about the mom-and-pop charity down on the corner. These were some of the most successful nonprofit mailers in America—groups such as the Humane Society of the United States, Common Cause, and the Christian Appalachian Project. In fact, most direct mail fundraisers do a downright poor job of thanking their donors. The donor acknowledgment practices of those big charities simply mirror what goes on throughout the independent sector.

Charities that cut costs by refraining from mailing thank-yous or by sending such cut-rate items as preprinted postcards are all missing the boat, because they can do so much better. But even worse is to defy the Golden Rule of Donor Acknowledgments.

The most heartwarming and informative thank-you copy will be wasted on a donor who already may have forgotten that he sent you a check. (If you doubt donors react this way, run a couple of focus groups, and ask donors what they think.) In fact, I'm so concerned about the widespread failure to heed the Golden Rule of Donor Acknowledgments that I'll offer a corollary: Send even a "bad" (that is, impersonal) thank-you if you can get it into the mail much faster than a "good" (that is, personal and specific) one!

Here, now, are a few other pointers for effective donor acknowledgments:

- Reassure your donors it was a good idea to send a gift. Don't let them suffer from buyer's remorse. Reinforce their original belief that your group is effective, caring, and worthy of their support.
- Be warm and friendly. If they're new donors, welcome them to the "family."
- Praise their generosity. Tell them how, by joining with other supporters, they're having a significant impact on your work.
- Reaffirm your gratitude at the end of the letter or in a P.S.
- Give examples of recent organizational successes they can feel proud of.

Most fundraisers believe it's advisable to suggest another gift in a thank-you package—and most of the time I agree with them. Normally this is a "soft ask" that no one could possibly interpret as arm-twisting. There are circumstances in which I don't think such an approach is advisable—the Bread for the World thank-you letter reproduced in Exhibit 17.1 is an excellent example—but it's often worth considering. For example, in emergencies and with important deadlines approaching, it might be unnatural not to ask for additional support. In any case, it's almost always a good idea to enclose a reply envelope, even if you're not soliciting an additional gift.

To explore some of the numerous possibilities opened up by thank-you packages, let's take a look at the diverse styles and approaches followed by those fifteen mailers who (eventually) thanked the Phantom Donor.

How Some of the Country's Top Fundraising Mailers Thank Their Donors

A #10 window envelope was far and away the preferred choice of the fifteen mailers. Not a single one used a closed-face (nonwindow) envelope, although CARE opted for a self-contained "fast-tab" envelope. There were also two postcards (from the Red Cross and from the National Organization for Women).

Of the envelope packages received, nearly half featured teasers. Nothing flashy, just a simple "thank you" in five out of the six cases. The sixth got fancier: "A special note of thanks."

Some direct mail pros argue that a thank-you is the best time to solicit another contribution—a "get 'em while they're hot" mentality. All of the thank-you packages sent to the Phantom (except for the two postcards) included a return envelope to be used for subsequent gifts. However, only seven of these thirteen mailers directly pitched for funds by including reply devices. The most aggressive approach was the attempt to seek an immediate upgrade by membership in a monthly giving club. Two environmental groups opted for this stratagem: Greenpeace USA and the National Audubon Society. Significantly, in both cases letter copy emphasized the long-term commitment needed in the day-to-day battle to save our environment.

Most of the packages consisted of copy that was short and to the point. Aside from the two postcards, the Phantom received six short-form receipts, one of which also incorporated a membership card. Of the seven actual letters, five were of the one-page variety. The exceptions were the two monthly sustainer packages: Greenpeace used a two-page letter, Audubon a three-pager.

One intriguing point about the two longer pieces was that these were the only letters that were not personalized. Both instead used a variation on the "Dear Supporter" salutation—ironically, a rather impersonal way to elicit a substantial upgrade.

Almost all the acknowledgments straightforwardly and profusely thanked the Phantom—from a simple "your gift makes a difference" to the gushy "you are special to us and we hold you in our hearts and minds." Religiously oriented groups were likely to add a "God bless you."

Generally the message was upbeat and gracious, reminding the Phantom Donor of the good work being accomplished by the group (to make her—or him—feel better about parting with fifteen bucks). Occasionally, though, the tone was more downbeat, and the Phantom was treated to a lecture on the ills faced by the organization. The Republican National Committee, for example, was up in arms about the "Clinton/Democrat tax and spend frenzy," while the World Wildlife Fund informed the Phantom that many species "are on the brink of extinction."

Four of the thirteen letter packages contained inserts. What was particularly striking was that all four were on the subject of planned giving. Each of these inserts incorporated a return coupon to request additional information. In two other instances—where a planned giving brochure was not enclosed—a checkoff box was included on the reply device to request further material.

Most of the Phantom's charities avoided sending premiums. The Billy Graham Evangelistic Association was a notable exception. As in previous acknowledgment packages, the Graham organization included a 300-page paperback book and a reprint from its monthly magazine. Only two other groups mailed premiums, apart from the Nature Conservancy's membership card. St. Joseph's Indian School sent a prayer card, and Father Flanagan's Boys' Home included an excerpt from a book by its executive director. The latter enclosed a "handy" wallet calendar that was "made in our own print shop."

Father Flanagan's also alerted the Phantom to be on the lookout for a future premium. The personalized copy declared, "In my next letter, because you are one of our family, I'm sending you an honorary certificate of citizenship." Two weeks later the certificate arrived—with another appeal for funds.

Despite bells and whistles and occasional high-pressure requests for additional donations, few donor acknowledgments generate even enough revenue to cover their costs. Nevertheless, savvy (if far from speedy) fundraising mailers go to all this trouble and expense, not just because it's thoughtful and polite to send thank-yous, but also for two reasons, which are obvious and easily confirmed by testing:

1. Thank-yous increase response to subsequent appeals.
2. Thank-yous increase donor loyalty.

And there's a third, more fundamental reason to invest in timely and appropriate donor acknowledgments:

3. Thank-yous help build long-term relationships with donors.

To give a better sense of what I mean, I'd like you to examine closely a thank-you package from another major fundraising mailer—not one on the Phantom's charity list.

Case Study: A Great Example of a Thank-You Letter

The Southern Poverty Law Center in Montgomery, Alabama, sent out a masterful donor acknowledgment package that consisted of an outer envelope and two notebook-sized pages, printed on one side only (see Exhibits 17.2 and 17.3). Many fundraisers insist you should include a self-addressed reply envelope in every communication with your donors, but there was none in this package (much less a personalized reply device that might generate a bounce-back gift). I'll bet, though, that this warm, informative acknowledgment generated gifts at least an order of magnitude greater than the few, paltry bounce-back contributions that might have resulted if the package were to include a reply envelope.

This package was mailed first class. Had it been mailed bulk rate instead (to save on postage), the Southern Poverty Law Center couldn't have used Bobby Person's name and address as the return address on the outer envelope. (Under postal regulations still in force in the United States at this writing, a nonprofit organization must correctly identify itself on the outer envelope to qualify for the nonprofit postal discount.) Why mail first class? With a first-class letter from a person unknown to the recipient, the package had an air of mystery about it and unquestionably received high readership—far higher, in all likelihood, than a letter identified as coming from the center would have garnered.

Clearly the Southern Poverty Law Center chose to invest in its future relationships with donors by spending a modest sum on thank-yous like these. You'd be well advised to consider whether this technique makes sense for your own organization. It probably does because the revenue generated from future appeals to new donors is likely to dwarf the investment you've made in acquiring and converting first-time donors to loyal donors through such techniques as this. And far more of your new donors are likely to respond to those future appeals (and more generously so) if they feel you've treated them like part of the family.

It's really that simple. Treat every one of your donors like Grandma or Uncle Paul, and your organization will reap the rewards for many years to come.

● ● ●

With that, we come to the end of Part Three. In Part Four, "The Letter Writer's Toolbox," you'll find a collection of practical tools you can put to immediate use as you craft your own fundraising letters.

Bobby Person
Route 1, Box 407
West End, North Carolina 27376

EXHIBIT 17.2 Thank-You Outer Envelope, Southern Poverty Law Center

Bobby Person
Route 1, Box 190
West End, North Carolina 27376

October 15, 1993

Ms. ⌐⌐⌐⌐ ⌐⌐⌐ ⌐.
⌐⌐⌐ ⌐⌐⌐⌐⌐⌐ ⌐⌐⌐.
⌐⌐⌐⌐⌐, CA 947⌐⌐

Dear Ms. ⌐⌐⌐⌐ ⌐ ,

    I understand from my friends at the Southern
Poverty Law Center and its Klanwatch Project in
Montgomery that you recently sent a gift to help in
their work.

    I wanted to show some appreciation for the work
the Center did for me and I wrote them a letter of
thanks. They asked if I would share my feelings
with you so that you might better understand that
their work touches the lives of real people in a
meaningful way. I was more than glad to help by
writing you directly.

    When I needed their help to protect me from
harassment from members of the Ku Klux Klan, they
spent hundreds of hours and several thousand
dollars to protect my family and me.

    Let me tell you about my case.

    I am a black person living in a small rural
North Carolina community and work as a guard at a
state prison. I wanted to advance myself and asked
my supervisor for permission to take the sergeant's
examination. No black man had ever been sergeant
of the prison guard.

    I did not know at the time that one of the
white guards was a Klansman. That night, a Klan
cross was burned in the dirt road in front of my
house. My wife and children were terrified. A few
nights later, several Klansmen wearing sheets and
paramilitary uniforms, and carrying guns, drove up
in front of my home and threatened to kill me. My
children were so frightened that they did not sleep
well for months. Later, shots were fired at the
guard tower at night from cars passing on the road.

EXHIBIT 17.3 Thank-You Letter, Southern Poverty Law Center

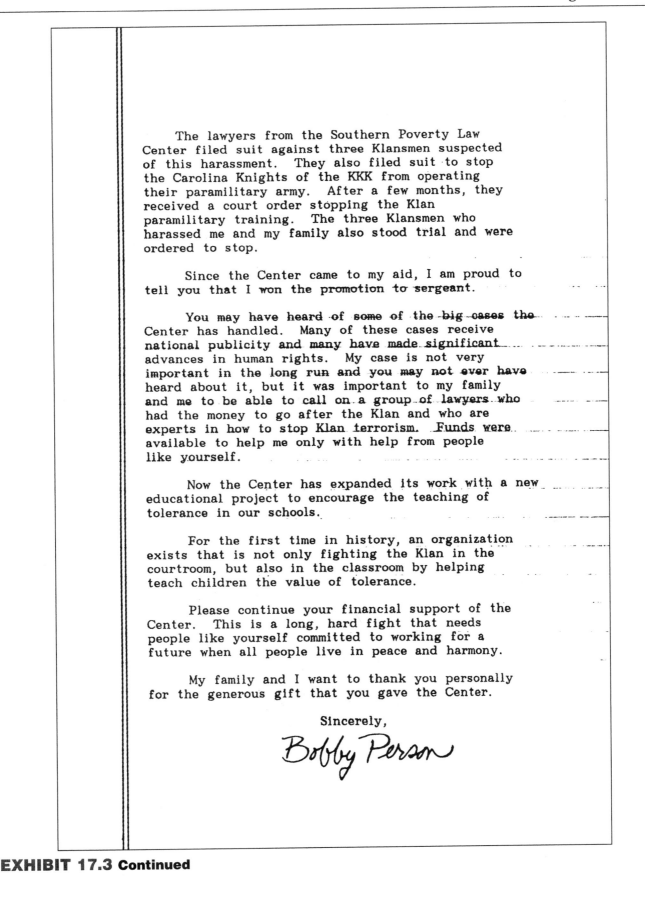

The lawyers from the Southern Poverty Law Center filed suit against three Klansmen suspected of this harassment. They also filed suit to stop the Carolina Knights of the KKK from operating their paramilitary army. After a few months, they received a court order stopping the Klan paramilitary training. The three Klansmen who harassed me and my family also stood trial and were ordered to stop.

Since the Center came to my aid, I am proud to tell you that I won the promotion to sergeant.

You may have heard of some of the big cases the Center has handled. Many of these cases receive national publicity and many have made significant advances in human rights. My case is not very important in the long run and you may not ever have heard about it, but it was important to my family and me to be able to call on a group of lawyers who had the money to go after the Klan and who are experts in how to stop Klan terrorism. Funds were available to help me only with help from people like yourself.

Now the Center has expanded its work with a new educational project to encourage the teaching of tolerance in our schools.

For the first time in history, an organization exists that is not only fighting the Klan in the courtroom, but also in the classroom by helping teach children the value of tolerance.

Please continue your financial support of the Center. This is a long, hard fight that needs people like yourself committed to working for a future when all people live in peace and harmony.

My family and I want to thank you personally for the generous gift that you gave the Center.

Sincerely,

Bobby Person

EXHIBIT 17.3 Continued

Part IV

The Letter Writer's Toolbox

This is the part where I invite you to steal my ideas as you might see fit. The resources that follow lay out for your unregulated use a bag full of treatments for the dread disease of writer's block:

- Sixty successful outer envelope teasers
- Fifty-four strong leads for fundraising letters
- Ninety ways to use the word *you* in a fundraising letter
- Sixty-three ways to handle awkward copywriting transitions
- Forty-one powerful ways to end a fundraising letter
- Fifty-eight ways to start a P.S. in a fundraising letter
- Fifteen ways how *not* to get results from your writing
- Ten other books to help you write successful fundraising letters

There are two ways to use these resources: (1) as an amusing assortment of copywriting ideas that will reassure you because they're so many and varied or (2) as a crutch you can lean on as you start writing an especially troublesome appeal.

Sixty Successful Outer Envelope Teasers

It's hard to make general statements about outer envelope teasers, much less lay down rules and regulations about how to write them. Instead, I'll do three things in this chapter: (1) list some of the many different kinds of teasers and show an example of each, (2) tell you about thirty of the teasers that have impressed me the most, and (3) list thirty all-time favorite teasers from five of my peers in the practice of raising money by mail. My hope in approaching the subject this way is to tickle your imagination. Perhaps I'll help lead you to write a few all-time favorite teasers for your own fundraising letters!

What You Can Accomplish with a Strong Teaser

To increase the likelihood the reader will open your appeal, you might write a teaser to fill any one of a number of needs—for example:

Function	Example
Describe the contents	*Membership Card Enclosed*
Establish urgency	*Your response needed within 10 days.*

Function	Example
Hint at advantages	*R.S.V.P.*
Flag the importance of the contents	*Membership Survey*
Start a story	*She was only 11 years old. She was as old as the hills.*
Offer a benefit	*Your Free Gift Enclosed*
Ask a question	*Would you spend $1 a day to save the life of a child?*
Pique curiosity	*What do these people have in common?*
Challenge the reader	*Take this simple quiz to learn your Health I.Q.*

There are both advantages and pitfalls in every one of these approaches. For example, the reader might answer a loud NO! to the question you pose, be totally unconvinced by your effort to establish urgency, or be miffed by the offer of a free gift. In other words, none of these approaches is guaranteed to work.

Nevertheless, teasers *can* deliver. Let's take a close look now at thirty of them that really do—at least as far as I'm concerned.

Thirty of My Own Favorite Teasers

My own all-time favorite outer envelope teaser from the fundraising field was one I didn't write. It's pictured at the top of Exhibit A.1. Judge for yourself whether it inspires *you*. It certainly intrigued a lot of other people. That teaser has been remailed for many years and has helped recruit hundreds of thousands of members for Handgun Control, Inc.

The best teaser I've ever written myself was the one that appears at the bottom of Exhibit A.1. It worked well, I believe, because the letter (which I didn't write) asked readers to do precisely what the envelope copy implied: to "give Nellie Red Owl a piece of their minds"—by jotting down a greeting or comment that could be read on the air of the Native American–run radio station that was the beneficiary of this appeal. In other words—and this is key, I believe—the teaser didn't just sucker readers into opening the envelope. It *delivered*.

Here are a few of my other recent favorites:

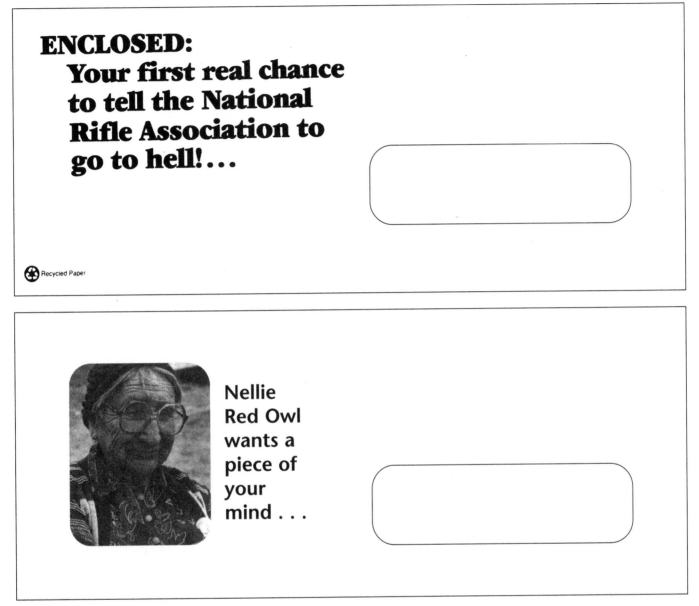

ENCLOSED:
Your first real chance
to tell the National
Rifle Association to
go to hell!...

Recycled Paper

Nellie
Red Owl
wants a
piece of
your
mind . . .

EXHIBIT A.1 Exemplary Outer Envelope Teasers

- From the National Republican Senatorial Committee (Washington, D.C.), rubber-stamped in red ink on an 11½ by 14½ inch brown kraft envelope bearing six postage stamps:

  PRE-PAID FEDERAL EXPRESS ENVELOPE ENCLOSED

- From the Smithsonian Institution (Washington, D.C.)—typeset in red ink on a white 6 by 9 inch window carrier next to a full-color illustration of a Native American ceremonial mask:

  Open Carefully . . . You may unleash a powerful spirit

- From Worldwatch Institute (Washington, D.C.)—in large blue type dominating a white Number 10 window envelope:

  "I read your <u>State of the World</u> every year."—Bill Clinton
  Maybe you should too . . .

- From KQED (San Francisco)—printed in blue and black ink on a 3⅞ by 7½ inch white window envelope:

  NOTICE OF ENROLLMENT:
  Membership card enclosed.
  Confirmation requested.

- From MADD (Mothers Against Drunk Driving, Irving, Texas)—typeset in red ink on a white Number 10 window envelope next to a second window through which a real penny shows:

  Because many people who sell alcohol think pennies are more important than human lives . . .

- From the Southern Poverty Law Center (Montgomery, Alabama)—typeset in bold black type in the corner card of a brown kraft Number 11 window carrier:

  Bill Moyers

- From the American Civil Liberties Union (New York)—typeset in black ink on a tan Number 10 window envelope, with the word "Don't" underlined in bold red:

  "We believe every American has the right to be different and not be punished for it." <u>Don't open this envelope unless you agree!</u>

- From Project HOPE (Millwood, Virginia)—a note handwritten in black ink above a headline in a broad yellow band stretching across the bottom of a 4 by 8 inch white window envelope:

  Critical that you read this today. W.B.W.
  URGENT: SOMALIA UPDATE

- From Common Cause (Washington, D.C.)—alternately typeset and laser-printed in blue, black, and red ink on a white personalized packet 9¼ by 13½ inches:

  DO NOT FORWARD
  CRITICAL INFORMATION PREPARED FOR:
  [my name and address]
  PETITIONS ENCLOSED FOR:
  PRESIDENT GEORGE BUSH
  SENATE MAJORITY LEADER GEORGE MITCHELL
  HOUSE SPEAKER TOM FOLEY
  IMMEDIATE RETURN REQUESTED BY:
  [date]

- From the Victory Fund (Washington, D.C.)—printed in blue and red on a white Number 10 window envelope:

  OK, THE ELECTION WENT OUR WAY. NOW WHAT?
  AN IMMODEST PROPOSAL ENCLOSED FOR:
  [my name and address]

- From the Sierra Club (San Francisco)—typeset in bold black and blue on a white Number 10 carrier:

  Your Sierra Club membership EXPIRES THIS MONTH!

- From Last Chance for Animals (Tarzana, California)—typeset in black and red ink above and below a photograph of a pathetic puppy showing through a large second window on a white Number 10 envelope:

  Would you go to jail to keep a puppy from being tortured?
  WE ARE!

- From the American Association of University Women (Washington, D.C.)—the latest example of an old chestnut that seems to work so often, typeset in an elegant face across the top of a window on a cream-colored Number 10 carrier:

The Favor of a Reply is Requested . . .

- From the New Forests Project (Washington, D.C.)—typeset in white and red type within and below a broad band of dark green across the front of a two-window Number 10 outer envelope (with seeds showing through the second window):

    FREE SEEDS ENCLOSED
    This miracle tree could mean a new life for the world's poor . . .
    NOTE: If no seeds are visible, tip the envelope.

- From In the Life/Media Network (New York)—printed in purple and gold across the front of a white Number 10 window envelope, alongside playful drawings and a shieldlike circular emblem featuring a Mickey Mouse hat:

    CHANGE THE FACE OF TELEVISION!
    THIS AIN'T NO MICKEY MOUSE CLUB

- From St. Jude Children's Research Hospital (Memphis, Tennessee)—handwritten in dark blue ink on the *back* of a white 3⅞ by 7½ inch window carrier:

    Would you give $10 . . . just $10 . . . to help save a child's life?

- From the National Audubon Society (New York)—set inside a band of red and blue on a perforated strip outlined in dashes above a personalized membership card that appears in an odd-sized window at the center of a 6 by 9 inch white outer envelope:

    PULL HERE FOR YOUR FREE BACKPACK
    (details inside)

- From the Sierra Club Legal Defense Fund (San Francisco)—handwritten and underlined with a scrawl in dark blue ink across the face of a gray 4 by 7½ inch window envelope:

    A personal reminder

- From Americans for a Balanced Budget (Falls Church, Virginia)—handwritten above the window on a white Number 10 envelope:

Have you heard about Bill Clinton's <u>NEW TAX</u>? Details Inside . . .

- From Feed the Children (Oklahoma City)—handwritten in red ink in the upper left-hand corner of a white Number 10 window outer envelope:

    What would you do with 500,000 pounds of BEANS?

- From the Nature Conservancy (Arlington, Virginia), on one of the most unusual and celebrated membership acquisition packages of recent years—printed in black ink in several different typefaces and at different angles, alongside fingers pointing to a full-color portrait of a startled-looking ostrich and my name and address showing through the window of a white 6 by 9 inch outer envelope:

    RELAX!
    Both of you.
    (A $10 nest egg will do it.)
    (Do not fold. Bumper sticker enclosed.)

- From the Democratic National Committee (Washington, D.C.)— "typed" upper left in black and printed in dark blue on the right on what appears to be a standard bluish Number 10 airmail envelope (with red and blue stripes around the perimeter):

    Bill Clinton
    430 South Capitol Street, SE
    Washington, DC 20003
    VIA AIR MAIL

- From the Coalition to Stop Gun Violence (Washington, D.C.)— typeset in huge red letters on a self-contained, 11 by 15 inch "door-mat" package beneath an official-looking address section that includes a personalized "Registered Survey Number":

    IMPORTANT SURVEY ON GUN CONTROL ENCLOSED

- From Habitat for Humanity International (Americus, Georgia)— typeset above the window on a bright red 6 by 9 inch outer envelope beneath a corner card reading only, "Rosalynn Carter":

    Christmas Card Enclosed . . .

- From the American Family Association (Tupelo, Mississippi)—printed in large blue letters across the face of a Number 11 white window envelope:

Here's your chance to help stop filth on television.

- From World Vision (Monrovia, California)—typeset in black in the upper left-hand corner of a closed-face white 5¾ by 8⅜ inch envelope:

  Enclosed: Important Information Regarding U.S. Government Grants

- From the Oakland Museum/Museum of California Foundation (Oakland, California)—set in contrasting typefaces in red and green inks on the front of a Number 10 white window outer envelope embellished with nondescript but elegant-looking designs in pale pink and continued on the back in simple red block letters:

  STEP INSIDE FOR A TASTE OF
  The Good Life
  YOUR FREE TICKETS FOR A PRIVATE TOUR ARE ENCLOSED

- From the People's Advocate, Inc. (Sacramento, California)—printed in black above the window on a white Number 10 outer envelope:

  Do you want to lose the Property Tax Exemption for your home?

Another Thirty All-Time Favorite Teasers

Taste in teasers is a function of style as well as the character and circumstances of the charities that use them. To give you a broader range of examples than my own files and taste will permit, I turned for help to my colleagues in the Association of Direct Response Fundraising Counsel (ADRFCO), the trade association for companies that provide direct mail fundraising services to nonprofit organizations. Several firms responded to my call for nominees for the All-Time Favorite Fundraising Envelope Teasers.

I received eighteen nominees from Charlene Divoky (Divoky & Associates). The following are the ones that teased me the most:

- Community Service Society of New York

  P.S. We named the duck Harold.

- Boston Public Library Foundation

Why don't woodpeckers get headaches?

- Northeast Animal Shelter

  The committee's decision is official . . . your Kind Human Award is enclosed.

- Community Service Society of New York

  Me? Sleep in a subway station?

- U.S. Committee for UNICEF

  Enclosed: The Life or Death Seed Catalog

- Northeast Animal Shelter

  She finally allowed herself to be rescued.

Michael P. Scholl (Direct Mail Decision Makers, Inc.) sent me twenty-five teaser candidates. Here are the ones I liked the most:

- Missionary Sisters of the Immaculate Conception

  How Sister Alice became GRANDMA

- Passionist Missions

  Father Carl . . . brutally murdered

- Missionary Servant of the Most Blessed Trinity

  One of the hardest letters I've ever had to write

- Guest House

  Fr. Bob is an Alcoholic and he's going through a private hell!

- Old Saint Mary's Church, San Francisco

  Rejoice with me . . .

- Missionary Sisters of the Immaculate Conception

  She arrived at the Grotto with tears in her eyes

Here are a few of the best teasers I received from Wendy Fisher (Mailworks):

- Little Brothers/Friends of the Elderly

  FACT: At 91, Emily Smithtown doesn't have a friend in the world. Not even one.

- Night Ministry/Youth Shelter Network

  Think kids are safer at home than on the street? Think again.

- Greater Chicago Food Depository

  FACT: Last year we distributed over 22 million pounds of food to hungry people.
  FACT: It wasn't enough.

- Illinois Citizens for Handgun Control

  Will you be killed by a handgun in the next 23 minutes?
  [BACK FLAP]: Someone will be.

- Little Brothers/Friends of the Elderly

  Come. Step with me for a minute into Emily's apartment.

- Dian Fossey Gorilla Fund

  She dared to have a dream—that one day her beloved mountain gorillas would be safe.
  Safe to roam their Viruna mountains in search of food . . . safe to give birth . . . rear their young . . . safe—so that their species can survive.
  Dian Fossey nurtured her dream . . . she died with that dream . . . But her beloved gorillas are still not safe.

Here are some verbal letter openers from Robert E. Hoagland (L. W. Robbins Associates):

- Joslin Diabetes Center

  They Were the Last Words Lisa's Parents Expected to Hear . . . And They Changed Her World Forever!

- Arkansas Children's Hospital Foundation

  What Has No Wings, Flies, and Is Called an Angel?

- Dana-Farber Cancer Institute/The Jimmy Fund

  "When it Comes to Courage, This Kid Is an All-Star!"

- American Red Cross of Massachusetts Bay

  Your Personal Emergency Relief Kit
  Open to Activate

- Bide-a-Wee Home Association

  The Cat Licked Her Face. And for a Moment, the Woman and the World Were Young Again.

Here are some of the teasers suggested by my colleague Bill Rehm (Mal Warwick & Associates):

- Toward Utility Rate Normalization

  They're at it again!
  California telephone customer alert

- Hyacinth Foundation

  My son was 29 years old when he died.

- Wellstone Alliance

  [HANDWRITTEN:] I need to know what <u>YOU</u> think.

- Shanti Project

  Can you remember where you were on June 5, 1981?

- Toward Utility Rate Normalization

  IMPORTANT NOTICE about your telephone bill
  Please read before paying

- American Red Cross/Bay Area

  ARE YOU PREPARED FOR FIRE?
  Checklist enclosed

- Toward Utility Rate Normalization

  WELCOME BACK!

Fifty-Four Strong Leads
for Fundraising Letters

1. Thank you . . . !

2. I'm writing you today . . .

3. You are among the first . . .

4. You may be surprised to learn . . .

5. Did you know that . . . ?

6. Don't you wish . . . ?

7. It's no secret that . . .

8. You've probably said to yourself . . .

9. Think about it for a moment.

10. Let's face it.

11. If you sincerely want to . . .

12. I wish you could have been with me when . . .

13. I was sure you'd want to know that . . .

14. I can't get the image out of my mind . . .

15. I still wake up in the middle of the night . . .

16. I've just returned from . . .

17. I need to hear from you this week about . . .

18. I don't want to waste words or paper . . .

19. I don't usually write such long letters . . .

20. We tried to reach you by phone . . .

21. According to our records, your membership has lapsed.

22. Will you please take a moment right now to renew your membership?

23. I want to tell you a story about . . .

24. You won't believe it.

25. As I was passing through _____ recently, I . . .

26. I've just returned from . . .

27. I want to tell you about a remarkable . . .

28. I'm writing to invite you . . .

29. I'd like to take just a few moments of your time to . . .

30. I hope you'll take a moment right now to . . .

31. Because you've been so generous . . .

32. I'm writing you this urgent letter today because . . .

33. It's been awhile since I heard from you . . .

34. I have exciting news for you!

35. I'm writing you today because _____ is [are] in grave danger.

36. Have you ever wondered . . . ?

37. Do you ever feel . . . ?

38. I want to share a recent experience with you.

39. I want to give you the latest information on . . .

40. I hope you'll be as excited as I am to learn . . .

41. Have you ever wanted to be part of . . . ?

42. Have you ever said to yourself . . . ?

43. If you've always wanted to . . .

44. Haven't you wondered how you could help . . . ?

45. It's no surprise that . . .

46. It's hard to believe, but . . .

47. I know you'll be interested to know that . . .

48. I know you'll want to be a part of this . . .

49. Let's be frank.

50. I have a secret.

51. You've been chosen . . .

52. If you've seen the recent headlines, you're well aware . . .

53. Someone you know . . .

54. I'd like to say it isn't so.

Ninety Ways to Use the Word "You" in a Fundraising Letter

1. Thank you for . . .
2. Thank you very much for . . .
3. Thank you again for . . .
4. As you know . . .
5. I'm writing you today . . .
6. I'm sure you'll agree that . . .
7. With your generous support,
8. Because you helped,
9. You are among the first . . .
10. You're the kind of person who . . .
11. I know that you . . .
12. Would you believe that . . . ?
13. As I wrote to you recently,
14. Did you know that . . . ?
15. I don't know about you, but I . . .
16. Will you spend just pennies a day to . . . ?
17. How many times have you said to yourself . . . ?
18. You're among the few I can count on to . . .
19. I was delighted to hear from you.

20. You're among our most generous supporters.

21. Now, at last, you can . . .

22. You're in for a pleasant surprise.

23. Have you ever wondered . . . ?

24. . . . may astonish you.

25. You may never forgive yourself if . . .

26. The benefits to you are substantial.

27. You can rely on . . .

28. You'll be joining the ranks of . . .

29. None of this would be possible without your generous help.

30. You owe it to yourself to explore this opportunity.

31. You've helped in the past, and your generosity . . .

32. Your membership gift . . .

33. You're one of our most generous supporters . . .

34. You've been with us for a long time, and . . .

35. As one of our newest members, you . . .

36. I want to tell you about . . .

37. It's people like you who . . .

38. I know, like me, you must feel . . .

39. You're such an important friend . . .

40. Through the years, you've been . . .

41. You've shown just how much you are . . .

42. You may be shocked . . .

43. You may be surprised . . .

44. I've noticed you haven't . . .

45. Working together, you and I . . .

46. You're one of the few people who truly understand . . .

47. You should be proud of what we've accomplished together.

48. With your special gift, _____ can . . .

49. Your gift can make the difference between . . .

50. You can help them [grow strong, live a better life] . . .

51. You helped prevent . . .

52. When _____ happened, you were there.

53. Have you ever felt as if . . . ?

54. Have you ever wished you . . . ?

55. Please believe me—you can . . .

56. Like me, you may . . .

57. I can tell you from my own experience . . .

58. I've seen firsthand how you . . .

59. When you join . . .

60. I'll be pleased to send you . . .

61. I need to hear from you by _____ . . .

62. I'll keep you informed . . .

63. I'll want to keep you involved . . .

64. It may seem to you . . .

65. You've helped so many people with . . . !

66. Now you can play a leadership role . . .

67. Can you believe . . . ?

68. Have you seen . . . ?

69. What would you think if . . . ?

70. Because of people like you . . .

71. You're just the kind of person who . . .

72. How can you, as a _____, . . . ?

73. You and others like you are _____'s only hope!

74. Have you ever noticed . . . ?

75. Can I rely on you to . . . ?

76. I hope you'll consider . . .

77. You're someone who . . .

78. You can rest assured that . . .

79. You may never again have an opportunity to . . .

80. You're not someone to stand by while . . .

81. Your gift really will make a difference.

82. What can you do? These ___*[number of]*___ things:

83. You too can be part of this project.

84. I want you by my side (again) at this critical time.

85. This is all possible because of you.

86. You probably had no idea . . .

87. Find out for yourself.

88. Here's a new opportunity for you.

89. For you, free of charge.

90. Reserved for you:

Sixty-Three Ways to Handle Awkward Copywriting Transitions

1. As I'm sure you'll understand,

2. But that's not all.

3. [Use subheads.]

4. But now, for the first time,

5. Today, more than ever,

6. Best of all,

7. Here's why:

8. Think of it:

9. One thing's for sure:

10. The truth is,

11. To show you what I mean,

12. I'm hoping you'll agree.

13. And there's more:

14. It's that simple!

15. It's now or never.

16. There's never been a better time.

17. Am I claiming too much? I don't think so.

18. That's why I'm writing you today.

19. In addition,

20. Not only that, but . . .

21. And . . .

22. Now,

23. Next,

24. [Indent paragraph]

25. Before I tell you . . .

26. As you can see,

27. Because it's people like you who . . .

28. Because there's no time to lose.

29. But wait, that's not all.

30. Why am I so concerned? Because . . .

31. Let me explain . . .

32. In a moment I'll tell you more about _____. But first . . .

33. And, most important of all, . . .

34. That's what _____ is all about.

35. It may seem hard to believe, but . . .

36. There's so much at stake!

37. Let me tell you more.

38. That's why I'm asking you to do three things right now.

39. The recent news from _____ is shocking, but I'm sure you know . . .

40. To clarify what I mean . . .

41. Now is the time to . . .

42. But wait: there's more.

43. Just imagine:

44. Consider the consequences:

45. In other words,

46. Put yourself in their place:

47. Time is of the essence.

48. Can you think of a better way to . . . ?

49. It's sad but true:

50. I know how you feel about _____ because you _____.

51. Will you help?

52. Are you willing to take the next step to . . . ?

53. Why wait?

54. It's clear that . . .

55. Despite the lack of media attention . . .

56. I think you'll agree that . . .

57. The truth hurts.

58. I know this isn't pleasant . . .

59. As you know very well . . .

60. Act now, and we'll . . .

61. If you really think about it . . .

62. Ask yourself:

63. Now that you know . . .

Forty-One Powerful Ways to End a Fundraising Letter

1. Thank you for caring so very much!

2. You may not know their names, but they'll carry thanks in their hearts for your kindness and generosity.

3. From the bottom of my heart, thank you!

4. Your investment will bear dividends for years to come.

5. I'm sure you'll be glad you did.

6. Isn't that what life is really all about?

7. So you can't lose!

8. Don't miss this unique opportunity!

9. It's up to you.

10. May I hear from you soon?

11. The future is in your hands.

12. And that can make all the difference in the world!

13. I'm counting on you!

14. In return, you'll have the satisfaction of knowing that . . .

15. Together, we will . . .

16. With your help, we'll . . .

17. The satisfaction you'll receive is indescribable.

18. Thank you for joining me in this . . .

19. I'm looking forward to hearing from you very soon.

20. Together, I know we can . . .

21. When you look back at this moment in history . . .

22. Please, if you feel the way I do, . . .

23. I can't think of a better gift to give our children and grandchildren than . . .

24. Thank you for your compassion.

25. I know you won't be disappointed.

26. Please, send your gift today.

27. And I promise to send you _____ just as soon as . . .

28. Thank you for taking the time to help.

29. I know I can count on you!

30. My warmest wishes to you.

31. You'll be so glad you decided to help!

32. You'll be proud to be part of _____!

33. The _____ are depending on you!

34. _____ won't forget you!

35. I can't thank you enough.

36. I believe you'll make the right choice.

37. Please act today!

38. This is your chance to . . .

39. With your help, _____ will have a chance to . . .

40. Please show them they're not alone!

41. The future of your children and your children's children hangs in the balance.

Fifty-Eight Ways to Start a P.S. in a Fundraising Letter

1. Thank you again for . . .
2. If you respond within the next X days, you'll receive . . .
3. If you send $X or more, you'll receive . . .
4. There's not much time.
5. The enclosed X are yours to keep—our gift to you.
6. Please use the enclosed X to . . .
7. If $X is too much for you to give at this time, will you consider a gift of $Y or $Z?
8. We need to _____ by _____, so please send your gift today.
9. Your gift of $_____ makes it possible for . . .
10. Please don't set this letter aside.
11. Remember, if you respond by . . .
12. Please take a look at the _____ I've enclosed for you.
13. As a special benefit for the first _____ people who respond, I'll . . .
14. And remember, your gift is tax deductible.
15. I've always regarded you as one of our strongest supporters, so . . .
16. Please don't wait.

17. Every day that goes by . . .

18. I hope I can count on receiving your gift in the next _____ days.

19. Please, as always, feel free to contact me at [telephone number] if you have any questions about . . .

20. If you decide not to join us in this crucial effort, I hope you'll take a moment to write and tell me why.

21. Just as soon as I return from _____, I'll let you know how . . .

22. I need to send that shipment of _____ in the next _____ days, so . . .

23. Don't forget: . . .

24. You've come through so many times in the past, and I hope I can count on you again now.

25. _____ need[s] your help today.

26. Did you know that . . . ?

27. If you act by . . .

28. Your gift of _____ will make it possible for _____ to get _____.

29. $_____ is just _____ per day!

30. For less than a cup of coffee a day,

31. I promised _____ that . . .

32. When I look into the eyes of . . .

33. Unless you and I act immediately,

34. Please know that your gift is _____'s only hope for _____.

35. Without your help, _____ doesn't stand a chance.

36. Won't you please take out your checkbook now and . . .

37. I hope I can count on you to respond by . . .

38. Take a moment right now to look at the enclosed _____. I'm sure you'll feel the same as I do:

39. I hope you'll enjoy—and use—the enclosed _____.

40. Remember, to reach our goal by _____, we need . . .

41. I can't stress enough how much your support will mean to us!

42. With your support, I can't . . .

43. It's members like you who . . .

44. There's no better time to . . .

45. Don't miss this chance to . . .

46. I'd like to hear your thoughts about . . .

47. Don't delay.

48. If your check and this letter have crossed in the mail,

49. What may seem a small gift to you can . . .

50. I know it's hard to imagine _____, but . . .

51. Put yourself in _____'s place for a moment.

52. All it takes to _____ is $_____!

53. If you and I don't do something right now,

54. If you won't help, who will?

55. Remember, every day that goes by without our help,

56. Please find it in your heart to give. Even just a little gift will help!

57. _____ need[s] to know that someone cares.

58. Thanks to friends like you,

Fifteen Ways How *Not* to Get Results

I can best approach the rules of copywriting through the back door, by advising you on how to avoid the most common errors I see. There are at least fifteen. They're described below, beginning with the five I believe cause the most trouble.

Chaotic Thinking

Effective writing begins (and ends) with clear, disciplined thought. As William Strunk Jr. and E. B. White put it so elegantly in *The Elements of Style:* "Design informs even the simplest structure, whether of brick and steel or of prose. You raise a pup tent from one sort of vision, a cathedral from another. This does not mean that you must sit with a blueprint always in front of you, merely that you had best anticipate what you are getting into." So before you lay a finger on the keyboard or position your pen on paper, *make up your mind what it is you want to communicate.* Decide where you want to go and how you'll get there. If necessary, outline the steps you'll take along the way. If you don't decide in advance what the point is, it's unlikely you'll get it across.

Hemming and Hawing

There may still be a place for slow and easy writing that meanders from point to point, but I think that approach went out of style with William Faulkner—and there is no room for such laziness when you're writing to achieve results. Get to the point—the quicker the better! Unless you can devise a clearly superior lead sentence, I suggest you start a letter with the words, "I'm writing to you today because . . . " That approach won't win a prize in a creative writing contest, but it does force you to communicate quickly and directly the result you're hoping to achieve with your letter. Creativity doesn't raise money, but directness does. If your writing doesn't get to the point, your readers' eyes and minds will wander off to more satisfying pursuits. Bluntness is usually a wiser and more productive course than subtlety.

Boring Leads

If you're faced with the task of writing a six-page letter or a ten-page memo, you'd better be sure your opening paragraph—and especially the opening sentence—is intriguing enough to pique your readers' interest. And that goes double for a letter intended to secure a gift or sell a product.

Writing that engages the reader often begins with a question, a challenge, a human interest story, a bold assertion, a familiar phrase turned on its head—or straightforward, unalloyed directness. The special circumstances and conditions of your writing assignment (or simple inspiration) may suggest that one of these approaches is ideal. But it may be enough simply to sum up the points you're going to make—if you state them dramatically enough and set the proper tone for the audience you're addressing—for example:

> I'm writing today to invite you to join me in launching a historic initiative with vast potential to improve the quality of life in our community.

For a general audience, that pompous lead might guarantee your letter will quickly make its way into the proverbial circular file. But for a highbrow group with a demonstrated commitment to your community and a connection to the person who signs the memo or the letter, the boldness of your claim may be captivating.

Run-On Sentences

Writing of any type suffers from overlong sentences; a letter to raise money or sell software can die a horrible death from this malady. If a sentence is longer than three typewritten lines, analyze it, looking for a way to break it down into two or three simpler and shorter sentences. Almost always, you'll get your point across more effectively if you do so.

Keep this in mind: a reader dedicated enough to tackle Proust or Joyce may be willing to concentrate hard enough to follow a tortured thought all the way to a long-overdue period. (Understandably, the period is sometimes known as a "full stop.") But *your* readers aren't likely to pay that much attention. Long sentences will test readers' limited attention span, and you'll come up the loser.

Failure to Use Visual Devices to Guide the Reader

A novelist who is highly skilled in moving the reader from one page to the next may be able to do so with the power of words alone. Most of us aren't so lucky, and our readers, who often have far more meager incentives to read on for page after page, are typically far less tolerant. To write effectively for impact, you'll probably need to make liberal use of subheads, bulleted or numbered series, boldfaced section headings, and other devices to break the monotony of gray, unbroken text. Only by providing your readers with clues that are visible at a glance can you make your writing actually *look* easy to read—and you'll substantially reinforce that impression by using short sentences and short paragraphs. Signals such as these send an important message to the reader: that you're writing for *her* benefit, not for your own.

Inconclusive (and Uninteresting) Endings

A strong appeal requires a forceful ending as well as a thought-provoking lead. It's not enough to sum up and repeat the strongest points made along the way. A letter should end on a high note: affirming the relationship between the signer and the recipient and relating the appeal to the organization's mission and the values that inspire it. End with something readers will remember.

Vague Language

Bad writing is full of excuses, qualifications, exceptions, and caveats. For example, a sales letter might begin:

> Most people agree, this product is one of the best things since the hula hoop.

Well, is it the best—or isn't it? If "most people" agree, then why not write instead:

> This incredible product will knock your socks off! Take it from me—it's the best thing since the hula hoop!

When a writer constantly relies on evasions, they signify fuzzy thinking. If you can't make your case in clear, unequivocal language, it's time to reexamine the reasoning that led you to conclude the case that you're presenting was defensible. Your readers won't become excited about helping you if your writing doesn't clearly convey what you want, and why, and when.

Overwriting

Inexperienced and insecure writers frequently overuse adjectives and adverbs, robbing their writing of clarity and impact. As Strunk and White wrote in the *Elements of Style,* "The adjective hasn't been built that can pull a weak or inaccurate noun out of a tight place." If you want to write for results, try doing so without using any adjectives at all. You can go back later and insert an adjective or two for the sake of precision or honesty. To the extent you exercise restraint, your readers will thank you—and they'll reward you with the ultimate gift to a writer: they'll go on reading.

Ten-Dollar Words

Like overwriting, the use of long, obscure, and highly technical language is a form of showing off. It's not necessary to write *cessation* when *end* will do, or use *communicate* when you can get the point across with *say* or *write*. Unfortunately, this sort of thing is all too common in writing today, and communication suffers as a result. Board chairs and chief executive officers are especially susceptible to this malady. Avoid it like any deadly (shall I say "communicable"?) disease.

"Business English"

The tendency to use widely accepted but grammatically incorrect—and often abysmally wordy—constructions is one of the afflictions of contemporary writing, and it infects a great deal of advertising and fundraising copy. Stay clear of abominations such as the following; choose their equivalents in acceptable English—or shun them altogether:

Avoid Using	*What to Use Instead*
"accordingly"	"so"
"along the lines of"	"like"
"and/or"	Leave this one to the lawyers!
"as to whether"	"whether"
"at this point in time"	"now" or "today"
"dialogue"	"talk"
"enclosed herewith"	"I'm sending you"
"etc."	Use *very* sparingly.
"finalize"	"finish"
"for the purpose of"	"for"
"implementation"	Just do it!
"in order to"	"To" will suffice.
"inasmuch as"	"because"
"in the event that"	"if"
"interface"	"work with" or "meet"
"make use of"	"use"
"owing to the fact that"	"because"
"per your request"	"as you asked"
"prioritize"	"set priorities"
"prior to"	"before"
"pursuant to"	"according to"
"quite" or "very"	Lilies sell better without gilt!
"results-wise"	"result is that"
"revert back"	"revert"

Avoid Using	What to Use Instead
"the foreseeable future"	How far away is that?
"with a view to"	"to"

Then there are all those words wasted because writers insist on doubling up, presumably out of some deep, hidden fear that they'll otherwise fail to get the point across. For example:

Avoid Using	What to Use Instead
"exact opposites"	"Opposites" will suffice.
"the reason is because"	Which is it: "the reason is"—or "because"? Choose one!
"final conclusion"	If it's the conclusion, isn't it final?
"actual experience"	As opposed to an unauthentic experience?
"continue on"	Is the alternative to "continue off"?
"end result"	Give me a break!

You get the point. From this time forward, I trust you'll be on guard against these boring and objectionable word wasters. While you're at it, please put the following words on your list of what to avoid:

Avoid Using	What to Use Instead
"hopefully"	Do you really hope so? Given the way this word is so frequently misused, I think that's unlikely. But if you really hope so, then *say* it!
"frankly"	This word is commonly used when its opposite is intended. It puts the reader on guard. So does, "To be honest with you."
"irregardless"	The correct word is "regardless."
"very unique"	If something's unique, it's one of a kind. Drop the "very."

Every one of these words and phrases is a violation of common sense. (Strunk and White comment, sometimes at greater length, about some of these examples in their *Elements of Style*.)

Stilted Language

Just because a word is grammatically correct and properly spelled and precisely expresses the thought you want to convey doesn't mean it's the *right* word. When you are seeking to achieve results, it's important to write as you speak, using familiar, everyday words. The best way to guard against problems of this sort is to give your writing a road test: read your letter aloud before you let anyone else see it. If you have trouble pronouncing a word or phrase, chances are it will trip up your reader too. Find another way to say what you've written.

Lack of Agreement

One of the most common violations of the rules of grammar is the writer's failure to decide in advance what point a sentence is to make. This confusion is often reflected in a mismatch between its subject and verb, or between a pronoun and its antecedent—for example:

> If members choose not to attend, you may obtain a discount instead.

There's nothing wrong with this sentence that a little forethought wouldn't have cured. Here is one possible approach:

> Members who choose not to attend are eligible for discounts.

This alternative wording is less likely to trip up the reader, who could easily do a doubletake on the original. The second version is also two words shorter, making it that much easier to read.

Dangling Modifiers

Closely related to the preceding problem, this common error typically arises from the same source: foggy thinking. I know of no way to describe it other than to use the grating language of the grammarian or to give examples:

> An example of the very best the community had to offer, the mayor awarded her the prize last year.

Loaded with valuable benefits, I thought the product was the best I could buy.

To avoid the confusion caused by mismatches like these, try revising them. Usually there are numerous acceptable alternatives. Here's one example of each:

The mayor awarded her the prize last year because she exemplified the very best the community has to offer.

It was simply loaded with valuable benefits—the best product I could buy, I thought.

You don't need to know what a modifier is: all you have to do is remember when you near the end of the sentence what you were writing about when you started it.

Overuse of the Passive Voice

There are times when the passive voice is unavoidable, or at least convenient—in the following, for instance:

The snowfall was unprecedented, but the streets were plowed clean in record time.

In this example, which is about streets and snow, not people, it's not important *who* plowed the streets (although the members of the street-plowing crew might have a different opinion). The point of the sentence is clear. Nothing is lost by the use of the passive voice. The corresponding active-voice statement is no clearer or more elegant than the passive one:

Snow accumulated to an unprecedented depth, but the crews plowed it clean in record time.

Usually, however, the passive voice detracts from the impact of a statement. The passive voice is frequently used to evade straightforward assertions of fact. Thus, it rarely helps sell products or obtain charitable gifts. Consider the following example:

> Voting members of the museum are required to attend one meeting per year to preserve their status and receive all these discounts.

That sentence reads like a passage from a rulebook, not a promise of benefits that might entice someone to join the museum. Try this instead:

> As a voting member of the museum, you'll receive all these discounts if you attend just one meeting per year.

Writing for results requires communicating conviction. The active voice helps the writer to be direct and permits the reader to grasp the point more quickly.

Atrocious Spelling

My mother always said that respect for spelling died in the 1950s when educators decided there was a better way to teach reading than by using phonetics. I think she was right. I know few Americans younger than I who can spell worth a damn. Fortunately, most of us who live by the word are likely to use one of the popular word-processing programs, all of which feature spell-checking utilities. I heartily recommend these devices as a partial answer for the spelling-impaired (only partial, because they won't pick up words that are correctly spelled but wrong in context). Using such a program requires only a few seconds, yet it may rescue you from years of mortification. Perhaps you don't care whether there are spelling errors in your copy, *but I do!*

For example, I will cast a dark eye on you if I catch you committing all-too-common spelling errors such as any of the following egregious examples:

- *except* (meaning "to exclude") instead of *accept* (meaning "to receive" or to "acknowledge")
- *it's* instead of *its* (when used as the possessive form of *it*)
- *affect* (meaning "to act on" or change something) instead of *effect* (meaning "to do" or "to bring about as a result")

- *loose* (as in "loose screw" or "loose clothing") instead of *lose* (as in "lose your keys")

● ● ●

If you heed the fifteen points just outlined and if you're faithful to Strunk and White's rules of grammar and vocabulary in *The Elements of Style* and Rudolf Flesch's "25 Rules of Effective Writing" from *How to Write, Speak and Think More Effectively*, you'll avoid most of the common mistakes that can prevent you from communicating effectively. You'll also be more likely to achieve the results you intend from your fundraising letters.

Ten Other Books to Help You Write Successful Fundraising Letters

You might be surprised just how many books have been published on the subject of letter writing. Books about letters that are effective or powerful—or tried and tested. Books of "classic" or "all-time great" letters. Books of model letters. Books about sales letters. Books about business letters. Even several books specifically devoted to fundraising letters—including several volumes of sample letters.

I've found very few of those books to be useful. In fact, some are dangerously misleading.

It's disappointing. The books by writers whose experience lies outside fundraising sometimes make suggestions inappropriate to this very peculiar field of ours. Some of the books written by people with extensive fundraising experience have fallen into the trap of dogmatism ("This worked for me once, so it's got to work for you" or "Long letters always outpull short ones"). And the collections of letters pose problems of their own, since the implication is that a letter published in a book of "good" letters is a "good" model for any fundraiser to follow under any circumstances.

The following list, arranged in alphabetical order by author, includes only the books I genuinely believe you'll find useful. It's a short list.

- Burnett, K. *Relationship Fundraising: A Donor-Based Approach to the Business of Raising Money.* London: White Lion Press, 1992. Ken Burnett is one of the world's leading practitioners of the art of raising money by mail. Many of us in the fundraising field speak about "building relationships with donors," but Burnett has systematically developed the techniques to bring this ideal down to earth.
- Caples, J. *Tested Advertising Methods.* (4th ed.) Englewood Cliffs, N.J.: Prentice Hall, 1974. John Caples virtually invented the field of direct response copywriting. His classic 1920s ad, "They laughed when I sat down to play the piano," is so well known it's become what is probably the only certifiable cliché in the business. Although Caples wrote space advertising in the main, not fundraising letters, the principles he developed through years of exhaustive testing are as applicable today—and in the writing of fundraising letters—as they were when he wrote his ads.
- Flesch, R. *How to Write, Speak and Think More Effectively.* New York: New American Library, 1963. Generations of Americans have turned to Rudolf Flesch for advice on effective writing and speaking. Much of his teaching is summed up in this wonderfully useful little volume, first copyrighted in 1946 but still readily available in paperback. Flesch's extensive and well-known findings on readability are threaded through the text, and it's chock-full of concrete and colorful examples. This book brims over with insight and useful advice—and it's a treasure chest of fascinating information for anyone intrigued by the dynamics of human language.
- Lautman, K. P., and Goldstein, H. *Dear Friend: Mastering the Art of Direct Mail Fund Raising.* (2d ed.) Rockville, Md.: Taft Group, 1991. This widely circulated manual, which covers the general topic of direct mail fundraising, is useful for the aspiring copywriter because of its heavy emphasis on the creation of the direct mail fundraising package. The book is filled with examples, along with commentary that makes them truly useful.
- Ogilvy, D. *Ogilvy on Advertising.* New York: Vintage Books, 1983. The late dean of the advertising industry was a direct marketer at heart and one of its most articulate and insightful writers. Reading Ogilvy's several useful books is one of the best possible ways for a fledgling copywriter to gain entry to the mysteries of writing fundraising letters.

- Smith, G. *Asking Properly: The Art of Creative Fundraising.* London: White Lion Press, 1996. Fundraising innovator George Smith is known around the world as one of the brightest lights in the business. This lively book, crammed with Smith's characteristic insight and wit, is an indispensable tool for the direct mail fundraising writer eager to learn how to think outside the box.

- Strunk, W., Jr., and White, E. B. *The Elements of Style.* (3d ed.) New York: Macmillan, 1979. If you write anything more than grocery lists and are intent on improving the quality of your work, *read this book.* I've commented on this indispensable little classic in Chapter Nine.

- Trenbeth, R. *The Membership Mystique.* Rockville, Md.: Fund-Raising Institute, 1986. This is a great resource for development professionals who want to fine-tune their membership development programs—or start one from scratch. Organizations without formal membership programs can learn a lot too. The book is crammed with examples that reflect a sophisticated understanding of copywriting. Out of print, but available in good fundraising libraries.

- Vögele, S. *Handbook of Direct Mail: The Dialogue Method of Direct Written Sales Communication.* Hemel Hempstead, U.K.: Verlag Moderne Industrie/Prentice Hall, 1992. I never thought I'd read, much less highly recommend, a dry direct marketing textbook translated from the German. But the German professor who wrote this insightful book was all the rage in European direct marketing circles for over a decade. Vögele is familiar to some Americans as the author of the eye-motion studies I wrote about in my earlier book, *999 Tips, Trends and Guidelines for Successful Direct Mail and Telephone Fundraising.* It's time now for Americans to start catching onto the wisdom of his dialogue method, which is a way of looking at direct mail that's based in large part on—but goes far beyond—the professor's eye-motion research. I've commented at length on Vögele's Dialogue Method in Chapter Two.

- Warwick, M. *Raising Money by Mail: Strategies for Growth and Financial Stability.* Berkeley, California: Strathmoor Press, 1995. Originally published in 1990 under the title *Revolution in the Mailbox: How Direct Mail Fundraising Is Changing the Face of American Society—And How Your Organization Can Benefit.* This book is my attempt to place direct mail fundraising in a larger context, spelling out the strategic potential and long-range impact of launching a direct mail fundraising program. The novice copywriter will find this book useful because it contains a great many sample fundraising letters, many of them reproduced in entirety, as well as my illustrated analysis of the components of a successful fundraising appeal.

A Final Word

You're unlikely to write a good fundraising appeal without understanding the dynamics of direct mail fundraising. If you're serious about this, you'll read up on the basics. For the grounding you need, I recommend three of the books listed above: Ken Burnett's *Relationship Fundraising,* Lautman and Goldstein's *Dear Friend,* and my own *Raising Money by Mail.* Read those three books cover to cover, understand them, apply the lessons they teach, and you'll be off to a great start in your direct mail fundraising career.

Index

CHAPTER FIVE

Exhibits 5.1, 5.2, 5.4, and 5.5 are used with permission by the San Francisco Conservatory of Music.

Exhibit 5.3 is used with permission by ICM Artists.

Exhibit 5.6 is used with permission by Campaign to Abolish Poverty.

CHAPTER SIX

Exhibit 6.1 is used with permission by Heal the Bay.

Exhibit 6.2, courtesy of the Million Mom March Foundation.

Exhibit 6.3 is used with permission by the Union of Concerned Scientists.

Exhibit 6.4 is used with permission by The National Council of La Raza.

Exhibit 6.5 is used with permission by Doctors of the World.

CHAPTER SEVEN

Exhibit 7.1 is used with permission by Mills-Peninsula Hospital Foundation.

CHAPTER EIGHT

Exhibits 8.1–8.6 are used with permission by St. Joseph's Indian School.

CHAPTER TEN

Exhibit 10.1 is used with permission by Bread for the World.

Exhibits 10.2 and 10.3 are used with permission by Western Pennsylvania Conservancy.

CHAPTER ELEVEN

Exhibit 11.1 is used with permission by Bread for the World.

Exhibits 11.2–11.16 are used with permission by Co-op America.

CHAPTER TWELVE

Exhibit 12.1 is used with permission by Bread for the World.

CHAPTER THIRTEEN

Exhibit 13.1 is used with permission by Bread for the World.

CHAPTER FOURTEEN

Exhibit 14.1 is used with permission by Bread for the World.

Exhibits 14.2–14.6 are used with permission by the San Francisco AIDS Foundation.

CHAPTER FIFTEEN

Exhibit 15.1 is used with permission by Bread for the World.

CHAPTER SIXTEEN

Exhibit 16.1 is used with permission by Bread for the World.

Exhibits 16.2–16.11 are used with permission by Peace Action.

Exhibit 16.12 is used with permission by Co-op America.

CHAPTER SEVENTEEN

Exhibit 17.1 is used with permission by Bread for the World.

Exhibits 17.2 and 17.3 are used with permission by Southern Poverty Law Center.

RESOURCE A

Exhibit A.1, copyright (c) Handgun Control, Inc. Used with permission.